Sports Injuries
Information
for Teens

TEEN HEALTH SERIES

First Edition

Sports Injuries Information for Teens

Health Tips about Sports Injuries and Injury Prevention

Including Facts about Specific Injuries, Emergency Treatment, Rehabilitation, Sports Safety, Competition Stress, Fitness, Sports Nutrition, Steroid Risks, and More

◆

Edited by Joyce Brennfleck Shannon

Omnigraphics

615 Griswold Street • Detroit, MI 48226

Bibliographic Note

Because this page cannot legibly accommodate all the copyright notices, the Bibliographic Note portion of the Preface constitutes an extension of the copyright notice.

Edited by Joyce Brennfleck Shannon

Teen Health Series

Karen Bellenir, *Managing Editor*
David A. Cooke, M.D., *Medical Consultant*
Elizabeth Barbour, *Permissions Associate*
Dawn Matthews, *Verification Assistant*
Laura Pleva Nielsen, *Index Editor*
EdIndex, Services for Publishers, *Indexers*

* * *

Omnigraphics, Inc.

Matthew P. Barbour, *Senior Vice President*
Kay Gill, *Vice President—Directories*
Kevin Hayes, *Operations Manager*
Leif Gruenberg, *Development Manager*
David P. Bianco, *Marketing Consultant*

* * *

Peter E. Ruffner, *Publisher*

Frederick G. Ruffner, Jr., *Chairman*

Copyright © 2004 Omnigraphics, Inc.

ISBN 0-7808-0447-3

Table of Contents

Part III: Sports Injuries That Commonly Affect Active Teens

Part IV: Rehabilitation And Physical Therapy

Part V: Preventing Sports Injuries In Teens

Part VI: Sports Nutrition For Young Adults

Part VII: Sport Safety Guidelines For Active Teens

Part VIII: Resources For Help And Additional Information

Preface

About This Book

Sports are an important part of life for many teens, and participation in a variety of activities can help establish a good foundation for life-long fitness. Unfortunately, injuries can happen. According to the Centers for Disease Control and Prevention, the highest rates of injuries related to sports and recreation seen in emergency departments are among teens. Appropriate medical care and adequate recovery are essential for reducing risks associated with injury and re-injury. Additionally, many injuries can be prevented through proper training, the use of correct equipment, adequate warm-up periods, adhering to game rules, and recognizing the importance of not playing through pain.

Sports Injuries Information For Teens reviews the special needs of teen athletes, injury rates for common sports, suggestions for sports safety, facts about handling competition stress, and tips for developing effective relationships with coaches. Diagnostic and treatment procedures for sports injuries from the field, to the emergency room, and through the rehabilitation process are described. Safety guidelines for individual and team sports, including baseball, basketball, football, gymnastics, soccer, skating, biking, skiing, snowboarding, and scuba diving are explained. Contact information for related national organizations is provided along with suggestions for additional reading.

How To Use This Book

This book is divided into parts and chapters. Parts focus on broad areas of interest; chapters are devoted to single topics within a part.

Part I: Basic Information About Sports Injuries In Teens discusses the specific needs of teen athletes, how to deal with injuries, and the risks of injury during practice or in competition for a variety of common sports.

Part II: Emergency Treatment Of Sports Injuries In Teens describes the on-field examination and assessment of injuries, what to expect in an emergency department, and common diagnostic procedures used to evaluate the nature and extent of injuries.

Part III: Sports Injuries That Commonly Affect Active Teens offers information about a variety of frequently occurring injuries. Topics include cuts, sprains, broken bones, concussions, repetitive stress injuries, and injuries to specific parts of the body.

Part IV: Rehabilitation And Physical Therapy presents facts about different types of therapies, the importance of rehabilitation, and guidelines for returning to sports activities after an injury.

Part V: Preventing Sports Injuries In Teens offers proven safety practices that prevent or reduce injuries in athletes. It provides information about pre-participation physicals, general fitness, exercise safety, handling the stress of competition, protective equipment, proper training, and the need for adequate sleep.

Part VI: Sports Nutrition For Young Adults discusses what and when to eat for best athletic performance, the importance of hydration, and the risks involved when using steroids.

Part VII: Sport Safety Guidelines For Active Teens reviews safety guidelines recommended by experts in specific sports to reduce the risk of injury. Guidelines are included for baseball and softball, basketball, football, gymnastics, track, soccer, tennis, skating and skateboarding, skiing and snowboarding, biking, and scuba diving.

Part VIII: Additional Help And Information includes a directory of national organizations able to provide information about sports injuries. Many of these organizations have web sites that offer a good beginning point for further research. A chapter of additional reading suggests other books on topics pertaining to sports injuries.

Bibliographic Note

This volume contains documents and excerpts from publications issued by the following government agencies: Centers for Disease Control and Prevention (CDC); National Center for Health Statistics; National Institute of Arthritis and Musculoskeletal and Skin Diseases (NIAMS); National Women's Health Information Center; and SafeUSA™.

In addition, this volume contains copyrighted documents and articles produced by the following organizations: Alabama Cooperative Extension System; American Academy of Family Physicians; American Academy of Orthopaedic Surgeons; American Academy of Otolaryngology-Head and Neck Surgery; American Academy of Podiatric Sports Medicine; American Association of Oral and Maxillofacial Surgeons; American College of Emergency Physicians; American College of Sports Medicine; American Council on Exercise®; American Dental Association; American Orthopaedic Foot and Ankle Society; American Orthopaedic Society for Sports Medicine; American Podiatric Medical Association; Dr. Jeffrey L. Halbrecht/Institute for Arthroscopy and Sports Medicine; National Athletic Trainers' Association; National Collegiate Athletic Association; National Safety Council; National Youth Sports Safety Foundation; Nemours Foundation; *Physician and Sportsmedicine*; Prevent Blindness America; Thomas Songer, PhD.; University of Pittsburgh Medical Center; and University of Pittsburgh Medical Center/Center for Sports Medicine.

Full citation information is provided on the first page of each chapter. Every effort has been made to secure all necessary rights to reprint the copyrighted material. If any omissions have been made, please contact Omnigraphics to make corrections for future editions.

Acknowledgements

In addition to the organizations listed above, special thanks are due to permissions associate Elizabeth Barbour and to managing editor Karen Bellenir.

Note From The Editor

This book is part of Omnigraphics' *Teen Health Series*. The series provides basic information about a broad range of medical concerns. It is not intended to serve as a tool for diagnosing illness, in prescribing treatments, or as a substitute for the physician/patient relationship. All persons concerned about medical symptoms or the possibility of disease are encouraged to seek professional care from an appropriate health care provider.

At the request of librarians serving today's young adults, the *Teen Health Series* was developed as a specially focused set of volumes within Omnigraphics' *Health Reference Series*. Each volume deals comprehensively with a topic selected according to the needs and interests of people in middle school and high school. If there is a topic you would like to see addressed in a future volume of the *Teen Health Series*, please write to:

Editor
Teen Health Series
Omnigraphics, Inc.
615 Griswold Street
Detroit, MI 48226

Our Advisory Board

The *Teen Health Series* is reviewed by an Advisory Board comprised of librarians from public, academic, and medical libraries. We would like to thank the following board members for providing guidance to the development of this series:

Dr. Lynda Baker, Associate Professor of Library and Information Science, Wayne State University, Detroit, MI

Nancy Bulgarelli, William Beaumont Hospital Library, Royal Oak, MI

Karen Imarisio, Bloomfield Township Public Library, Bloomfield Township, MI

Karen Morgan, Mardigian Library, University of Michigan-Dearborn, Dearborn, MI

Rosemary Orlando, St. Clair Shores Public Library, St. Clair Shores, MI

Medical Consultant

Medical consultation services are provided to the *Teen Health Series* editors by David A. Cooke, M.D. Dr. Cooke is a graduate of Brandeis University, and he received his M.D. degree from the University of Michigan. He completed residency training at the University of Wisconsin Hospital and Clinics. He is board-certified in internal medicine. Dr. Cooke currently works as part of the University of Michigan Health System and practices in Brighton, MI. In his free time, he enjoys writing, science fiction, and spending time with his family.

Part One

Basic Information About Sports Injuries In Teens

Chapter 1

Adolescent Athletes Have Special Needs

More young people enjoy sports than ever before. Athletic participation has increased in grade schools, high schools, and community programs.

Adolescent athletes have special needs. Because their bodies are growing, they often require different coaching, conditioning, and medical care than more mature athletes. It is important to examine the special requirements of young athletes to better prepare them for the competitive pressures and physical injuries that can come with increased sports activity.

Statistics demonstrate the increased popularity of sports among young people. Fifty percent of boys and 25 percent of girls between the ages of eight and sixteen compete in an organized sports program sometime during the year. Three-fourths of junior high schools and middle schools have competitive interscholastic sports programs. At the high school level, there are 32 male and 27 female competitive sports with 7,000,000 high school students participating. Beyond organized sports programs, millions more compete and participate in physical education classes, church and community intramural programs, and other recreational athletic activities.

About This Chapter: Text in this chapter is from "The Young Athlete," © February 2002 American Academy of Orthopaedic Surgeons. Reprinted with permission from Your Orthopaedic *Connection*, the patient education website of the American Academy of Orthopaedic Surgeons located at http://orthoinfo.aaos.org.

A host of factors has contributed to the awakening of interest in health, conditioning, and sports. The media impact on youth has elevated talented college and professional athletes to heroic levels. The multimedia message on these sports heroes may confuse young athletes by creating unrealistic expectations. The early return to competition by professional athletes following an injury creates the impression that athletes often heal faster than the rest of us. However, peer pressure and the economic and social forces exerted on school coaches to win may lead to decisions that are not truly in the best interests of adolescent athletes' health, growth, and development.

> **✔ Quick Tip**
>
> Many sports injuries in adolescent athletes, particularly elbow and knee injuries, are caused by excessive, repetitive stress on immature muscle-bone units. Such repetitive overuse can cause fractures, muscle tears, or bone deformity. Fortunately, such injuries are uncommon, and usually prolonged pain is an early warning sign.

Adolescent Athletes Are Different

The growing athlete is not merely a smaller version of the adult. There are marked differences in coordination, strength, and stamina between a youth and an adult. In young athletes, bone-tendon-muscle units, growth areas within bones, and ligaments experience uneven growth patterns, leaving them susceptible to injury.

Increases in body size may be due to fat and not muscle, causing marked differences in strength. Too often unfair competition occurs between boys of 100 pounds of baby fat and peach fuzz versus 200 pounds of muscle and mustache.

Grade school students are less likely to suffer from severe injury because they are smaller and slower than older athletes; when they collide or fall, the forces on their musculoskeletal system are usually not high enough to cause injury. On the other hand, high school athletes are bigger, faster, stronger, and capable of delivering tremendous forces in contact sports.

Coaches bear a prime responsibility in developing their athletes and watching for early signs of physical problems (such as pain or limp). They often recognize severe injuries because their athletes show signs of pain and can't continue playing.

Coaches may have more difficulty spotting less severe injuries, however, because the pain is low grade and the athlete often ignores it. Repeat injuries may turn into overuse conditions which can put the athlete on the sidelines for the rest of the season.

Coaches, parents, and players should provide protection for the adolescent athlete through proper conditioning, prompt treatment of injuries, and rehabilitation programs. Conditioning programs usually strive to make the young athlete physically fit by improving muscle strength, endurance, flexibility, and cardiorespiratory fitness.

The coaches and parents also are responsible for creating a psychological atmosphere that fosters self-reliance, confidence, cooperation, trust, and a positive self-image. Adolescent athletes must learn to deal with success and defeat in order to place events in a proper perspective. Some coaches and parents go too far in analyzing player performance. The promotion of the "win at all costs" ethic has both short-term and long-term detrimental effects on impressionable young people.

Soft Tissue Injuries

Fortunately major sports-related injuries are rare in young people. Little sports time is lost from sports injuries due to minor trauma involving soft tissues. Moreover, sports injuries occur more frequently in physical education classes and free-play sports than in organized team sports. Minimal safety precautions and supervision can prevent many injuries.

Sprains

Almost one-third of all sports injuries are classified as sprains. A sprain is a partial or complete tear of a ligament, which is a tough band of fibrous connective tissue that connects the ends of bones and stabilizes the joint. Symptoms include the feeling that a joint is loose or unstable; an inability to bear weight because of pain; loss of motion; the sound or feeling of a pop or snap when the injury occurred; and swelling. However, not all sprains produce pain.

Strains

A strain is a partial or complete tear of a muscle or tendon. Muscle tissue is made up of cells that contract and make the body move. A tendon consists of tough connective tissue that attaches muscles to bones.

> **♣ It's A Fact!!**
>
> About 95% of sports injuries are due to minor trauma involving soft tissues—bruises, muscle pulls, sprains (ligaments), strains (muscles and tendons), and cuts or abrasions.

Contusions

The most common sports injury contusions (bruises) rarely cause a student athlete to be sidelined. Bruises result when a blunt injury causes underlying bleeding in a muscle or other soft tissues.

Spinal Cord Injuries

Although spinal cord injuries in sports are rare, ten percent of all spinal injuries occur during sports, primarily diving, surfing, and football. They can range from a sprain to paralysis in the arms and legs (quadriplegia) to death. Participants in contact sports can minimize the risk of minor neck spinal injuries—sprains and pinched nerves—by doing exercises to strengthen their neck muscles.

Skeletal Injuries

A sudden, violent collision with another player, an accident with sports equipment, or a severe fall can cause skeletal injuries in the growing athlete, including fractures.

Fractures constitute a low five to six percent of all sports injuries. Most of these breaks occur in the arms and legs. Rarely are the spine and skull fractured.

More common, however, are stress fractures and ligament-bone disruptions that occur because of continuing overuse of a joint. The main symptom of a stress fracture is pain. Frequently, initial x-rays do not show any signs of a stress fracture so the athlete is permitted to return to the same activity. Unfortunately the pain often returns or continues, but the athlete keeps playing. The most frequent places stress fractures occur are the tibia (the larger leg bone below the knee), fibula (the outer and thinner leg bone below the knee), and foot.

Little League elbow can result when a pitcher's repetitive throwing puts too much pressure on the elbow bone's growth centers. This painful condition results from overusage of muscles and tendons or from an injury to the cartilage surfaces in the elbow.

Diagnosis And Treatment

Diagnosis of any sports-related orthopaedic injury should be made promptly by orthopaedic surgeons, physicians who specialize in the care of the musculoskeletal system. The physician usually will ask the young athlete how the injury occurred, then follow with questions about the type of pain—whether it is a stabbing pain, a dull ache, or throbbing—the location of the pain, and the sport in which the athlete was involved.

During the physical examination, the orthopaedist will ask the athlete to move the affected area to determine whether the student's motion has been affected. The orthopaedist will gently touch the area to observe for obvious skeletal abnormalities. X-rays or other radiographic tests may be ordered, depending on the athlete's condition and the doctor's need for additional information.

✔ Quick Tip

Prompt treatment for soft tissue injuries usually consists of rest, applying ice, wrapping with elastic bandages (compression), and elevating the injured arm, hand, leg, or foot. This usually limits discomfort and reduces healing time. Proper first aid will minimize swelling and help the physician establish an accurate diagnosis.

Orthopaedic surgeons have been in the forefront of treating musculoskeletal system injuries and have a long tradition of caring for adolescent athletes. In the last two decades, they have analyzed and clarified young athletes' psychological needs, conditioning, training, and susceptibility to physical injury. They provide early and comprehensive care of orthopaedic injuries. This can help student athletes heal and return to competition with less chance of repeated injury.

Treatment varies according to the patient's condition, but it may include bed rest, elevation, compression bandages, crutches, cast immobilization, or physical therapy.

Female Athletes

Female involvement in sports has increased tremendously at the high school level—by 700% over the last 15 years. Although early studies indicated that female

✎ **Weird Words**

Contusion: The bruise that results when a blunt injury causes underlying bleeding in a muscle or other soft tissue.

Fibula: The outer and thinner leg bone below the knee.

Ligament: A tough band of fibrous connective tissue that connects the ends of bones and stabilizes the joint.

Orthopaedic Surgeon or Orthopaedist: A medical doctor with extensive training in the diagnosis, and non-surgical and surgical treatment of the musculoskeletal system, including bones, joints, ligaments, tendons, muscles, and nerves.

Sprain: A partial or complete tear of a ligament.

Strain: A partial or complete tear of a muscle or tendon.

Tendon: Tough connective tissue that attaches muscles to bones.

Tibia: The larger leg bone below the knee.

athletes needed to train at lower levels of intensity than male athletes, it appears that this was more a social than a physiological problem. Today's female athlete is able to train and frequently compete at levels that rival many of the best male athletes. Although there are differences in performance that are sex-related, athletic injuries are related more to the player's sport than sex.

Risk And Benefits

Sports activity by young people is generally safe with low risks and high benefits. The major goal should be enjoyable participation. Exposure to competitive and noncompetitive sports encourages the development of fitness, motor skills, social skills, and life-long appreciation for sports.

☞ **Remember!!**

In adolescent athletes, bone-tendon-muscle units, and ligaments experience uneven growth patterns, leaving them susceptible to injury.

Chapter 2

Injuries Are Not Accidents

Injuries occur as the result of energy transfer that is delivered in excess of a threshold. The first basic principle in injury epidemiology is the understanding of what injuries are and, in some sense, what they are not. In general, injuries occur when humans encounter energy forces that are larger than the body's normal tolerance levels for energy absorption. The level of energy encountered exceeds a threshold.

Get to know your local engineer or physicist, because injuries occur as the result of energy transfers. All injuries can be characterized from the perspective of a transfer of energy that exceeds a threshold. We deal with all forms of physical energy every day, whether mechanical (motion), thermal (heat), or other forms. Normally, we can withstand most shifts in energy forces. However, there are selected times when our personal thresholds for tolerance of energy transfer are exceeded and an injury occurs.

As an example, when we drive in an automobile, our bodies assume the rate of speed of the vehicle. When a crash occurs, the body is suddenly slowed, and energy transfers between the victim, his/her car, and the object struck (a

About This Chapter: Text in this chapter is excerpted from "Ten Basic Principles of Injury Epidemiology," by Thomas Songer, Ph.D., Department of Epidemiology, University of Pittsburgh Graduate School of Public Health. © Thomas Songer. Reprinted with permission.

tree, another car, etc.). Injuries arise when our threshold to withstand this energy transfer is exceeded.

Energy Transfer And Injuries

If the energy transfer is localized in one area, the likely outcome may be a penetrating injury. If the energy transfer is dispersed over a broad area, the result will often be a non-penetrating injury. In situations involving thermal energy transfer, the result will be a burn. And so on, depending upon the mode of energy involved.

Most injuries (74%) arise from the transfer of physical or mechanical energy. This is due to the frequency in which we come into contact with events and vehicles that involve mechanical energy. The leading causes of death from mechanical energy transfer are injuries from motor vehicle accidents, firearms, and falls.

Injuries Do Not Occur By Chance

♣ **It's A Fact!!**

Causes Of Injuries

- Energy transfers that exceed our abilities for compensation

- Types of energy that can cause injury

  - Mechanical
  - Electric
  - Radiation
  - Thermal
  - Chemical

Types of Injuries

- Penetrating
- Non-Penetrating
- Compression
- Burn

Many injury professionals feel that injuries are not accidents. This has been a common slogan spoken by injury research professionals. It originated some time ago to counteract the perception that injuries occurred by chance. In the past, many persons in the lay public and many legislators regarded injuries as accidents; events that you had little control over. This thought probably arose from the publicity that natural disasters receive.

However, it is now well recognized that nearly all injuries are not the result of random events. There are distinct patterns and circumstances that characterize their occurrence. We understand that injuries most often occur to certain risk groups and are fairly predictable (whether it be to certain persons, at certain times, or in common locations).

In this light, many persons in the injury field refer to automobile accidents as crashes rather than accidents. In reality, it does not matter whether or not crashes or accidents is the most appropriate term. What is important is the recognition that injury events often have identifiable characteristics, and that we may be able to prevent future injuries by intervening on one or more of these characteristics.

Injury Surveillance Systems Form The Basis For Injury Control

Injury surveillance or monitoring systems are important for they provide us knowledge on how many injuries occur, when they occur, and to whom they occur! This information lays the foundation for efforts to reduce injuries in the future.

All of the injury control measures that quickly come to mind, e.g. seat belts, airbags, helmets, were implemented after it became apparent that injuries were occurring in relatively high numbers and that we needed to do something about it.

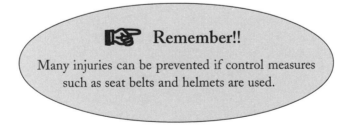

☞ Remember!!

Many injuries can be prevented if control measures such as seat belts and helmets are used.

Chapter 3

Dealing With Sports Injuries: An Overview

Just getting started in football, basketball, soccer, or some other sport and worried about sports injuries? Don't sweat it. Think of it as just another part of playing by the rules—but this rulebook is the one that keeps you from getting hurt. The first rule here is the most important one: the best way to deal with sports injuries is to prevent them. Prevention includes knowing the rules of the game you're playing, using the proper equipment, and playing safe.

But you've practiced with your team, played it safe on the field, and still suffered an injury. Don't worry, it's not the end of the world—just the beginning of a healing process. Read on to find out what this process is and how you can deal with a sports injury.

What Are Sports Injuries?

You probably have lots of friends who play sports, either on a team or on their own. You may belong to a gym or go in-line skating on the weekends. Although you probably know the risks of falling down and breaking an arm or leg, you may not be aware of the other kinds of injuries that can occur.

About This Chapter: Text in this chapter is from "Dealing With Sports Injuries." This information was provided by KidsHealth, one of the largest resources online for medically reviewed health information written for parents, kids, and teens. For more articles like this one, visit www.KidsHealth.org. or www.TeensHealth.org. © 2002 The Nemours Center for Children's Health Media, a division of The Nemours Foundation. Reprinted with permission.

Sports injuries are injuries that typically occur while participating in organized sports, competitions, training sessions, or organized fitness activities. These injuries may occur in teens for a variety of reasons, including improper training, lack of appropriate footwear or safety equipment, and rapid growth during puberty.

Sports Injuries On Your Body

You may think of your back or your arms and legs as the only places where you could get hurt while playing, but you can get a sports injury anywhere on your body, including your face, neck, head, sex organs, hands, and feet.

Head And Neck Injuries

Head injuries include concussions, contusions, fractures, and hematomas. A concussion is a violent jarring or shock to the head that causes a temporary jolt to the brain. If severe enough, or recurrent, concussions can cause brain damage but fortunately this is not common in teens. A hematoma is a bleeding or pooling of blood between the tissue layers covering the brain or inside the brain. All of these injuries can be caused by impact to the head from a fall, forceful shaking of the head, a blow to the head, or whiplash. Whiplash is an injury to the neck caused by an abrupt jerking motion of the head.

✔ Quick Tip

Who's At Risk?

Playing sports involves a certain amount of risk for sports-related injuries. Twice as many males as females suffer sports-related injuries. This is due, in part, to the types of sports males and females play. Collision or contact sports have higher injury rates—football, basketball, baseball, and soccer account for about 80% of all sports-related emergency room visits for children between 5 and 14 years of age. While teens and young adults experience injuries related to the force they can generate and the intensity of play, children in this age group are less proficient at assessing risks and have less coordination, slower reaction times and less accuracy than adults.

Source: From *Sports- and Recreation-Related Injuries*, Centers for Disease Control and Prevention (CDC), October 10, 2002.

> ### ✔ Quick Tip
>
> Always wear helmets for contact sports and when doing activities like biking and rollerblading to prevent head injuries. Neck injuries are among the most dangerous. You can hurt your neck through a sudden traumatic injury in sports like mountain climbing, skydiving, horseback riding, gymnastics, diving, rugby, judo, or boxing.

Neck injuries include strains, fractures, contusions, and sprains. Most neck injuries are caused by impact to the head or neck sustained during a fall or a blow. Your neck can also be injured a little at a time. Too much strain on your neck can cause increasing pain, sometimes only on one side of your neck. Sometimes you may feel only a slight pain when you move a certain way.

If the injury is severe and there is a chance that the neck might be injured, it's very important to keep the injured person still with their head held straight while someone calls for emergency medical help. If the person is lying on the ground, do not try to move them. Never try to move someone who may have a neck injury—a mishandled neck fracture could lead to permanent paralysis or even death.

How do these injuries happen? Serious head and neck injuries occur most often in athletes who participate in contact sports (like football or rugby) or sports with the potential for falling accidents, such as horseback riding.

Foot Injuries

Foot injuries can include ligament strains, stress fractures, heel bruises, and bursitis. Because your feet support all of your weight and must absorb a lot of force over and over again, they can be particularly susceptible to injury. Another reason some teens may suffer foot injuries is because of differences in their feet. For example, some people have flat feet or high arches. These differences don't mean that sports should be avoided, but it does mean that precautions, such as a special shoe insert, may be needed.

Sex Organs

When it comes to injuries to the sex organs, guys usually suffer more trauma than girls because the penis and testicles are outside the body and lack natural protection during contact sports. Guys should always wear

✎ Weird Words

There are two general types of sports injuries. The first type is called an acute traumatic injury.

Acute Traumatic Injuries: Usually involve a single blow from a single application of force—like getting a cross-body block in football.

Acute traumatic injuries include the following:

Fracture: A crack, break, or shattering of a bone.

Bruise (known medically as a contusion): Caused by a direct blow, which may cause swelling and bleeding in muscles and other body tissues.

Strain: A stretch or tear of a muscle or tendon, the tough and narrow end of a muscle that connects it to a bone.

Sprain: A stretch or tear of a ligament, the tissue that supports and strengthens joints by connecting bones and cartilage.

Abrasion: A scrape.

Laceration: A cut in the skin that is usually deep enough to require stitches.

The second type of sports injury is called an overuse or chronic injury.

Chronic Injuries: Those that happen over a period of time. Chronic injuries are usually the result of repetitive training, such as running, overhand throwing, or serving a ball in tennis. These include:

Stress Fractures: Tiny cracks in the bone's surface often caused by repetitive overloading (such as in the feet of a basketball player who is continuously jumping on the court).

Tendinitis: Inflammation of the tendon caused by repetitive stretching.

Bursitis: An inflammation of the bursa, which is a small sac, in the shoulder, elbow, or knee (these joints all contain several bursa).

Often overuse injuries seem less important than acute injuries. You may be tempted to ignore that aching in your wrist or that soreness in your knees, but always remember that just because an injury isn't dramatic doesn't mean it's unimportant or will go away on its own. If left untreated, a chronic injury will probably get worse over time.

athletic supporters, or in some sports a cup, to protect the genitals from serious injury.

Injuries to the uterus or ovaries are rare, but breast injuries are common complaints among teen girls. As the breasts develop, they can often be sore, and a blow from a softball or a jab from an elbow, for example, can be painful. Girls should wear supportive sports bras while playing sports or exercising.

Back Injuries

Back injuries include sprains, fractures, contusions, and strains and are caused by twists or overexertion of back muscles during bending or lifting movements. These injuries can occur in contact sports like football and ice hockey or in weight lifting, figure skating, gymnastics, dancing, baseball, and basketball.

Hand Injuries

Hand injuries include fractures, dislocations, and sprains and often occur in contact sports such as football, lacrosse, and hockey. Hand injuries can result from a fall that forces the hand or fingers backward, a forceful impact to the hands, or a direct blow.

Taking Care Of Sports Injuries

If your pain progressively increases with activity (what sports medicine doctors call an upward crescendo) and causes any limping or loss of range of motion, you need to see a doctor as soon as possible.

What kinds of pain should you be on the lookout for? Any injury that results in swelling, numbness, intense pain or tenderness, stiffness, or loss of flexibility should be taken seriously.

You should also know the difference between soreness and chronic pain. Soreness is temporary, but chronic pain continues over a greater length of time. For example, it's not always necessary to see a doctor right away if your shoulder is sore, but you should schedule an appointment if the pain is worsening at any time or if it persists for a week or more.

Injuries Can Be Prevented

Estimates suggest that half of all childhood sports-related injuries can be prevented, and steps can be taken to reduce risks in all types of recreational activities:

- To avoid unnecessary injuries, all children and adolescents should have a physical exam before starting new sports activities.

- Participate in activities that are supervised by an experienced or trained coach who understands and enforces game rules.

- If starting a new exercise program, set realistic goals and start with frequencies and intensities appropriate to your current physical condition (based on consultation with your physician) and injury-history.

- Ensure that playing fields and environments are safe and well-maintained (e.g. well-maintained playing fields free of tripping hazards, holes, exposed sprinklers, broken glass).

- Make sure you are properly outfitted for the sport in which you plan to participate—proper protective gear (helmet, shin guards, knee pads); shoes that fit well and are appropriate for the sport; clothing that is not too loose so it won't become tangled. In some sports, mouth guards and face protection can help prevent traumas to the face, head, eyes, and mouth, which are among the most common types of injuries.

- Stretch and warm-up before playing.

- Do not play through pain. If you are injured, see your doctor. Follow all the doctor's orders for recovery, and get the doctor's okay before returning to play. Playing again too soon can lead to a more serious and long-lasting injuries.

- Have a first aid kit available at all times.

- Learn skills to prevent injuries specific to your sport (e.g. learn how to safely stop or fall while inline skating).

- For children's team sports, be sure to match and group children based on skill level, weight, and physical maturity—especially for contact sports.

Source: From *Sports- and Recreation-Related Injuries*, Centers for Disease Control and Prevention (CDC), October 10, 2002.

The most important thing to do when you suspect you are injured is to stop doing whatever sport has caused the injury right away and go see a doctor. For more severe or complicated injuries, it may be best to see a doctor who specializes in sports medicine.

The doctor will examine your injury and use diagnostic tools such as x-rays and magnetic resonance imaging (MRI) to determine the extent of your injury. MRI allows doctors to see soft tissues more clearly than x-rays or CT scans do.

Once the doctor knows the full extent of your injury, he or she usually will start with conservative treatment techniques such as rest and ice to help decrease swelling. Pain relief and anti-inflammatory medicines such as ibuprofen (like Motrin) may be prescribed. Splints, casts, and surgery also may be needed, depending on the injury.

One of three things will happen next. Your doctor may recommend that you not play while you heal, that you play and use a protective device (a knee brace or wrist guard, for example), or that you undergo rehabilitation (physical therapy). Sports medicine doctors won't let you play if you are at risk for getting another injury or aggravating an injury you are recovering from.

When Can You Play Again?

If your doctor has asked you to stop playing, your number one question is probably "When can I play sports again?" This depends on your specific injury, so make sure you discuss this with your doctor. There are things you can do while injured to stay fit, but make sure you check with your doctor first. These activities include using stationary cycles, swimming, water therapy, and rowing machines.

Your rehabilitation program will also help you stay fit as you recover. Rehabilitation, or rehab, is the process that gets you back in shape and ready for action again. Rehab may be part of your treatment program and can include exercise, manual therapy from a physical therapist (a specialist who is trained to help you recover from a sports injury), and technology such as ultrasound. Ultrasound equipment is used to heat the injured area. This heat relieves pain, promotes healing, and increases your range of motion.

Playing Safe

What can you do to protect yourself from getting hurt again? Use protective gear—such as helmets for contact sports like football—that is appropriate to the specific sport.

♣ It's A Fact!!

Sports-related injuries are the leading cause of emergency room visits for 12–17-year-olds.

Source: From *Sports- and Recreation-Related Injuries*, Centers for Disease Control and Prevention (CDC), October 10, 2002.

When you return to play, you might need some new protective gear, including modified shoes (such as those with inserts or arch supports or those designed for use in a particular sport), tapings (tape used to wrap a knee, for example, to provide extra support), knee and elbow braces, and mouth guards. These devices help support and protect your body part from strains, direct blows, and possible reinjury.

To help prevent reinjury, be sure to warm up adequately before practice and games. Remember to take it slow when you first get back into your sport and gradually build back up to your preinjury level.

Also, know your limits. If the previously injured part (or any body part) begins to hurt, stop immediately and rest. Don't delay in seeking medical attention if the pain persists. It's your body's way of telling you something is not right.

So, play, but play safe. Try to learn from your experience and do the things that can help you avoid getting hurt again.

For More Information About Sports Injuries

CDC/National Center for Injury Prevention and Control

Mailstop K65
4770 Buford Highway NE
Atlanta, GA 30341-3724
Phone: 770-488-1506
Fax: 770-488-1667
Website: www.cdc.gov/ncipc
E-mail: CHCINFO@cdc.gov

American Academy of Pediatrics
141 Northwest Point Boulevard
Elk Grove Village, IL 60007-1098
Phone: 847-434-4000
Fax: 847-434-8000
Website: www.aap.org
E-mail: cfc@aap.org

National Athletic Trainers' Association
2952 Stemmons Frwy.
Dallas, TX 75247-6196
Phone: 214-637-6282
Fax: 214-637-2206
Website: www.nata.org
E-mail: webdude@nata.org

National Safety Council
1121 Spring Lake Drive
Itasca, IL 60143-3201
Phone: 630-285-1121
Fax: 630-285-1315
Website: www.nsc.org
E-mail: info@nsc.org

☞ **Remember!!**

Be smart—know the rules, use proper equipment, warm-up, and play safe to avoid sports-related injury.

Chapter 4

Am I Playable?

You want to do your best, make your coach and parents proud of you, and not let your team down. You are in a very important game, one you think you can't afford to miss or lose, but you are injured.

While many professional athletes play while injured or in severe pain, they are being paid millions for their performance and do so under the guidance of an entire medical staff who have evaluated the risks of staying in the game and the potential for permanent injury.

Most athletes do not have the same resources available to them. How do you know when you really have to be taken out of the game?

Symptoms That Indicate You Must Be Referred For Medical Attention

Pain is an indication that you are injured and need medical attention. Do not try to play through it or walk it off. You must be evaluated by a medical professional to determine the extent of your injury. Other symptoms that indicate you must have medical attention include:

About This Chapter: Text in this chapter is from "Am I Playable?—Tips for Athletes." This material is reprinted with permission of the National Youth Sports Safety Foundation, One Beacon Street, Suite 3333, Boston, Massachusetts 02108, www.nyssf.org. © 1999 National Youth Sports Safety Foundation.

- Swelling

- Loss of range of motion in a joint

- Dizziness

- Ringing in the ears

- Headache

- Limping

- Localized tenderness or pain

- Nausea and vomiting

- Drowsiness, memory loss, or altered consciousness

- Stumbling or lack of co-ordination

- Weakness in the arms or legs

- Persisting back or neck pain

- Open wound

- Seizure

♣ It's A Fact!!

What Are The Risks Of Staying In The Game And Playing Injured?

You may:

- Increase the severity of the injury

- Delay recovery time

- Cause permanent damage to your body which may end your sports career

☞ Remember!!
Be smart, use good judgment. Take care of your body and stay in sports for life!

Chapter 5

Three-Year Study Of Injuries To High School Athletes

More than half of injuries to high school athletes in nine sports were found to occur during practice sessions, according to a study released by the National Athletic Trainers' Association (NATA). The three-year project investigated injuries in selected high school sports over a three-year period (1995 to 1997 academic years). Findings from this extensive research of nearly 250 schools appeared in the September 1999 issue of the *Journal of Athletic Training*.

The NATA-funded study was conducted by John W. Powell, PhD, ATC. It focused on characterizing the risk of injury associated with 10 popular high school sports by comparing the relative frequency of injury and selected injury rates among sports, as well as the participation conditions within each sport. The sports studied were baseball (boys), softball (girls), football (boys), field hockey (girls), soccer (both), basketball (both), volleyball (girls) and wrestling (boys). The data came from 246 certified athletic trainers (ATCs) representing different sized schools across various geographic regions of the country. During the study, 23,566 reportable injuries occurred, and an average of 6,000 students were injured at least once each year.

About This Chapter: Text in this chapter is from a September 21, 1999 National Athletic Trainers' Association Press Release titled, "NATA Releases Results of Three-Year Study of Injuries to High School Athletes." It is reprinted with permission from the National Athletic Trainers' Association (NATA), © 1999 NATA.

The results of this study showed these interesting discoveries:

- An average of 55.5 percent of the reported injuries occurred during practice sessions.

- Only boys (59.3 percent) and girls' (57 percent) soccer showed a larger proportion of reported injuries in games than practices.

- Football had the highest rate of injury per 1,000 athlete exposures (8.1), while volleyball showed the lowest rate (1.7).

- The largest proportion of fractures came from boys' baseball (8.8 percent), basketball (8.6 percent), soccer (8.5 percent), and softball (8.4 percent).

✔ **Quick Tip**
The findings of this study indicate the best way to minimize the risk of injury in young athletes is to provide participation opportunities that are under the blanket of a well-designed and operational injury prevention program.

- More than 73 percent of injuries restricted players fewer than eight days.

- The highest frequency of knee injuries appeared in girls' soccer (19.4 percent), while baseball was the lowest (10.5 percent).

- The largest proportion of surgeries reported among the ten sports was for girls' basketball (4.0 percent) and the lowest was field hockey (1.2 percent).

- Of the injuries requiring surgery, 60.3 percent were to the knee.

- Field hockey was the only sport where sprains and strains accounted for less than 50 percent of the total injuries.

"Injury prevention programs should be in place for both practices and games," said Dr. Powell. "Although sports injuries cannot be entirely eliminated, consistent and professional evaluation of yearly injury patterns can provide focus for the development and evaluation of injury prevention strategies."

Dr. Powell identified four key points based on the data:

1. Each sport has an inherent risk based on the nature of the game and activities of the players;

2. Injury prevention programs should be in place for practice sessions, as well as games;

3. The prevention of reinjury through daily injury management is a critical component of an injury prevention program;

4. Sex differences in knee surgery patterns are specific to the sport being considered.

The NATA has as one of its goals, to increase the awareness of the need for more certified athletic trainers (ATCs) at the high school setting. ATCs are highly educated and skilled professionals specializing in the prevention, treatment, and rehabilitation of injuries. As this study indicates, injuries can be better minimized by involving more ATCs in high school sports programs. The American Medical Association (AMA) recognizes athletic training as an allied healthcare profession and recommends the use of ATCs in all high school athletic programs.

☞ Remember!!

Every sport has a risk of injury. You can reduce your risk of injury by always following sports injury prevention guidelines during both practice and games.

Chapter 6

Practice Injury Rate Across 16 Sports

Figures 6.1 and 6.2 compare the practice injuries across 16 sports without regard to severity. Comparisons of injury rates between sports are difficult because each sport has its own unique schedule and activities. If such comparisons are necessary, it may be best to use the game data for which the intensity variable is most consistent.

Figures 6.3 and 6.4 examine two measures of severity found in the NCAA Injury Surveillance System (ISS), time loss and injuries that required surgery. These practice data are presented to assist in decision regarding appropriate medical coverage for a sport; however, each severity category has some limitations that should be considered.

1. Time Loss. Figure 6.3 evaluates the practice rates of reported injuries that caused restricted or loss of participation of seven days or more. Limitation to this type of severity evaluation include:

a. An injury that restricts participation in one sport may not restrict participation in another.

b. Injuries that occur at an end of the season can only be estimated with regard to time.

*2. **Injuries That Require Surgery.** Figure 6.4 evaluates the practice rates of reported injuries that required either immediate or post-season surgery. Limitations to this severity evaluation include:*

a. The changing nature of surgical techniques and how they are applied.

b. The assumption that all sports had access to the same quality of medical evaluation.

c. Injuries can occur that may be categorized as severe, such as concussions, which may not require surgery.

☞ Remember!!

It is difficult to compare injury rates between sports; however, injury rate statistics do assist athletes and coaches as they strive to prevent sports injuries.

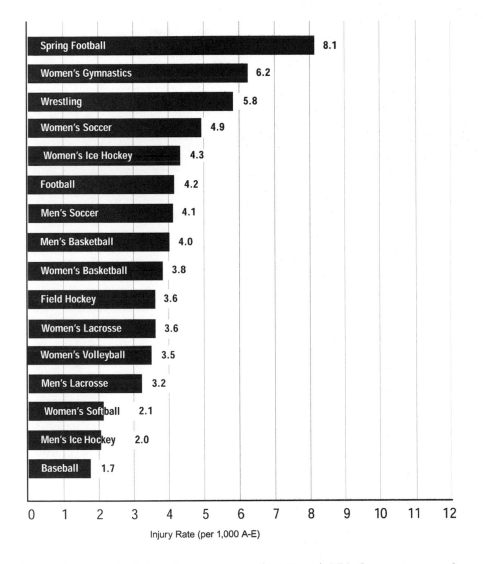

Figure 6.1. Practice Injury Rate Summary (All Sports). This figure represents the average practice injury rate (expressed as injuries per 1,000 athlete-exposures) for all sports analyzed in the ISS in the 2001-2002 season.

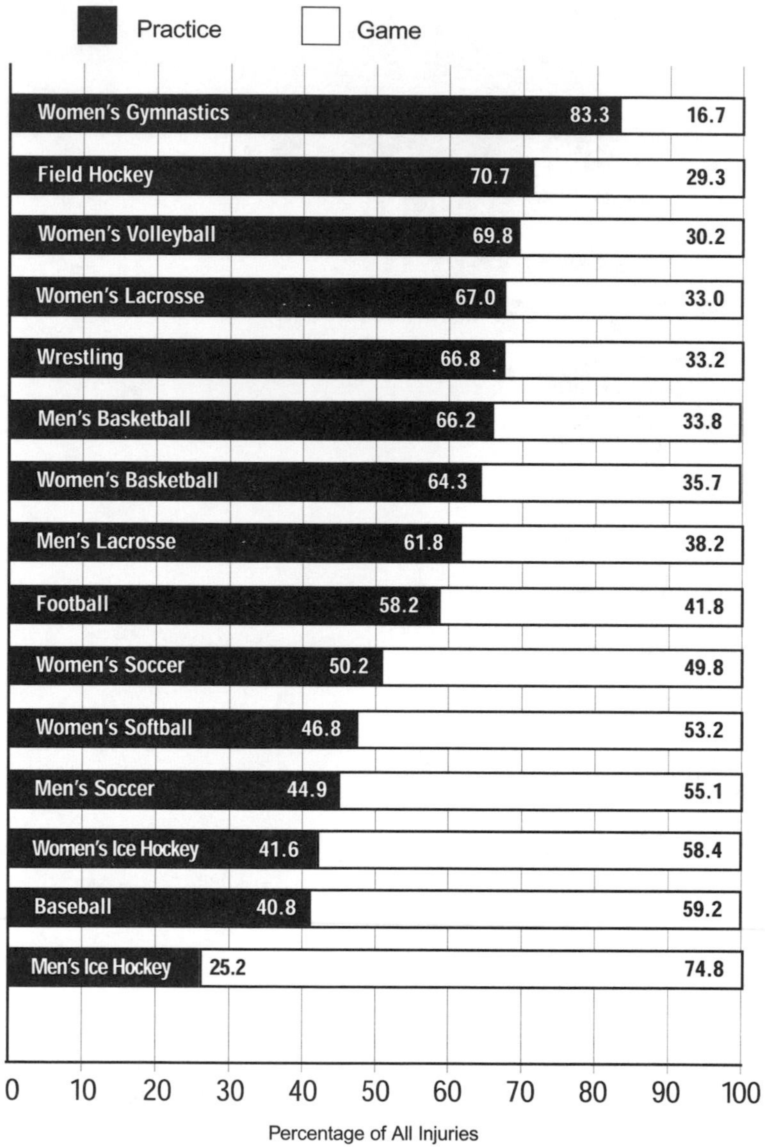

Figure 6.2. *Percentage Of All Injuries Occurring In Practices And Games. This figure represents the percentage of all injuries that occurred in practices and in games in the 2001–2002 season. The relatively few injuries that occurred in the weight room were not included in the practice and game percentages. It should be noted that these calculations are based only on the absolute number of injuries and do not take exposures into consideration.*

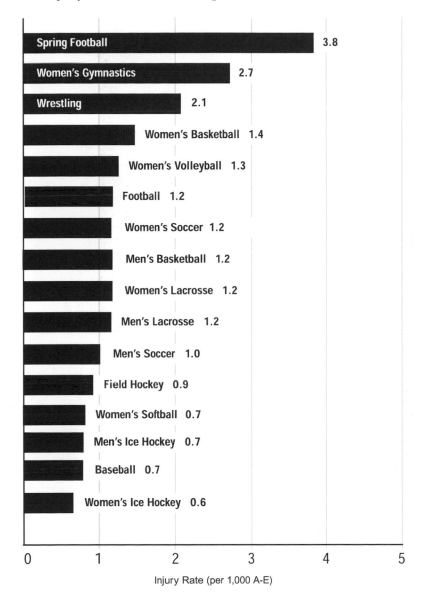

Figure 6.3. Severity—Practice Injuries Resulting In 7+ Days Of Time Loss (Injury Rate). This figure represents a measure of injury severity (time loss) in practice across all sports analyzed in the ISS in the 2001–2002 season. Specifically, the rate of all injuries that caused restricted or missed participation for seven or more days are reported.

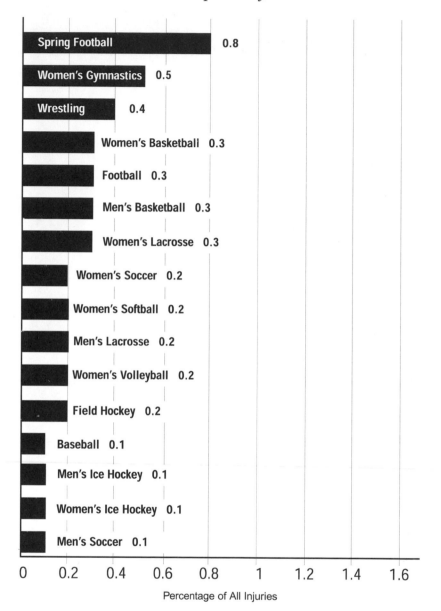

Figure 6.4. Severity—Practice Injuries Requiring Surgery (Injury Rate). This figure represents the practice rate of reported injuries requiring surgery across all sports analyzed in the ISS in the 2001–2002 season.

Chapter 7

Game Injury Rate Across 16 Sports

Figures 7.1 and 7.2 compare the game injuries across 16 sports without regard to severity. Comparisons of injury rates between sports are difficult because each sport has its own unique schedule and activities. If such comparisons are necessary, it may be best to use the game data for which the intensity variable is most consistent.

Figures 7.3 and 7.4 examine two measures of severity found in the NCAA Injury Surveillance System (ISS), time loss and injuries that required surgery. These game data are presented to assist in decision regarding appropriate medical coverage for a sport; however, each severity category has some limitations that should be considered.

*1. **Time Loss**. Figure 7.3 evaluates the game rates of reported injuries that caused restricted or loss of participation of seven days or more. Limitation to this type of severity evaluation include:*

a.   An injury that restricts participation in one sport may not restrict participation in another.

About This Chapter: Text in this chapter is from "Game Comparison Across 16 Sports," excerpted from *2002-2003 NCAA Sports Medicine Handbook*, August 2002, Appendix B–NCAA Injury Surveillance System Summary. Reprinted with permission of the NCAA. This material is subject to periodic review and change.

b. Injuries that occur at an end of the season can only be estimated with regard to time.

2. Injuries That Require Surgery. Figure 7.4 evaluates the game rates of reported injuries that required either immediate or post-season surgery. Limitations to this severity evaluation include:

a. The changing nature of surgical techniques and how they are applied.

b. The assumption that all sports had access to the same quality of medical evaluation.

c. Injuries can occur that may be categorized as severe, such as concussions, which may not require surgery.

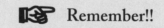 **Remember!!**

The NCAA Injury Surveillance System (ISS) was developed in 1982 to provide current and reliable data on injury trends in intercollegiate athletics. For further information:

NCAA Injury Surveillance System
P.O. Box 6222
Indianapolis, IN 46206
Phone: 317-917-6960
Fax: 317-917-6336
Website: www1.ncaa.org

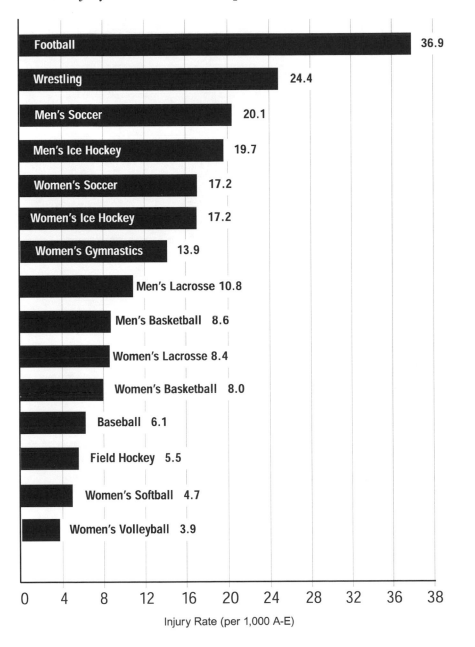

Figure 7.1. Game Injury Rate Summary (All Sports). This figure represents the average game injury rate (expressed as injuries per 1,000 athlete-exposures) for all sports analyzed in the ISS in the 2001–2002 season.

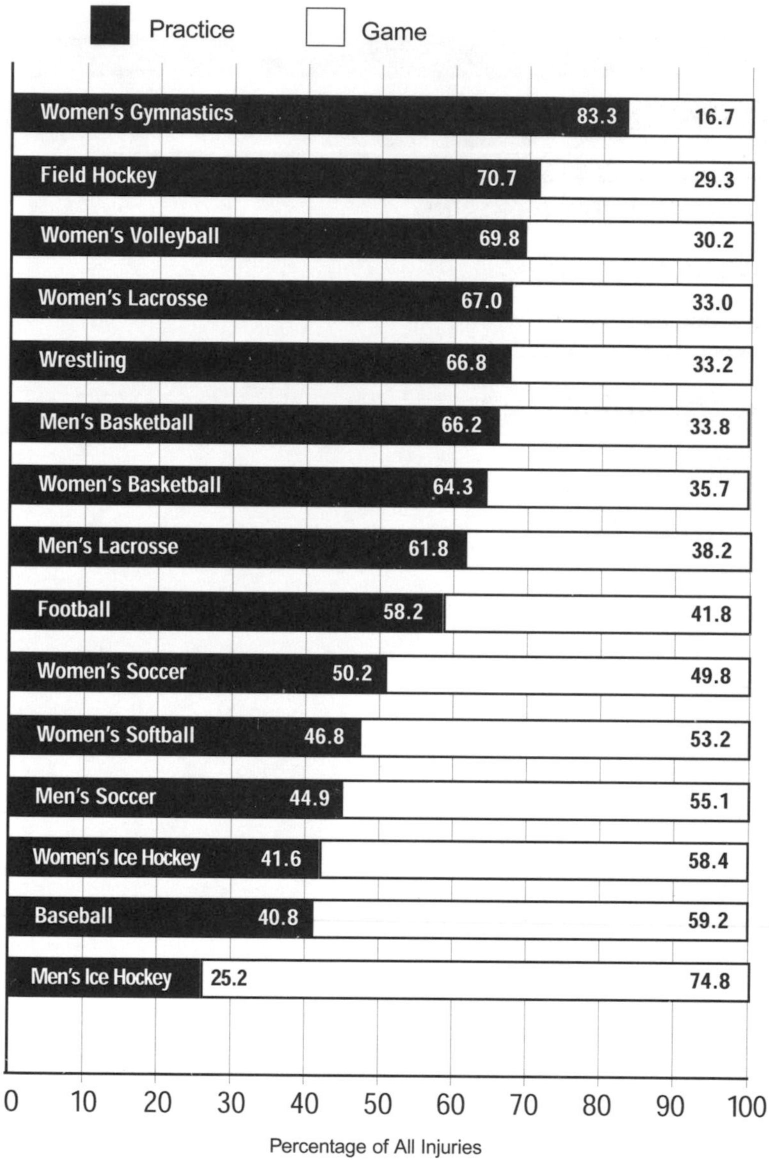

Practice	Game

	Practice	Game
Women's Gymnastics	83.3	16.7
Field Hockey	70.7	29.3
Women's Volleyball	69.8	30.2
Women's Lacrosse	67.0	33.0
Wrestling	66.8	33.2
Men's Basketball	66.2	33.8
Women's Basketball	64.3	35.7
Men's Lacrosse	61.8	38.2
Football	58.2	41.8
Women's Soccer	50.2	49.8
Women's Softball	46.8	53.2
Men's Soccer	44.9	55.1
Women's Ice Hockey	41.6	58.4
Baseball	40.8	59.2
Men's Ice Hockey	25.2	74.8

0   10   20   30   40   50   60   70   80   90   100

Percentage of All Injuries

Figure 7.2. Percentage Of All Injuries Occurring In Practices And Games. This figure represents the percentage of all injuries that occurred in practices and in games in the 2001–2002 season. The relatively few injuries that occurred in the weight room were not included in the practice and game percentages. It should be noted that these calculations are based only on the absolute number of injuries and do not take exposures into consideration.

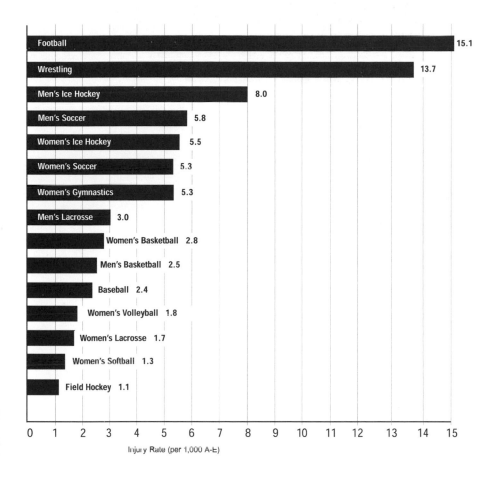

Figure 7.3. Severity—Game Injuries Resulting In 7+ Days Of Time Loss (Injury Rate). This figure also represents the time-loss variable across all sports. Specifically, the game rate of injuries that caused restricted or missed participation for seven or more days is reported.

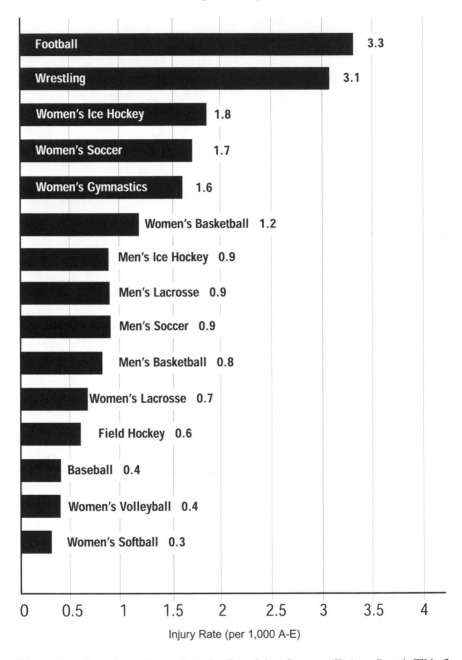

Figure 7.4. *Severity—Game Injuries Requiring Surgery (Injury Rate). This figure represents the game rate of reported injuries requiring surgery.*

Part Two

Emergency Treatment Of Sports Injuries In Teens

Chapter 8

On-Field Examination Of The Conscious Athlete

In Brief

The on-site physician at an athletic event must be able to recognize life-threatening conditions, provide initial care for all conditions, and direct transport if needed. Preparation is critical for avoiding catastrophe; it involves establishing communication and protocol beforehand, as well as developing a mental checklist for assessing injuries. After ensuring an adequate airway, breathing, and circulation, the examiner determines the patient's level of consciousness, mental status and symptoms, and assesses for neck injury. The physician may then need to prepare for emergency transport or for further evaluation on the sidelines.

Evaluation Of The Conscious Athlete

The initial on-field evaluation of a conscious athlete determines the presence of a serious or life-threatening condition. Obtain a brief history and perform a screening physical examination. The athlete should not be allowed to sit up or walk until neck injury has been excluded.

About This Chapter: The text in this chapter is reprinted with permission from Stuart, MJ, "On-field examination and care: An emergency checklist." *The Physician and Sportsmedicine* 1998, 26 (11), 51-55. © 1998 The McGraw-Hill Companies. All rights reserved. Reviewed in June 2003 by David A. Cooke, MD, Diplomate, American Board of Internal Medicine.

Mental status. Assess orientation to person, place, time, and situation (ask the athlete to describe the circumstance of the injury). Check for retrograde amnesia (loss of memory of events immediately before the injury).

Symptoms. Ask about pain, headache, dizziness, nausea, blurred or double vision, and numbness, tingling, or electric-shock sensations in the extremities.

Mechanism of injury. Serious neck injuries (cervical spine fractures and dislocations) are most commonly caused by an axial load to the head with the spine in a flexed position (impact to the top of the head with the chin down).

Rule out neck injury. The athlete should not sit up or walk unless he or she has: no neck pain or tenderness; no pain, feeling of numbness, or tingling sensations in the arms or legs; normal sensation to touch on the chest, arms, hands, legs, and feet; and normal motor function on both sides (can make a fist, bend the elbow, lift the arm, curl the toes, move the ankle up and down, bend the knee, and lift the leg).

> ✔ **Quick Tip**
> On-field examinations of sports injuries are essential to proper treatment and fast recovery. If you are injured, listen carefully and cooperate with the people who are helping you. This is the quickest way to return to play.

Regional physical exam. Briefly examine the area of the athlete's complaint. Check for deformity, swelling, bleeding, tenderness, and active range of motion.

Postural symptoms. Have the athlete sit up, and reassess for dizziness, nausea, pain, or other symptoms. When an athlete sits up, he or she should always do so under his or her own power, rather than be pulled up by helpful bystanders. It is often at this point that the athlete decides not to get up, and the injury is shown to be more serious than previously suspected.

Move to sidelines. If there is no evidence of head, neck, or spine trauma, unstable fractures, or uncontrolled bleeding, the athlete can be helped carefully off the field. If these serious injuries remain a possibility, the athlete should be transported off the field on a spine board.

Helping the athlete to the sidelines may require splinting of an injured extremity and/or assistance with walking to avoid weight bearing. Obtain a more detailed history and physical examination on the sidelines or in the locker room or training room.

Injury Severity

The initial assessment of injury severity will guide further evaluation and treatment (Table 8.1). Mild injuries are treated on site according to first-aid principles. Moderate injuries may preclude immediate return to play. Referral to a specialist is indicated for dental or eye trauma or if there is any question about the type or severity of an injury. Severe injuries require prompt transport to a medical facility for further assessment and care.

Life-threatening injuries demand relevant resuscitation efforts and emergency transportation to the most appropriate trauma care facility available. These conditions include respiratory arrest or irregular breathing, severe chest or abdominal pain, excessive bleeding from a major artery, suspected spinal injury, head injury with prolonged loss of consciousness, fractures or dislocations with no pulse, and any signs of shock or internal hemorrhage.

Suggested Readings

Allman FL, Crow RW: On-field evaluation of sports injuries, in Griffin LY (ed): *Orthopaedic Knowledge Update: Sports Medicine.* Rosemont, IL, American Academy of Orthopaedic Surgeons, 1994, pp 141-149.

☞ Remember!!

An Orderly, Logical Assessment

The first responder at the scene of an athletic injury needs to be able to recognize a life-threatening condition, provide emergency care, and facilitate transportation to a medical facility when indicated. An orderly, logical primary assessment on the field can help identify serious conditions promptly and guide further evaluation and treatment.

Table 8.1. Classification Of Injury Severity

Type Of Injury	Degree Of Injury			
	Mild	Moderate	Severe	Life-Threatening
Skin or penetrating	Abrasion; superficial laceration	Deep laceration without neurovascular or articular involvement	Deep laceration with neurovascular or articular involvement	Major artery laceration
Musculoskeletal	Sprain, strain, or contusion without swelling or loss of motion	Sprain, strain, or contusion with some swelling, pain, and limitation of motion	Sprain, strain, or contusion with marked swelling, pain, and limitation of motion; fracture or dislocation	
Brain or spinal cord	Head trauma with transient confusion (complete resolution in less than 15 minutes)	Concussion with symptoms more than 15 minutes but without loss of consciousness	Concussion with retrograde amnesia or loss of consciousness	Head injury with prolonged loss of consciousness; cervical spine injury with spinal cord involvement
Miscellaneous	Blister	Dental injury		Cardiac arrest; respiratory failure, or airway obstruction

Fox K: Emergency procedures, in Anderson MK, Hall SJ (eds): *Sports Injury Management*. Baltimore, Williams & Wilkins, 1995, pp 57-101.

Hunter-Griffin LY: Emergency assessment of the injured athlete, in *Athletic Training and Sports Medicine*. Park Ridge, IL, American Academy of Orthopaedic Surgeons, 1991, pp 156-166.

Magee DJ: Emergency sports assessment, in Magee DJ: *Orthopedic Physical Assessment*, ed 3. Philadelphia, WB Saunders, 1997, pp 727-757.

—Michael J. Stuart, MD

Dr. Stuart is an associate professor of orthopedic surgery and the co-director of the Mayo Clinic Sports Medicine Center in Rochester, Minnesota.

Dr. Howe, the Emergencies Series editor, is the team physician at Western Washington University in Bellingham and an editorial board member of *The Physician and Sportsmedicine*.

Chapter 9

Meet The Lifesavers: An Introduction To Emergency Medical Services

If you, or someone you know, is ever sick or injured and needs emergency help, remember—there are lots of people who are specially trained to help you get better! Meet some of them here.

Emergency Medical Technicians

Emergency medical technicians, sometimes called EMTs, have different amounts of training depending on their job. Sometimes EMTs are dispatchers who answer calls for help and send ambulances and rescue vehicles to the scene of the emergency. Other EMTs drive the ambulance, assist with rescues, and perform basic emergency medical care.

Paramedics

Paramedics are EMTs with the highest level of training. They are able to perform many medical procedures at the scene of the emergency or in the ambulance on the way to the hospital. Using a radio to communicate, paramedics often get instructions from a doctor at the emergency room or at the base station (the paramedic's headquarters.)

Emergency Nurses

If you were a patient in the emergency room, an emergency nurse would probably the first person you'd see. One of the nurse's jobs is to ask you questions about your problem and to help decide when you can see the doctor. Emergency nurses are specially trained to help treat emergency patients.

Emergency Physicians

Emergency physicians are doctors who are specially trained to take care of a certain type of patient—emergency patients. Doctors who are specially trained are often called specialists. Emergency physicians specialize in helping people who are injured in accidents or who become sick very suddenly such as someone who is having a heart attack or has a very high fever.

✔ Quick Tip
If you are unsure of who is treating you, it is always all right to ask.

Others

Police officers and fire fighters are some of the other people that might help you especially if you had to be rescued.

In Case Of Emergency: Dial 9-1-1

1. **Dial 9-1-1** or your local emergency number. If you don't know the emergency number, dial O for the operator.

2. **Tell** the dispatcher about what happened. Be calm and speak slowly.

    -   Explain the type of emergency.

    -   Give your name and the phone number of the telephone you are using.

    -   Give the exact address of the emergency.

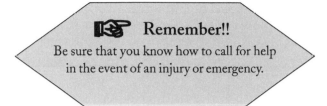

Remember!!
Be sure that you know how to call for help
in the event of an injury or emergency.

3. You'll have to **answer questions** like:

   - Is anyone hurt? How many victims? Is the injured person conscious? Are they breathing? Can the injured people talk?

   - Can they move? Is there a fire? Is anyone trapped?

4. **Listen** to the instructions the dispatcher gives you.

5. **Don't hang up** until the dispatcher tells you to. Don't leave the scene of the emergency until help arrives.

Chapter 10

The Emergency Department: What To Expect

Medical emergencies are unpredictable—people don't expect to have one. You can ease the anxiety of a visit to an emergency department by learning some basic facts.

"First, it's important to know that emergency medicine over the past 30 years has evolved into a state-of-the-art, technologically advanced, fully recognized medical specialty," said Dr. Russell Harris of the American College of Emergency Physicians. "Today's emergency physicians are highly educated and trained to handle all kinds of emergency situations and to provide the best possible care."

Arrival

If you arrive by ambulance or are unconscious you will be assigned a patient bed immediately and will be treated. If someone else drives you to the emergency department, you will first enter the waiting room, where your medical condition will be assessed.

Triage

Most likely, a nurse will determine the severity of your condition based on your symptoms and will check your vital signs, including temperature, heart rate, and blood pressure. This process is called triage.

Additional information will also be obtained, such as your name, address, and medical history, and someone will prepare a chart. Anyone who comes to an emergency department will not be turned away regardless of their ability to pay or insurance coverage.

"There are many reasons a trip to the emergency department can take longer than a visit to the doctor's office," said Dr. Harris. Unlike a doctor's office, where appointments are spread out, many emergency patients may arrive at once. Also unlike a doctor's office, patients often must wait for the results of x-rays or tests. You can help make the time pass more quickly and speed your treatment by planning ahead. Take along a book or something to occupy your attention. If possible, bring along someone to remain at your bedside. Also, bring any up-to-date medical records, including lists of medications and allergies and any advance directives such as a living will.

> ### ☞ Remember!!
>
> Keep in mind that the severity of your injury will determine how quickly you are treated in the emergency department. Life-threatening injuries and illnesses are treated before other perhaps painful, but non-life-threatening injuries.

Examination

Once you are placed in an examination area, an emergency physician will examine you, possibly ordering tests (e.g., x-ray, blood, electrocardiogram) and your vital signs will be monitored. Nurses and other assistants will also assist you during your visit.

Treatment

If you are critically ill or require constant intravenous medications or fluids, you may be admitted to the hospital. Otherwise, an emergency physician will discuss your diagnosis and treatment plan with you before you are discharged. You may also receive written instructions regarding medications, medical restrictions, or symptoms that may require a return visit.

"Every year almost 100 million people seek care in the nation's emergency departments, making the ED American's health care safety net—available 24 hours a day, 7 days a week—treating patients from all walks of life—rich and poor, young and old, insured and uninsured," added Dr. Harris.

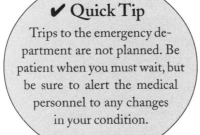

✔ **Quick Tip**
Trips to the emergency department are not planned. Be patient when you must wait, but be sure to alert the medical personnel to any changes in your condition.

Chapter 11

Common Diagnostic Procedures For Injuries Teen Athletes Experience

Athletes who suffer a moderate to severe injury should see an orthopaedist to receive a professional diagnosis and the necessary proper medical care. Prompt medical care following a sports-related injury can limit the extent of damage and significantly reduce the recovery period. Some commonly used diagnostic tools and treatment procedures follow.

Non-Invasive Diagnostic Procedures

Clinical Examination is done to assess the history of an injury, as well as the structure and function of the injured area. Orthopaedists conduct an exam to determine how the injury occurred, the degree of pain and swelling, the stability of the joint, and the range of motion. This information helps the physician determine the site, extent, and nature of an injury.

Computerized Tomography (CT) is a computerized diagnostic imaging tool used to obtain information about the body. The information is presented as an image generated by a computer that synthesizes x-rays obtained from many different directions. CT is particularly useful for detecting hidden bone injuries or soft tissue masses that may not be detected by simple x-ray.

Magnetic Resonance Imaging (MRI) is another computerized procedure in which the patient's body is placed in a magnetic field. The effects of the field on the tissue can then be measured. This technique does not involve radiation like conventional x-rays or CT scans and can provide a very accurate and detailed image of an injured area.

Ultrasound Imaging uses sound waves to produce images that aid physicians in the diagnosis of injuries. This does not involve the use of radiation, but generally is not as specific as the MRI. Ultrasound is frequently used to assess rotator cuff injuries.

> ✔ **Quick Tip**
> Anytime you need medical treatment, make sure you understand what will happen during diagnostic procedures so that you can cooperate and get the test results that will help the doctor make treatment decisions.

X-Ray Machines use electromagnetic radiation x-rays to create an image of an injury. X-rays are helpful in determining the extent of injuries primarily to the bone and, to some extent, the soft tissue.

Invasive Diagnostic Procedures

Arthrography involves injecting a contrast dye into a joint and taking an x-ray to determine the exact site and extent of an injury within the joint. It is typically used when there is a suspicion of a ruptured ligament or torn cartilage in the knee or a torn rotator cuff in the shoulder. It may be performed on other joints as well.

Arthroscopy involves inserting a fiber optic device connected to a camera through a small incision to examine the interior of a joint. Arthroscopy is frequently used to confirm the surgeon's clinical diagnosis and then to perform surgical procedures if they are indicated in the joint.

Surgical Treatment

Arthroplasty is a surgical procedure used to help stabilize or improve the function of a joint. In some cases, arthroplasty refers to procedures used to repair torn ligaments or the capsule around a joint, as in the shoulder to tighten the capsule for a shoulder that dislocates. It also may refer to the use of artificial materials such as metal alloys or plastics to create a new or artificial joint to help restore the range of motion and functional strength to the joint.

Arthroscopy is a common procedure used both for diagnostic and surgical procedures. It can be used to repair or remove torn cartilage or remove bone or cartilage fragments from the joint and assist in repairing certain ligament injuries. Arthroscopy is the least invasive form of surgery and is often performed on an outpatient basis.

Open Repair Reconstructive Surgery is a procedure that requires a larger incision than arthroscopy so that the orthopaedist can assess and repair a serious injury. Open surgery is commonly used to repair ligament injuries around the joint and bone fractures that require the insertion of screws and metal plates.

Immobilization

Immobilization is a common treatment for sports-related injuries. Immobilization helps an injury settle and allows the healing process to begin. Immobilization helps control the blood supply to the injury which reduces pain and swelling. Methods of immobilization include the use of hard casts, soft casts, splints, slings and leg immobilizers.

Hard casts are made of plaster or plastic and are used to immobilize serious injuries including broken bones and severe sprains.

Soft casts (bandage wraps) are used to provide compression to an injury which helps control and reduce swelling.

Splints and slings are often used to immobilize injuries to the upper body including the arms and shoulders. Splints and slings hold an injury stationary until the range of motion returns to the joint.

Leg immobilizers are devices that immobilize the leg after a knee injury. As with other immobilization techniques, the leg immobilizers help an injury settle and speed healing.

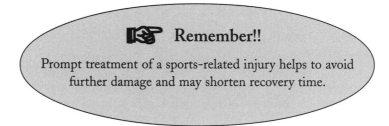

☞ Remember!!

Prompt treatment of a sports-related injury helps to avoid further damage and may shorten recovery time.

Chapter 12

Family Member Presence In The Emergency Department

Main Points

- Family member presence in an emergency department is the practice of allowing a patient's family member to stay in the treatment area while a patient is resuscitated or undergoes a medical procedure.

- Hospital policy determines whether or not a family member can be present during a medical procedure. Most hospitals that allow family member presence require a nurse or social worker to remain with the family member, especially during a resuscitation, to explain what is happening.

- The presence of family members generally is well-received in controlled environments, although the practice is new and its role in emergency medicine remains controversial.

- Family presence during labor and delivery is routine at most hospitals, while other hospitals are experimenting with it. Like all new concepts, family presence has its supporters and critics.

About This Book: The text in this chapter is from, "Family Member Presence in the Emergency Department," © 2003 American College of Emergency Physicians®, reprinted with permission. The American College of Emergency Physicians is a national medical society representing more than 19,000 physicians who specialize in emergency medicine.

- Care of the patient is the primary goal of emergency physicians, nurses, and technicians, as well as the patient's family.

- Family presence should never be forced on either the family or the emergency staff.

What Is Family Member Presence In The Emergency Department?

Family member presence generally refers to the practice of having a patient's family members remain in the treatment area during various medical or surgical procedures, such as resuscitation. Exactly which actions or procedures define this practice vary and are specific to each emergency department. Many hospitals have always allowed family members to remain with their children or spouses during emergency department visits for minor problems.

Should Family Members Remain During Resuscitations Or Emergency Procedures?

Yes and no. The acceptability of family members under such circumstances is based on the family's wish to remain with their loved one, the opinions of medical personnel, the reactions of family members and patients, the nature of the emergency, and the hospital's policy.

Just as the science of medicine is constantly changing, so too is the relationship between health care personnel and patients and their families. Patients and family members who in the past simply accepted the treatment plans prescribed by their physicians, now are invited to participate in all aspects of their medical care. With this increased involvement in medical decision-making has come a related increase in the presence of families during the actual delivery of medical care.

> **✔ Quick Tip**
> If you are a patient in the emergency department, you may ask for a family member to be with you during medical procedures. Sometimes one of the staff members will stay with you during a procedure if it is not appropriate for a family member to stay.

In most hospitals that allow family presence, family members do not ask to remain; they simply are never asked to leave. In other hospitals, a family member may simply request to stay in order to remain. In some circumstances, medical personnel may sense uneasiness in family members and ask them to step outside to help them leave without feeling guilt for abandoning their loved one. Family members should never be forced to remain in the treatment area.

The views of medical personnel about the presence of family can affect the appropriateness of this practice. Optimal care of the patient is the first goal of emergency physicians, nurses, and technicians, as well as the patient's family.

Therefore, if emergency personnel are sufficiently uncomfortable with the presence of family members—to the point it might impact their performance—then family members should not be present. Just as it should not be forced on a patient's family, it should not be forced on an emergency medical team.

The nature of a patient's problem also can dictate the appropriateness of family presence. For example, procedures which unduly expose the patient may prove embarrassing to both family members and patients. Some hospitals regulate family presence based on the criticality of the patient or intervention, limiting the presence of family members to only minor procedures on stable patients. Other emergency departments adopt the opposite philosophy, based on the belief that the more unstable the patient, the greater the need for family members to be present.

A survey of 400 parents, published in the July 1999 issue of *Annals of Emergency Medicine* found that most would want to be present when invasive procedures are performed on their children, with parental desire decreasing as procedural invasiveness increased.

Does The Presence Of Family Members Help?

The impact of family members in the treatment area is difficult to study objectively. To date, there is limited evidence that family members may relieve anxiety in children undergoing minor medical procedures. Although there are no data showing that a family member's presence has impacted a patient's response to treatment, particularly in critical cases, there is good evidence the practice has beneficial effects on family members themselves. In fact, relatives who have remained with loved ones during care have expressed great appreciation for the efforts of emergency teams, better understanding that truly dedicated efforts were made, and more rapid closure with patients who don't survive. Almost universally, studies questioning family members who have remained in treatment areas during resuscitations or procedures have strongly favored the practice.

✔ Quick Tip

The actions of family members can affect the feasibility of family presence. Those who remain in a room quietly, or stand at a bedside and soothe or encourage a loved one, will not be a distraction to an emergency team. However, outbursts of hysterical behavior, physical interference with medical actions, or other types of disruptive behavior may require a family member to leave the room. Similarly, if a patient is agitated by the presence of a family member, then that person should leave.

Are There Any Downsides To Family Member Presence?

Like everything in medicine, nothing is absolute. There can be drawbacks to the presence of family members during resuscitations and emergency procedures. For example, family members remaining with patients have collapsed during relatively minor procedures; some have been seriously injured, requiring medical assistance and care themselves. Even such medically mundane activities as insertion of intravenous catheters or simple laceration repairs have produced episodes of fainting in parents or spouses. Unfortunately, in some high-profile cases, people have successfully sued hospitals and health care providers over these instances.

In other cases, family members have witnessed actions they felt were below the standard of care and used this as a basis for legal actions. Health care providers, and emergency department personnel in particular, are at higher risk for such claims as a result of the nature of emergency medicine. Such instances are rare, although even a single event can discourage a hospital from permitting the practice.

The presence of family members can also present a problem in teaching centers. Instruction of inexperienced students or physicians in training programs must be done tactfully when relatives are present at the bedside.

How Do Emergency Departments Decide To Permit Family Member Presence?

The presence of family members in emergency departments is a relatively new practice. Although the presence of families has always been the standard at some hospitals, it has only been in the past 5 years that it has been openly discussed in the medical literature.

Except in hospitals that have policies against it, the decision whether to allow relatives to remain often is made on a case-by-case basis. All the factors presented above must be considered, as well as the personalities and preferences of family members and medical personnel.

Research in this area has demonstrated that physicians and nurses with the most experience with this practice tend to favor its use in emergency departments, while those with limited or no experience would rather avoid it. As expected, residents in training are also more opposed to having family members present during a procedure than are attending emergency physicians.

Like all new concepts, family presence has its supporters and critics. Some physicians believe it should be mandated in every department, while others believe it should be prohibited. With strong feelings and good supporting arguments on both sides of this issue, it's not surprising there is no universal approach to family presence in all hospitals.

What Happens When Disagreement Occurs?

Occasionally, family members and medical personnel may disagree over the appropriateness of their presence. If time permits, or it involves an upcoming procedure, then discussions can be held with hospital personnel. However, in emergency situations, this generally is not an option, and decisions must be made in a timely fashion.

The first priority in any such disagreement is the patient's care. Delays in care should not occur because of arguments about relatives remaining in the room. If a family member must be removed from a treatment area, often the need for such a drastic measure can be addressed after the patient is stabilized. However, these disagreements are rare, and generally there is time for a brief discussion to resolve both family member and medical personnel concerns.

In most instances, an open dialogue between the attending physician and the family will lead to a rapid resolution of the disagreement or an agreeable compromise. Even when medical personnel feel strongly it is inappropriate for family members to be present, assurance the family will be permitted to return to the bedside as soon as the procedure is completed often alleviates concerns.

Are There Any Rules To Govern Family Member Behavior During A Resuscitation?

The only behavioral rule governing family presence is no interference with the care of the patient. Disruptive behavior, whether verbal or physical, will not be permitted under any circumstances in any emergency resuscitation. If a family member does not feel he or she can maintain control, he or she can ask to be escorted from the resuscitation area but permitted to return at any time their condition changes.

Lack of interference does not imply lack of interaction. Provided it does not impede access to the patient, family members generally are encouraged to speak with, touch, comfort, and soothe emergency patients as appropriate. Emergency personnel will provide guidance as to the degree of physical interaction that will be helpful. Questions of emergency staff are encouraged, because this helps family members understand what is happening. The timing of such questions or the length of answers will vary depending on the status of the medical procedure.

How Should Family Members Decide Whether To Remain?

Family members generally do not have to make a formal decision about remaining during a resuscitation or emergency procedure; they simply follow their instincts. It's a personal decision. Frequently, some family members want to stay and others do not. In fact, it's common for some family members to remain in the treatment area, some to remain in the waiting area, and still others to wander between the two. There are advantages and disadvantages to both approaches. What's important is for emergency personnel to make family members feel comfortable with whatever decision they make.

☞ **Remember!!**

Providing the best care for the patient is to goal of the emergency room staff. Family members can be an important part of helping the patient when they work with the emergency room staff.

Chapter 13

Nonfatal Activity-Related Injuries Treated in Emergency Departments

Each year in the United States, an estimated 30 million children and adolescents participate in organized sports,[1] and approximately 150 million adults participate in some type of nonwork-related physical activity.[2] Engaging in these activities has numerous health benefits but involves a risk for injury. The Centers for Disease Control and Prevention (CDC) analyzed data from the National Electronic Injury Surveillance System All Injury Program (NEISS-AIP) to characterize sports- and recreation-related injuries among the U.S. population. This chapter summarizes the results of that analysis, which indicate that during July 2000-June 2001 an estimated 4.3 million nonfatal sports- and recreation-related injuries were treated in U.S. hospital emergency departments. Injury rates varied by sex and age and were highest for boys aged 10-14 years. Effective prevention strategies, including those tailored to specific activities and those aimed at children, adolescents, and adults, are needed to reduce sports- and recreation-related injuries in the United States.

About This Chapter: Text in this chapter is excerpted from "Nonfatal Sports- and Recreation-Related Injuries Treated in Emergency Departments–United States, July 2000-June 2001," *MMWR Weekly*, August 23, 2002; 51 (33); 736-740, Centers for Disease Control and Prevention (CDC).

NEISS-AIP is operated by the U.S. Consumer Product Safety Commission (CPSC) and collects data on initial visits for all types and causes of injuries treated in U.S. emergency departments.

Sports- and recreation-related injuries included those occurring during organized and unorganized activities, whether work-related or not. An injury was defined as bodily harm resulting from exposure to an external force or substance. Each case was classified into one of 39 mutually exclusive sports- and recreation-related groups based on an algorithm that considered both the consumer products involved (e.g., bicycles or accessories, swings or swing sets, or in-line skating [activity, apparel, or equipment]), and the narrative description of the incident.

During July 2000-June 2001, an estimated 4.3 million sports- and recreation-related injuries were treated in U.S. hospital emergency departments, comprising 16% of all unintentional injury-related ED visits (Tables 13.1 and 13.2). The percentage of all unintentional injury-related ED visits that were sports- and recreation-related was highest for persons aged 10-14 years (51.5% for boys, 38.0% for girls), and lowest for persons aged greater than 45 years (6.4% for men, 3.1% for women). The overall rate of sports- and recreation-related injuries was 15.4 per 1,000 population (Table 13.1 and 13.2). Rates were highest among persons aged 10-14 years (75.4 for boys, 36.3 for girls). Among all ages, rates were higher for males than for females.

> ## ♣ It's A Fact!!
>
> The most frequent injury diagnoses from June 2000 – July 2001 were
>
> - strains/sprains (29.1%),
> - fractures (20.5%),
> - contusions/abrasions (20.1%), and
> - lacerations (13.8%;).
>
> The body parts injured most commonly were
>
> - ankles (12.1%),
> - fingers (9.5%),
> - face (9.2%),
> - head (8.2%), and
> - knees (8.1%).
>
> Of an estimated 350,734 persons with sports- and recreation-related head injuries, approximately 199,050 had a brain injury diagnosed (i.e., diagnosis of concussion or internal injury). Overall, 2.3% of persons with sports- and recreation-related injuries were hospitalized.

Types of sports- and recreation related activities in which persons were engaged when injured varied by age and sex. For males aged 10-19 years, football-, basketball-, and bicycle-related injuries were most common. For females aged 10-19 years, basketball-related injuries ranked highest. For persons aged 20-24 years, basketball- and bicycle-related injuries ranked among the three leading types of injuries. Exercise (e.g., weight lifting, aerobics, stretching, walking, jogging, and running) was the leading injury-related activity for women 20 years and over and ranked among the top four types of injuries for men 20 years and over.

Editorial Note

This report indicates that an estimated 4.3 million sports- and recreation-related injuries are treated each year in U.S. emergency departments (EDs). These injuries occur among all population groups and account for more ED visits annually than injuries involving motor-vehicle occupants (3.5 million).

The findings in this report are subject to at least five limitations.

1. First, injury rates were based on the U.S. population; data on exposure time or frequency of participation were not collected. Because of the lack of exposure data, these estimates cannot be used to compare relative risks for different sports or for different age groups or sexes.

2. Second, NEISS-AIP captures only injuries treated in hospital emergency departments.

3. Third, it could not be determined whether a sports- and recreation-related injury was a new injury or an aggravation of an injury sustained previously.

4. Fourth, NEISS-AIP narrative descriptions do not provide detailed information about injury circumstances (e.g., whether or not the activity was organized, whether the injury occurred during training or competition, or whether protective equipment was used).

5. Finally, NEISS-AIP is designed to provide national estimates but not state or local estimates.

Table 13.1. Number and percentage* of males with nonfatal unintentional sports- and recreation-related injuries treated in emergency departments by rank, activity, and age group.

Age Rank	10-14 yrs No. (%)	15-19 yrs No. (%)	20-24 yrs No. (%)
1	Football 144,907 (18.7)	Basketball 168,691 (25.9)	Basketball 85,056 (29.1)
2	Bicycle 123,764 (16.0)	Football 138,689 (21.3)	Bicycle 29,112 (9.9)
3	Basketball 117,807 (15.2)	Bicycle 52,937 (8.1)	Football 26,439 (9.0)
4	Baseball 47,546 (6.1)	Soccer 30,222 (4.6)	Exercise 17,504 (6.0)
5	Skateboarding 39,271 (5.1)	Combative 28,616 (4.4)	ATV 13,520 (4.6)
6	Soccer 29,049 (3.7)	Baseball 26,679 (4.1)	Soccer 11,061 (3.8)
7	Scooter 25,752 (3.3)	Exercise 24,892 (3.8)	Combative 10,859 (3.7)
8	Playground 20,994 (2.7)	Skateboarding 23,476 (3.6)	Softball 10,294 (3.5)
Other***	226,848 (29.2)	156,228 (24.0)	88,898 (30.4)
Total	775,938	650,430	292,743

*Numbers are national estimates of nonfatal sports-and recreation-related injuries for each age group.

***Comprises 31 other sports and recreation categories.

☞ **Remember!!**

Studies and statistics are only helpful if we apply what we learn. Don't become a sports-related injury statistic. Sports-related injuries may be prevented by using safety equipment and following the rules of the game.

> ### ✔ Quick Tip
> The benefits of physical activity are substantial; however, persons engaging in such activity should be aware of their risk for injury.

Table 13.2. Number and percentage* of females with nonfatal unintentional sports- and recreation-related injuries treated in emergency departments by rank, activity, and age group.

Age Rank	10-14 yrs No. (%)	15-19 yrs No. (%)	20-24 yrs No. (%)
1	Basketball 53,130 (14.9)	Basketball 37,674 (18.1)	Exercise 10,202 (13.2)
2	Bicycle 38,889 (10.9)	Gymnastics 21,865 (10.5)	Bicycle 7,429 (9.6)
3	Soccer 28,137 (7.9)	Soccer 19,865 (9.6)	Basketball 60,777 (7.8)
4	Gymnastics 23,183 (6.5)	Softball 17,040 (8.2)	Gymnastics 5,307 (6.9)
5	Softball 19,886 (5.6)	Volleyball 12,202 (5.9)	Softball 4,017 (5.2)
6	Scooter 16,127 (4.5)	Exercise 10,652 (5.1)	Horseback 3,035 (3.9)
7	Playground 16,000 (4.5)	Bicycle 10,275 (4.9)	Misc. ball games 3,016** (3.9)
8	Trampoline 13,610 (3.8)	Football 6,711 (3.2)	Swimming 2,826** (3.7)
Other***	146,988 (41.3)	71,376 (34.4)	35,507 (45.9)
Total	355,950	207,660	77,416

*Numbers are national estimates of nonfatal sports-and recreation-related injuries for each age group.

**Estimates might be unstable because the coefficient f variation is greater than 30%.

***Comprises 31 other sports and recreation categories.

This report was based on data contributed by T. Schroeder, MS, C. Downs, A. McDonald, MA, and other staff of the Div. of Hazard and Injury Data Systems, U.S. Consumer Product Safety Commission; and with the assistance of L. Doll, PhD, E. Sogolow, PhD, G. Ryan, PhD, National Center for Injury Prevention and Control, CDC.

References

1. National Institute of Health. *Conference on sports injuries in youth: surveillance strategies, 1991.* Bethesda, Maryland: National Institute of Health, 1992; NIH publication no. 93-3444.

2. CDC. *2000 Behavioral Risk Factor Surveillance System.* Available at: http://www.cdc.gov/brfss.

3. CDC. National estimates of nonfatal injuries treated in hospital emergency departments–United States, 2000. *MMWR* 2001;50:340-6.

4. Thompson RS, Rivara FP, Thompson DC. A case-control study of the effectiveness of bicycle safety helmets. *N Engl J Med* 1989;320:1361-7.

5. Janda DH, Bir C, Kedroske B. A comparison of standard vs. breakaway bases: an analysis of a preventative intervention for softball and baseball foot and ankle injuries. *Foot & Ankle International* 2001;22:810-6.

6. Burt CW, Overpeck MD. Emergency visits for sports-related injuries. *Ann Emerg Med* 2001;37:301-8.

7. Warner M, Barnes PM, Fingerhut LA. Injury and poisoning episodes and conditions: *National Health Interview Survey*, 1997. Vital Health Stat 2000;10(202).

8. U.S. Department of Health and Human Services. Healthy people 2010, 2nd ed. *With understanding and improving health and objectives for improving health* (2 vols). Washington, DC: U.S. Department of Health and Human Services, 2000.

Part Three

Sports Injuries That Commonly Affect Active Teens

Chapter 14

Cuts, Scrapes, And Stitches

How Should I Clean A Wound?

The best way to clean a cut, scrape, or puncture wound (such as from a nail) is with cool water. You can hold the wound under running water or fill a tub with cool water and pour it from a cup over the wound.

Use soap and a soft washcloth to clean the skin around the wound. Try to keep soap out of the wound itself because soap can cause irritation. Use tweezers that have been cleaned in isopropyl alcohol to remove any dirt that remains in the wound after washing.

Even though it may seem that you should use a stronger cleansing solution (such as hydrogen peroxide or an antiseptic), these things may irritate wounds. Ask your family doctor if you feel you must use something other than water.

Should I Use A Bandage?

Leaving a wound uncovered helps it stay dry and helps it heal. If the wound isn't in an area that will get dirty or be rubbed by clothing, you don't have to cover it.

About This Chapter: Text for this chapter is reprinted with permission from *Cuts, Scrapes, and Stitches: Caring For Wounds*, an AAFP Family Health Facts brochure, 2002. Copyright © American Academy of Family Physicians. All Rights Reserved.

If it's in an area that will get dirty (such as your hand) or be irritated by clothing (such as your knee), cover it with an adhesive strip (Band-Aid) or with sterile gauze and adhesive tape. Change the bandage each day to keep the wound clean and dry.

Certain wounds, such as scrapes that cover a large area of the body, should be kept moist and clean to help reduce scarring and speed healing. Bandages used for this purpose are called occlusive or semiocclusive bandages. You can buy them in drug stores without a prescription. Your family doctor will tell you if he or she thinks this type of bandage is best for you.

Should I Use An Antibiotic Ointment?

Antibiotic ointments (such as Bacitracin) help healing by keeping out infection and by keeping the wound clean and moist. A bandage does pretty much the same thing. If you have stitches, your doctor will tell you whether he or she wants you to use an antibiotic ointment. Most minor cuts and scrapes will heal just fine without antibiotic ointment, but it can speed healing and help reduce scarring.

What Should I Do About Scabs?

Nothing. Scabs are the body's way of bandaging itself. They form to protect wounds from dirt. It's best to leave them alone and not pick at them. They will fall off by themselves when the time is right.

When Should I Call My Doctor?

You can close small cuts yourself with special tape, called butterfly tape, or special adhesive strips, such as Steri-Strips.

Call your doctor if your wound is deep, if you can't get the edges to stay together, or if the edges are jagged. Your doctor may want to close your wound with stitches or skin adhesive. These things can help reduce the amount of scarring.

How Do I Take Care Of Stitches?

You can usually wash an area that has been stitched in one to three days. Washing off dirt and the crust that may form around the stitches helps reduce scarring. If the wound drains clear yellow fluid, you may need to cover it.

Your doctor may suggest that you rinse the wound with water and rebandage it in 24 hours. Be sure to dry it well after washing. You may want to keep the wound elevated above your heart for the first day or two to help lessen swelling, reduce pain, and speed healing.

Your doctor may also suggest using a small amount of antibiotic ointment to prevent infection. The ointment also keeps a heavy scab from forming and may reduce the size of a scar.

Stitches are usually removed in 3 to 14 days, depending on where the cut is located. Areas that move, such as over or around the joints, require more time to heal.

What Is Skin Adhesive?

Skin adhesive (such as Dermabond) is a new way to close small wounds. Your doctor will apply a liquid film to your wound and let it dry. The film holds the edges of your wound together. You can leave the film on your skin until it falls off (usually in 5 to 10 days).

It's important not to scratch or pick at the adhesive on your wound. If your doctor puts a bandage over the adhesive, you should be careful to keep the bandage dry. Your doctor will probably ask you to change the bandage every day.

Don't put any ointment, including antibiotic ointment, on your wound when the skin adhesive is in place. This could cause the adhesive to loosen and fall off too soon. You should also keep your wound out of direct light (such as sunlight or tanning booth lamps).

Keep an eye on your wound. If the skin around your wound becomes very red and warm to touch, or if the wound reopens, call your doctor.

Do I Need A Tetanus Shot?

Tetanus is a serious infection you can get after a wound. The infection is also called lockjaw, because stiffness of the jaw is the most frequent symptom.

To prevent tetanus infection when the wound is clean and minor, you'll need a tetanus shot if you haven't had at least three doses before or haven't had a dose in the last 10 years.

When the wound is more serious, you'll need a tetanus shot if you haven't had at least 3 doses before or if you haven't had a shot in the last 5 years. The best way to avoid tetanus infection is to talk to your family doctor to make sure your shots are up to date.

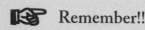 **Remember!!**

Call Your Family Doctor If Any Of The Following Things Occur

- The wound is jagged.

- The wound is on your face.

- The edges of the cut gape open.

- The cut has dirt in it that won't come out.

- The cut becomes tender or inflamed.

- The cut drains a thick, creamy, grayish fluid.

- You start to run a temperature over 100° F.

- The area around the wound feels numb.

- You can't move comfortably.

- Red streaks form near the wound.

- It's a puncture wound or a deep cut and you haven't had a tetanus shot in the past 5 years.

- The cut bleeds in spurts, blood soaks through the bandage or the bleeding doesn't stop after 10 minutes of firm, direct pressure.

Chapter 15

Strains And Sprains

What Causes A Sprain?

A sprain can result from a fall, a sudden twist, or a blow to the body that forces a joint out of its normal position. This results in an overstretch or tear of the ligament supporting that joint. Typically, sprains occur when people fall and land on an outstretched arm, slide into base, land on the side of their foot, or twist a knee with the foot planted firmly on the ground.

Where Do Sprains Usually Occur?

Although sprains can occur in both the upper and lower parts of the body, the most common site is the ankle. Ankle sprains are the most common injury in the United States and often occur during sports or recreational activities. Approximately 1 million ankle injuries occur each year, and 85 percent of them are sprains.

The talus bone and the ends of two of the lower leg bones (tibia and fibula) form the ankle joint (see Figure 15.1). This joint is supported by several lateral (outside) ligaments and medial (inside) ligaments. Most ankle sprains happen when the foot turns inward as a person runs, turns, falls, or

About This Chapter: Text in this chapter is from "Questions and Answers About Sprains And Strains," National Institute of Arthritis and Musculoskeletal and Skin Diseases (NIAMS), March 1999.

✎ Weird Words

Acute: An illness or injury that lasts for a short time and may be intense.

Chronic: An illness or injury that lasts for a long time.

Femur: The upper leg or thigh bone, which extends into the hip socket at its upper end and down to the knee at its lower end.

Fibula: The thin, outer bone of the leg that forms part of the ankle joint at its lower end.

Inflammation: A characteristic reaction of tissues to disease or injury. It is marked by four signs: swelling, redness, heat, and pain.

Joint: A junction where two bones meet.

Ligament: A band of tough, fibrous tissue that connects two or more bones at a joint and prevents excessive movement of the joint.

Muscle: Tissue composed of bundles of specialized cells that contract and produce movement when stimulated by nerve impulses.

Range Of Motion: The arc of movement of a joint from one extreme position to the other. Range-of-motion exercises help increase or maintain flexibility and movement in muscles, tendons, ligaments, and joints.

Sprain: An injury to a ligament—a stretching or a tearing. One or more ligaments can be injured during a sprain. The severity of the injury will depend on the extent of injury to a single ligament (whether the tear is partial or complete) and the number of ligaments involved.

Strain: An injury to either a muscle or a tendon. Depending on the severity of the injury, a strain may be a simple overstretch of the muscle or tendon, or it can result in a partial or complete tear.

Tendons: Tough, fibrous cords of tissue that connect muscle to bone.

Tibia: The thick, long bone of the lower leg (also called the shin) that forms part of the knee joint at its upper end and the ankle joint at its lower end.

lands on the ankle after a jump. This type of sprain is called an inversion injury. One or more of the lateral ligaments are injured, usually the anterior talofibular ligament. The calcaneofibular ligament is the second most frequently torn ligament.

The knee is another common site for a sprain. A blow to the knee or a fall is often the cause; sudden twisting can also result in a sprain (see Figure 15.2).

Sprains frequently occur at the wrist, typically when people fall and land on an outstretched hand.

What Are The Signs And Symptoms Of A Sprain?

The usual signs and symptoms include pain, swelling, bruising, and loss of the ability to move and use the joint (called functional ability). However, these signs and symptoms can vary in intensity, depending on the severity of the sprain. Sometimes people feel a pop or tear when the injury happens.

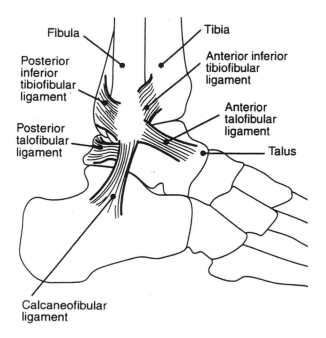

Figure 15.1. Lateral View Of The Ankle

Doctors use many criteria to diagnose the severity of a sprain. In general, a grade I or mild sprain causes overstretching or slight tearing of the ligaments with no joint instability. A person with a mild sprain usually experiences minimal pain, swelling, and little or no loss of functional ability. Bruising is absent or slight, and the person is usually able to put weight on the affected joint. People with mild sprains usually do not need an x-ray, but one is sometimes performed if the diagnosis is unclear.

A grade II or moderate sprain causes partial tearing of the ligament and is characterized by bruising, moderate pain, and swelling. A person with a moderate sprain usually has some difficulty putting weight on the affected joint and experiences some loss of function. An x-ray may be needed to help the doctor determine if a fracture is causing the pain and swelling. Magnetic resonance imaging is occasionally used to help differentiate between a significant partial injury and a complete tear in a ligament.

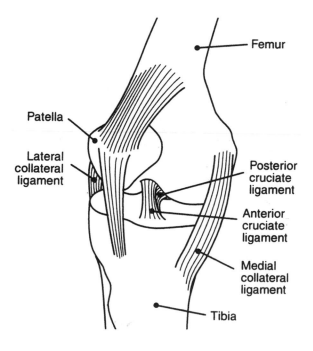

Figure 15.2. Lateral View Of The Knee

✔ Quick Tip

When To See A Doctor For A Sprain

- You have severe pain and cannot put any weight on the injured joint.

- The area over the injured joint or next to it is very tender when you touch it.

- The injured area looks crooked or has lumps and bumps (other than swelling) that you do not see on the uninjured joint.

- You cannot move the injured joint.

- You cannot walk more than four steps without significant pain.

- Your limb buckles or gives way when you try to use the joint.

- You have numbness in any part of the injured area.

- You see redness or red streaks spreading out from the injury.

- You injure an area that has been injured several times before.

- You have pain, swelling, or redness over a bony part of your foot.

- You are in doubt about the seriousness of the injury or how to care for it.

People who sustain a grade III or severe sprain completely tear or rupture a ligament. Pain, swelling, and bruising are usually severe, and the patient is unable to put weight on the joint. An x-ray is usually taken to rule out a broken bone. When diagnosing any sprain, the doctor will ask the patient to explain how the injury happened. The doctor will examine the affected joint and check its stability and its ability to move and bear weight.

What Causes A Strain?

A strain is caused by twisting or pulling a muscle or tendon. Strains can be acute or chronic. An acute strain is caused by trauma or an injury such as a blow to the body; it can also be caused by improperly lifting heavy objects or overstressing the muscles. Chronic strains are usually the result of overuse—prolonged, repetitive movement of the muscles and tendons.

Where Do Strains Usually Occur?

Two common sites for a strain are the back and the hamstring muscle (located in the back of the thigh). Contact sports such as soccer, football, hockey, boxing, and wrestling put people at risk for strains. Gymnastics, tennis, rowing, golf, and other sports that require extensive gripping can increase the risk of hand and forearm strains. Elbow strains sometimes occur in people who participate in racquet sports, throwing, and contact sports.

What Are The Signs And Symptoms Of A Strain?

Typically, people with a strain experience pain, muscle spasm, and muscle weakness. They can also have localized swelling, cramping, or inflammation, and with a minor or moderate strain, usually some loss of muscle function.

♣ It's A Fact!!

RICE Therapy

Rest

Reduce regular exercise or activities of daily living as needed. Your doctor may advise you to put no weight on an injured area for 48 hours. If you cannot put weight on an ankle or knee, crutches may help. If you use a cane or one crutch for an ankle injury, use it on the uninjured side to help you lean away and relieve weight on the injured ankle.

Ice

Apply an ice pack to the injured area for 20 minutes at a time, 4 to 8 times a day. A cold pack, ice bag, or plastic bag filled with crushed ice and wrapped in a towel can be used. To avoid cold injury and frostbite, do not apply the ice for more than 20 minutes.

Compression

Compression of an injured ankle, knee, or wrist may help reduce swelling. Examples of compression bandages are elastic wraps, special boots, air casts, and splints. Ask your doctor for advice on which one to use.

Elevation

If possible, keep the injured ankle, knee, elbow, or wrist elevated on a pillow, above the level of the heart, to help decrease swelling.

Patients typically have pain in the injured area and general weakness of the muscle when they attempt to move it. Severe strains that partially or completely tear the muscle or tendon are often very painful and disabling.

How Are Sprains And Strains Treated?

Reduce Swelling And Pain

Treatment for sprains and strains is similar and can be thought of as having two stages. The goal during the first stage is to reduce swelling and pain. At this stage, doctors usually advise patients to follow a formula of rest, ice, compression, and elevation (RICE) for the first 24 to 48 hours after the injury. The doctor may also recommend an over-the-counter or prescription nonsteroidal anti-inflammatory drug, such as aspirin or ibuprofen, to help decrease pain and inflammation.

For people with a moderate or severe sprain, particularly of the ankle, a hard cast may be applied. Severe sprains and strains may require surgery to repair the torn ligaments, muscle, or tendons. Surgery is usually performed by an orthopaedic surgeon.

It is important that moderate and severe sprains and strains be evaluated by a doctor to allow prompt, appropriate treatment to begin. A person who has any concerns about the seriousness of a sprain or strain should always contact a doctor for advice.

Begin Rehabilitation

The second stage of treating a sprain or strain is rehabilitation, whose overall goal is to improve the condition of the injured part and restore its function. The health care provider will prescribe an exercise program designed to prevent stiffness, improve range of motion, and restore the joint's normal flexibility and strength. Some patients may need physical therapy during this stage.

When the acute pain and swelling have diminished, the health care provider or physical therapist will instruct the patient to do a series of exercises several times a day. These are very important because they help reduce swelling, prevent stiffness, and restore normal, pain-free range of motion. The health care provider can recommend many different types of exercises, depending on the injury. For example, people with an ankle sprain may be told to rest their heel on the floor and write the alphabet in the air with their big toe. A patient with an injured knee or foot will work on weight-bearing and balancing exercises. The duration of the program depends on the extent of the injury, but the regimen commonly lasts for several weeks.

Another goal of rehabilitation is to increase strength and regain flexibility. Depending on the patient's rate of recovery, this process begins about the second week after the injury. The health care provider or physical therapist

☞ Remember!!
Prevention Of Sprains And Strains

There are many things people can do to help lower their risk of sprains and strains.

- Maintain a healthy, well-balanced diet to keep muscles strong.

- Maintain a healthy weight.

- Practice safety measures to help prevent falls (for example, keep stairways, walkways, yards, and driveways free of clutter, and salt or sand icy patches in the winter).

- Wear shoes that fit properly.

- Replace athletic shoes as soon as the tread wears out or the heel wears down on one side.

- Do stretching exercises daily.

- Be in proper physical condition to play a sport.

- Warm up and stretch before participating in any sports or exercise.

- Wear protective equipment when playing.

- Avoid exercising or playing sports when tired or in pain.

- Run on even surfaces.

will instruct the patient to do a series of exercises designed to meet these goals. During this phase of rehabilitation, patients progress to more demanding exercises as pain decreases and function improves.

The final goal is the return to full daily activities, including sports when appropriate. Patients must work closely with their health care provider or physical therapist to determine their readiness to return to full activity. Sometimes people are tempted to resume full activity or play sports despite pain or muscle soreness. Returning to full activity before regaining normal range of motion, flexibility, and strength increases the chance of reinjury and may lead to a chronic problem.

The amount of rehabilitation and the time needed for full recovery after a sprain or strain depend on the severity of the injury and individual rates of healing. For example, a moderate ankle sprain may require 3 to 6 weeks of rehabilitation before a person can return to full activity. With a severe sprain, it can take 8 to 12 months before the ligament is fully healed. Extra care should be taken to avoid reinjury.

Where Can People Find More Information About Sprains And Strains?

National Institute of Arthritis and Musculoskeletal and Skin Diseases Information Clearinghouse
NIAMS/National Institutes of Health
1 AMS Circle
Bethesda, MD 20892-3675
Phone: 301-495-4484
TTY: 301-565-2966
Fax: 301-718-6366
Website: www.niams.nih.gov
E-mail: niamsinfo@mail.nih.gov

The clearinghouse provides information on arthritis and musculoskeletal and skin diseases. Additional information and updates can also be found on the NIAMS Web site.

American Academy of Orthopaedic Surgeons
6300 North River Rd.
Rosemont, IL 60018-4262
Toll-Free: 800-346-AAOS (2267)
Fax On Demand: 800-999-2939
Website: www.aaos.org

The academy provides education and practice management services for orthopaedic surgeons and allied health professionals. It also serves as an advocate for improved patient care and informs the public about the science of orthopaedics. The orthopaedist's scope of practice includes disorders of the body's bones, joints, ligaments, muscles, and tendons. For a single copy of an AAOS brochure, send a self-addressed stamped envelope to the address above or visit the AAOS website.

The NIAMS gratefully acknowledges the assistance of James S. Panagis, M.D., M.P.H., of NIAMS; Jo A. Hannafin, M.D., Ph.D., of the Hospital for Special Surgery, New York, NY; and Harold B. Kitaoka, M.D., of the Mayo Clinic, Rochester, MN, in the preparation and review of this information.

Chapter 16

The Facts About Fractures And Broken Bones

How Do Bones Break?

Bones are made up of bone cells, proteins (say: pro-teens), and minerals (say: min-er-ulls), like calcium. Sound like something you might have read on the side of a cereal box or vitamin bottle? That's because your diet has a big effect on the strength and health of your bones.

Your bones are tough stuff—but even tough stuff can break. Like a wooden pencil, bones bend under some strain (too forceful bending) and once the pressure is too sudden or too much, they might snap. You can break a bone by falling off a skateboard or if your sister's bike falls over on you in just the right way.

When a bone breaks it is called a fracture (say: frak-chur). There's more than one way to break or fracture a bone. A break can be anything from a

About This Chapter: Text in this chapter is from "The Facts About Fractures and Broken Bones." This information was provided by KidsHealth, one of the largest resources online for medically reviewed health information written for parents, kids, and teens. For more articles like this one, visit www.KidsHealth.org, or www.TeensHealth.org. © 2001 The Nemours Center for Children's Health Media, a division of The Nemours Foundation. Reprinted with permission.

✎ **Weird Words**

Doctors describe fractures in the following ways:

- A **complete fracture** is when the bone has broken into two pieces.

- A **greenstick fracture** is when the bone cracks on one side only, not all the way through (like when you bend a living stick on a tree).

- A **single fracture** is when the bone is broken in one place.

- A **comminuted (say: kah-mih-noot-ed) fracture** is when the bone is broken into more than two pieces or crushed.

- A **bending fracture**, which only happens in kids, is when the bone bends but doesn't break.

- An **open fracture** is when the bone is sticking through the skin.

hairline fracture (a thin break in the bone) to the bone being broken into two or more pieces.

What Happens When You Break A Bone?

It hurts! It's different for everyone, but the pain is often like the deep ache you get from a super bad stomachache or headache. Some people may experience sharper pain—especially with an open fracture. And if the fracture is small, a kid may not feel much pain at all. Sometimes, a kid won't even be able to tell that he broke a bone!

Breaking a bone is a big shock to your whole body. It's normal for you to receive strong messages from parts of your body that aren't anywhere close to the fracture. You may feel dizzy, woozy, or chilly from the shock. A lot of people cry for a while. Some people pass out until their body has time to adjust to all the signals it's getting. And other people don't feel any pain right away because of the shock of the injury (say: in-jurr-ee). Injury is another word for hurt. A broken bone is an injury.

✔ **Quick Tip**

If you think you or someone else has broken a bone, the most important things to do are to:

- stay calm

- make sure the person who is hurt is as comfortable as possible

- tell an adult

- if there are no adults around, call 911, or the emergency number in your area

The worst thing for a broken bone is to move it. This will hurt the person and it can make the injury worse! In the case of a broken arm or leg, a grown-up may be able to cushion or support the surrounding area with towels or pillows.

One super-important tip: if you're not sure what bone is broken or you think the neck or back is broken, do not try to move the injured person until a trained medical professional has arrived!

What Does The Doctor Do?

The first thing on the doctor's list (after making sure that there aren't any problems, like bleeding, that need attention right away) is to look at the bone to figure out what type of fracture it is.

The doctor will need to take x-rays. These are special pictures used to view parts of the body not easily seen from the outside. X-rays give the doctor a map of the fracture so that he or she can set the bones back in their normal position.

With breaks in larger bones, or more than two pieces, the doctor may put a metal pin in your bone to help set it. Don't worry—you'll be given some medicine so you won't feel a thing. And when your bone has healed, the doctor will remove the pin.

After your bone has been set, the next step is usually putting on a cast, the special bandage that will keep the bone in place for the 1 to 3 months it will take for the break to mend. Casts are made of bandages soaked in plaster, which harden to a tough shell (that's why they last so long!). Sometimes casts are made of fiberglass or plastic—and some are even waterproof, which means you can still go swimming and get it wet! And sometimes they come in cool colors or patterns that you can choose.

How Do Broken Bones Heal?

Your bones are natural healers. At the location of the fracture, your bones will produce lots of new cells and tiny blood vessels that rebuild the bone. These cells cover both ends of the broken part of the bone and close up the break (sort of like your mom or dad sews a rip in your pants) until it's as good as new.

What Should You Do When The Cast Comes Off?

Just when you thought the worst was over and your bone was healed, here comes the doctor with a noisy saw! This isn't the same kind of saw your mom or dad has in your garage or basement. This kind of saw can cut through your cast without cutting your skin. It won't hurt, but it might tickle a bit! Once the cast is off, the injured area will probably look and feel pretty weird. Some things you may notice about the place where the cast was include:

- pale, dry, or flaky skin

- hair that looks darker

- the area (muscles especially) look smaller or weaker

☞ **Remember!!**

How can you be sure you don't break any more bones? Your body talks with more than its mouth. Listen to it! Some of the easiest ways to prevent broken bones include:

- Always play it safe! Use safety helmets, pads, and the right gear to stay in one piece when you are biking, in-line blading, or riding on your scooter.

- Your body needs to build up or it will break down. Take your time training. As far as your body is concerned, warm-ups and cool-downs are as important as the main activity—don't skip them.

- Feed your bones the calcium and vitamin D they need to stay strong.

Don't worry. This is all temporary. If you follow your doctor's instructions, you'll be 100% before you know it.

Your doctor will give you special exercises to do. Remember, the muscles around the break have been on a major vacation and need time to get with the program, too! Be careful with the area. Don't play games or sports that might use that body part until your doctor says it's okay.

You can ask the doctor what foods, like milk or yogurt, might make your bones feel well and stay strong.

Chapter 17

Growth Plate Injuries Affect Teen Athletes

What Is The Growth Plate?

The growth plate, also known as the epiphyseal plate or physis, is the area of growing tissue near the end of the long bones in children and adolescents. Each long bone has at least two growth plates: one at each end. The growth plate determines the future length and shape of the mature bone. When growth is complete—sometime during adolescence—the growth plates close and are replaced by solid bone.

Who Gets Growth Plate Injuries?

These injuries occur in children and adolescents. The growth plate is the weakest area of the growing skeleton, weaker than the nearby ligaments and tendons that connect bones to other bones and muscles. In a growing child or teen, a serious injury to a joint is more likely to damage a growth plate than the ligaments that stabilize the joint. An injury that would cause a sprain in an adult can be associated with a growth plate injury in a child or teen.

Injuries to the growth plate are fractures. They comprise 15 percent of all childhood fractures. They occur twice as often in boys as in girls, with the

About This Chapter: Text in this chapter is from "Questions and Answers About Growth Plate Injuries," National Institute of Arthritis and Musculoskeletal and Skin Diseases (NIAMS), October 2001, NIH Publication No. 02-5028.

greatest incidence among 14- to 16-year-old boys and 11- to 13-year-old girls. Older girls experience these fractures less often because their bodies mature at an earlier age than boys. As a result, their bones finish growing sooner, and their growth plates are replaced by stronger, solid bone.

Approximately half of all growth plate injuries occur in the lower end of the outer bone of the forearm (radius) at the wrist. These injuries also occur frequently in the lower bones of the leg (tibia and fibula). They can also occur in the upper leg bone (femur) or in the ankle, foot, or hip bone.

✎ Weird Words

Epiphysis: The end of a bone.

Growth Plate (also known as the epiphyseal plate or physis): The area of growing tissue near the end of the long bones in children and adolescents. Each long bone has at least two growth plates: one at each end.

Manipulation: When a doctor puts bones or joints back into their correct position using his hands.

Metaphysis: The shaft of a long bone.

Orthopaedic Surgeon: A doctor who specializes in bone and joint problems.

What Causes Growth Plate Injuries?

While growth plate injuries are caused by an acute event, such as a fall or a blow to a limb, chronic injuries can also result from overuse. For example, a gymnast who practices for hours on the uneven bars, a long-distance runner, or a baseball pitcher perfecting his curve ball can all have growth plate injuries.

In one large study of growth plate injuries in children, the majority resulted from a fall, usually while running or playing on furniture or playground equipment. Competitive sports, such as football, basketball, softball, track and field, and gymnastics, accounted for one-third of all injuries. Recreational activities, such as biking, sledding, skiing, and skateboarding, accounted for one-fifth of all growth plate fractures, while car, motorcycle, and all-terrain-vehicle accidents accounted for only a small percentage of fractures involving the growth plate.

Whether an injury is acute or due to overuse, a child or teen who has pain that persists or affects athletic performance or the ability to move or put pressure on a limb should be examined by a doctor. A child or teen should never be allowed or expected to work through the pain.

Children and teens who participate in athletic activity often experience some discomfort as they practice new movements. Some aches and pains can be expected, but their complaints always deserve careful attention. Some injuries, if left untreated, can cause permanent damage and interfere with proper growth of the involved limb.

Although many growth plate injuries are caused by accidents that occur during play or athletic activity, growth plates are also susceptible to other disorders, such as bone infection, that can alter their normal growth and development.

How Are Growth Plate Fractures Diagnosed?

After learning how the injury occurred and examining the child, the doctor will use x-rays to determine the type of fracture and decide on a treatment plan. Because growth plates have not yet hardened into solid bone, they don't show on x-rays. Instead, they appear as gaps between the shaft of a long bone, called the metaphysis, and the end of the bone, called the epiphysis. Because injuries to the growth plate may be hard to see on x-ray, an x-ray of the noninjured side of the body may be taken so the two sides can be compared. Magnetic resonance imaging (MRI), which is another way of looking at bone, provides useful information on the appearance of the growth plate. In some cases, other diagnostic tests, such as computed tomography (CT) or ultrasound, will be used.

What Kind Of Doctor Treats Growth Plate Injuries?

For all but the simplest injuries, the doctor may recommend that the injury be treated by an orthopaedic surgeon (a doctor who specializes in bone and joint problems in children and adults). Some problems may require the services of a pediatric orthopaedic surgeon, who specializes in injuries and musculoskeletal disorders in children.

How Are Growth Plate Injuries Treated?

As previously indicated, treatment depends on the type of fracture. Treatment, which should be started as soon as possible after injury, generally involves a mix of the following:

Immobilization

The affected limb is often put in a cast or splint, and the child is told to limit any activity that puts pressure on the injured area.

Manipulation Or Surgery

If the fracture is displaced, the doctor will have to put the bones or joints back in their correct positions, either by using his or her hands (called manipulation) or by performing surgery (open reduction and internal fixation). After the procedure, the bone will be set in place so it can heal without moving. This is usually done with a cast that encloses the injured growth plate and the joints on both sides of it. The cast is left in place until the injury heals, which can take anywhere from a few weeks to two or more months for serious injuries. The need for manipulation or surgery depends on the

> ✔ **Quick Tip**
> ## Signs That Require A Visit To The Doctor
>
> - Inability to continue play because of pain following an acute or sudden injury
>
> - Decreased ability to play over the long term because of persistent pain following a previous injury
>
> - Visible deformity of the child's arms or legs
>
> - Severe pain from acute injuries that prevent the use of an arm or leg.
>
> Adapted from *Play It Safe, a Guide to Safety for Young Athletes* of the American Academy of Orthopaedic Surgeons.

location and extent of the injury, its effect on nearby nerves and blood vessels, and the child's age.

Strengthening And Range-Of-Motion Exercises

These treatments may also be recommended after the fracture is healed.

Long-Term Follow-Up

Long-term follow-up is usually necessary to monitor the child's recuperation and growth. Evaluation includes x-rays of matching limbs at 3- to 6-month intervals for at least 2 years. Some fractures require periodic evaluations until the child's bones have finished growing. Sometimes a growth arrest line may appear as a marker of the injury. Continued bone growth away from that line may mean that there will not be a long-term problem, and the doctor may decide to stop following the patient.

What Is The Prognosis For Growth In The Involved Limb Of A Child With A Growth Plate Injury?

About 85 percent of growth plate fractures heal without any lasting effect. Whether an arrest of growth occurs depends on the following factors, in descending order of importance:

- **Severity of the injury**—If the injury causes the blood supply to the epiphysis to be cut off, growth can be stunted. If the growth plate is shifted, shattered, or crushed, a bony bridge is more likely to form and the risk of growth retardation is higher. An open injury in which the skin is broken carries the risk of infection, which could destroy the growth plate.

- **Age of the child**—In a younger child, the bones have a great deal of growing to do; therefore, growth arrest can be more serious, and closer surveillance is needed. It is also true, however, that younger bones have a greater ability to remodel.

- **Which growth plate is injured**—Some growth plates, such as those in the region of the knee, are more responsible for extensive bone growth than others.

• **Type of growth plate fracture**—Of the five fracture types, Types IV and V are the most serious. Treatment depends on the above factors and also bears on the prognosis.

☞   Remember!!

The most frequent complication of a growth plate fracture is premature arrest of bone growth. The affected bone grows less than it would have without the injury, and the resulting limb could be shorter than the opposite, uninjured limb. If only part of the growth plate is injured, growth may be lopsided and the limb may become crooked.

Growth plate injuries at the knee are at greatest risk of complications. Nerve and blood vessel damage occurs most frequently there. Injuries to the knee have a much higher incidence of premature growth arrest and crooked growth.

For More Information About Growth Plate Injuries

National Institute of Arthritis and Musculoskeletal and Skin Diseases (NIAMS)
National Institutes of Health
1 AMS Circle
Bethesda, MD 20892-3675
Toll-Free: 877-22-NIAMS (266-4267)
Phone: 301-495-4484 or
Fax: 301-718-6366
TTY: 301-565-2966
Website: www.niams.nih.gov
E-mail: niamsinfo@mail.nih.gov

NIAMS provides information on arthritis and rheumatic disease and bone, muscle, joint, and skin diseases. It distributes patient and professional education materials and refers people to other sources of information. Additional information and updates can also be found on the NIAMS website.

American Academy of Orthopaedic Surgeons

6300 North River Rd.
Rosemont, IL 60018-4262
Toll-Free: 800-346-AAOS (2267)
Fax On Demand: 800-999-2939
Website: www.aaos.org

The academy provides education and practice management services for orthopaedic surgeons and allied health professionals. It also serves as an advocate for improved patient care and informs the public about the science of orthopaedics. The orthopaedist's scope of practice includes disorders of the body's bones, joints, ligaments, muscles, and tendons. For a single copy of an AAOS brochure, send a self-addressed stamped envelope to the address above or visit the AAOS website.

American Academy of Pediatrics

141 Northwest Point Boulevard
Elk Grove Village, IL 60007-1098
Phone: 847-434-4000
Fax: 847-434-8000
Website: www.aap.org
E-mail: cfc@aap.org

The American Academy of Pediatrics (AAP) and its member pediatricians dedicate their efforts and resources to the health, safety, and well-being of infants, children, adolescents, and young adults. Activities of the AAP include advocacy for children and youth, public education, research, professional education, and membership service and advocacy for pediatricians.

American Orthopaedic Society for Sports Medicine

6300 N. River Road, Suite 500
Rosemont, IL 60018
Toll-Free: 877-321-3500
Phone: 847-292-4900
Fax: 847-292-4905
Website: www.sportsmed.org
E-mail: aossm@aossm.org

The society is an organization of orthopaedic surgeons and allied health professionals dedicated to educating health care professionals and the general public about sports medicine. It promotes and supports educational and research programs in sports medicine, including those concerned with fitness, as well as programs designed to advance knowledge of the recognition, treatment, rehabilitation, and prevention of athletic injuries.

Chapter 18

Concussions

When a cartoon character gets bonked on the head, stars appear. Although it may be amusing to watch in a cartoon, it's not so funny when it happens in real life. Seeing stars, feeling goofy or dazed, and possibly being rendered unconscious are all symptoms of a brain injury called a concussion.

What Is A Concussion?

The brain is made of soft tissue and is cushioned by spinal fluid. A tough, leathery outer covering called the dura surrounds the delicate brain—and both the brain and dura are encased in the hard, protective skull.

A concussion is a temporary loss of brain function due to an injury. When someone suffers a concussion or closed head injury, the brain shifts inside the skull. This can result in a sudden—usually temporary—disruption in a person's mental abilities.

A concussion is usually the result of a direct blow, such as an object hitting the head.

About This Chapter: Text in this chapter is from "Concussions." This information was provided by KidsHealth, one of the largest resources online for medically reviewed health information written for parents, kids, and teens. For more articles like this one, visit www.KidsHealth.org or www.TeensHealth.org. © 2002 The Nemours Center for Children's Health Media, a division of The Nemours Foundation. Reprinted with permission.

But concussions can also occur from other types of injuries—such as a football tackle or the sudden stopping of a vehicle during a crash—that violently jar or shake the head and neck. Because there isn't a lot of room for movement between the brain and the layers of tissue that protect it, if the brain is forcefully shifted within the skull during an injury, its delicate structures and blood vessels can be damaged—and normal brain functions may be interrupted.

Concussions and other brain injuries such as contusions (bruising of the brain) are fairly common. About every 15 seconds, someone in the United States has a brain injury. According to the Centers for Disease Control and Prevention (CDC), almost 1.5 million brain injuries are reported every year in the United States.

Most people with concussions recover just fine with appropriate treatment. Some people, however, develop long-term disabilities or even die as a result of serious head injuries.

What Causes A Concussion?

The most common cause of concussions in teens is car accidents, whether between two cars or between a car and another object such as a tree

✎ Weird Words

Concussion: A temporary loss of brain function due to an injury, usually from a direct blow to the head.

Dura: Tough, leathery outer covering surrounding the brain.

Postconcussion Syndrome: When a person has not recovered from a concussion within a few months, or the same physical, cognitive, and emotional difficulties start weeks or months after the brain injury and last for longer periods of time, maybe permanently.

or telephone pole. Most of these accidents involve speeding or driving while under the influence of alcohol.

The next most common cause of concussion is sports injury. High-contact sports such as football, boxing, and hockey pose a higher risk of head injury, even with the use of protective headgear. Other causes include falls and physical violence, such as fighting. Guys are more likely to get concussions than girls.

What Are The Signs and Symptoms?

The symptoms of a concussion depend upon how severe the injury to the brain is. Although loss of consciousness (passing out) is often associated with concussions, a person can have a head injury that results in a mild concussion and never lose consciousness.

♣ It's A Fact!!

The most important thing to remember if you suspect that someone has had a concussion is to get medical attention immediately.

What Is Postconcussion Syndrome?

A person who has had a concussion and has not recovered within a few months is said to have postconcussion syndrome (PCS). PCS is not always present immediately after a brain injury. Sometimes it starts weeks or months later. Someone with PCS may have the same physical, cognitive, and emotional difficulties described earlier, such as poor memory, headaches, dizziness, and irritability, but they last for longer periods of time and may be permanent.

People who have continuing problems after a concussion should see a doctor who may refer them to a rehabilitation specialist for additional help.

Some people, such as boxers or football players, may suffer repeated concussions because of their activities. People who damage their brains repeatedly can have permanent brain damage if they try to resume their normal routine—or in the case of athletes, their sport—too quickly.

What Do Doctors Do?

If a doctor suspects that you may have a concussion, he or she will get many clues by talking to you about the head injury and your symptoms. The doctor may ask you more than once what seem like silly questions—such as who you are, where you are, what day of the week it is, and who the president is—but these questions are asked to check your level of consciousness and your memory and concentration abilities.

The doctor will perform a thorough examination of your nervous system, including testing your balance, coordination of movement, and reflexes. You may even be asked to do some activity such as running in place for a few minutes to see how well your brain functions after a physical workout.

Your doctor may order a CT scan (a special brain x-ray) or an MRI (a special non-x-ray brain image) to rule out bleeding or other serious injury involving the brain.

If you are released from the hospital soon after a concussion, the doctor will give you a list of instructions that may include such things as having a parent wake you up at least once during the night. If someone cannot be easily awakened, becomes increasingly confused, or has other symptoms such as continued vomiting after a head injury, it may mean there is a more severe problem, and that person should seek medical care right away.

✔ **Quick Tip**

Symptoms of a concussion may include:

- "seeing stars" and feeling dazed, dizzy, or lightheaded

- having trouble remembering things (such as what happened directly before and after the injury occurred—this is not uncommon, even with mild concussions)

- nausea or vomiting

- headaches

- blurred vision and sensitivity to light

- difficulty concentrating, thinking, or making decisions

- feeling anxious or irritable for no apparent reason

- feeling overly tired

- coordination and balance may be off (you might have problems with physical tasks you could normally do, such as catching a ball)

The doctor will probably recommend that you take acetaminophen or other aspirin-free medications for headaches. He or she may tell you to take things easy if you're in school or if you have a job. Depending on how severe your injury is, you may have to carry a lighter homework load or even cut back on the time you spend in class or at work.

After a concussion, the brain needs time to heal. It's important to wait until all symptoms of a concussion have cleared up before returning to normal activities. The amount of time a person needs to recover depends on how long his symptoms persist, and a person should be followed closely by his doctor. Healthy teens can usually resume their normal activities within a few weeks, but keep in mind that each situation is different.

✔ **Quick Tip**

Anyone with a recent concussion is at increased risk for a second concussion if they are injured again (even with less force).

Can Concussions Be Prevented?

Some accidents can't be avoided. However, you can do a lot to prevent a concussion by taking proper precautions in situations where you might injure your head.

Always wear a seat belt in a car. If you drive, be aware and attentive at all times, and always obey speed limits, signs, and safe-driving laws to reduce the chances of having an accident. Driving rules and regulations were created to protect everyone. Never use alcohol or other drugs when you're behind the wheel—this is not only illegal, but makes your reaction time slower and impairs your judgment, making you much more likely to have an accident if you drive under the influence.

Wearing appropriate headgear and safety equipment when biking, blading, skateboarding, playing contact sports, and doing other activities can significantly reduce your chances of having a concussion. By using a bike helmet, for instance, you can reduce your risk of having a concussion by about 85%.

Taking good care of yourself after a concussion is essential. If you reinjure your brain during the time it is still healing, it will take even more time to completely heal. Each time a person has a concussion, it does additional damage. Having multiple concussions over a period of time has the same effect on a person as being knocked unconscious once for several hours.

☞ **Remember!!**
If you use care and common sense in all of your daily activities, you have a much better chance of avoiding a concussion. The best thing you can do to protect your head is to use your head!

Chapter 19

Know The Score On Facial Sports Injuries

Playing catch, shooting hoops, bicycling on a scenic path, or just kicking around a soccer ball have more in common than you may think. On the up side, these activities are good exercise and are enjoyed by thousands of Americans. On the down side, they can result in a variety of injuries to the face.

Many injuries are preventable by wearing the proper protective gear, and your attitude toward safety can make a big difference. However, even the most careful person can get hurt. When an accident happens, it's your response that can make the difference between a temporary inconvenience and permanent injury.

When Someone Gets Hurt

- Ask "Are you all right?" Determine whether the injured person is breathing and knows who and where they are.

- Be certain the person can see, hear, and maintain balance. Watch for subtle changes in behavior or speech, such as slurring or stuttering. Any abnormal response requires medical attention.

- Note weakness or loss of movement in the forehead, eyelids, cheeks, and mouth.

About This Chapter: Text in this chapter is from "Know the Score on Facial Sports Injuries," reprinted from www.entnet.org with permission of the American Academy of Otolaryngology—Head and Neck Surgery Foundation. Copyright © 2003. All rights reserved.

- Look at the eyes to make sure they move in the same direction and that both pupils are the same size.

- If any doubts exist, seek immediate medical attention.

When Medical Attention Is Required, What Can You Do?

- Call for medical assistance (911).

- Do not move the victim, or re-move helmets or protective gear.

- Do not give food, drink, or medication until the extent of the injury has been deter-mined.

- Remember HIV—be very careful around body fluids. In an emergency protect your hands with plastic bags.

> ✎ **Weird Words**
>
> Hematoma: A blood clot or collection of blood beneath the mucus membrane.
>
> Larynx (voicebox): A complex organ consisting of cartilage, nerves, and muscles with a mucous membrane lining all encased in a protective tissue (cartilage) framework.
>
> Otolaryngologist: A doctor who specializes in surgery to the head and neck including facial plastic surgery.

- Apply pressure to bleeding wounds with a clean cloth or pad, unless the eye or eyelid is affected or a loose bone can be felt in a head injury. In these cases, do not apply pressure but gently cover the wound with a clean cloth.

- Apply ice or a cold pack to areas that have suffered a blow (such as a bump on the head) to help control swelling and pain.

- Remember to advise your doctor if the patient has HIV or hepatitis.

Facial Fractures

Sports injuries can cause potentially serious broken bones or fractures of the face. Common symptoms of facial fractures include:

- swelling and bruising, such as a black eye

- pain or numbness in the face, cheeks, or lips

- double or blurred vision

- nosebleeds

- changes in teeth structure or ability to close mouth properly

It is important to pay attention to swelling because it may be masking a more serious injury. Applying ice packs and keeping the head elevated may reduce early swelling.

If any of these symptoms occur, be sure to visit the emergency room or the office of a facial plastic surgeon (such as an otolaryngologist—head and neck surgeon) where x-rays may be taken to determine if there is a fracture.

Upper Face

When you are hit in the upper face (by a ball for example) it can fracture the delicate bones around the sinuses, eye sockets, bridge of the nose, or cheek bones. A direct blow to the eye may cause a fracture, as well as blurred or double vision. All eye injuries should be examined by an eye specialist (ophthalmologist).

Lower Face

When your jaw or lower face is injured, it may change the way your teeth fit together. To restore a normal bite, surgeries often can be performed from inside the mouth to prevent visible scarring of the face; and broken jaws often can be repaired without being wired shut for long periods. Your doctor will explain your treatment options and the latest treatment techniques.

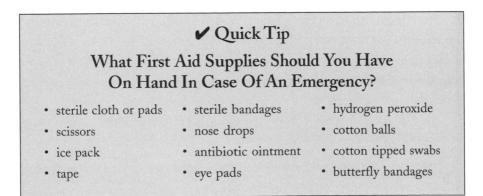

✔ Quick Tip

What First Aid Supplies Should You Have On Hand In Case Of An Emergency?

• sterile cloth or pads	• sterile bandages	• hydrogen peroxide
• scissors	• nose drops	• cotton balls
• ice pack	• antibiotic ointment	• cotton tipped swabs
• tape	• eye pads	• butterfly bandages

Soft Tissue Injuries

Bruises, cuts, and scrapes often result from high speed or contact sports, such as boxing, football, soccer, ice hockey, bicycling skiing, and snowmobiling. Most can be treated at home, but some require medical attention.

Bruises

Also called contusions, bruises result from bleeding underneath the skin. Applying pressure, elevating the bruised area above the heart, and using an ice pack for the first 24 to 48 hours minimizes discoloration and swelling. After two days, a heat pack or hot water bottle may help more. Most of the swelling and bruising should disappear in one to two weeks.

Cuts And Scrapes

The external bleeding that results from cuts and scrapes can be stopped by immediately applying pressure with gauze or a clean cloth. When the bleeding is uncontrollable, you should go to the emergency room.

Scrapes should be washed with soap and water to remove any foreign material that could cause infection and discoloration of the skin. Scrapes or abrasions can be treated at home by cleaning with 3% hydrogen peroxide and covering with an antibiotic ointment or cream until the skin is healed. Cuts or lacerations, unless very small, should be examined by a physician. Stitches may be necessary, and deeper cuts may have serious effects. Following stitches, cuts should be kept clean and free of scabs with hydrogen peroxide and antibiotic ointment. Bandages may be needed to protect the area from pressure or irritation from clothes. You may experience numbness around the cut for several months. Healing will continue for 6 to 12 months. The application of sunscreen is important during the healing process to prevent pigment changes. Scars that look too obvious after this time should be seen by a facial plastic surgeon.

Nasal Injuries

The nose is one of the most injured areas on the face. Early treatment of a nose injury consists of applying a cold compress and keeping the head

higher than the rest of the body. You
should seek medical attention in the
case of:

- breathing difficulties
- deformity of the nose
- persistent bleeding
- cuts

Bleeding

Nosebleeds are common and usually short-lived. Often they can be controlled by squeezing the nose with constant pressure for 5 to 10 minutes. If
bleeding persists, seek medical attention.

> ### ♣ It's A Fact!!
>
> You should get immediate medi-
> cal care when you have:
>
> - deep skin cuts
> - obvious deformity or fracture
> - loss of facial movement
> - persistent bleeding
> - change in vision
> - problems breathing and/or swallowing
> - alterations in consciousness or facial movement

Bleeding also can occur underneath the surface of the nose. An otolaryn-
gologist/facial plastic surgeon will examine the nose to determine if there is
a clot or collection of blood beneath the mucus membrane of the septum (a
septal hematoma) or any fracture. Hematomas should be drained so the pressure does not cause nose damage or infection.

Fractures

Some otolaryngologists (head and neck specialists) set fractured bones
right away before swelling develops, while others prefer to wait until the
swelling is gone. These fractures can be repaired under local or general anesthesia, even weeks later.

Ultimately, treatment decisions will be made to restore proper function
of the nasal air passages and normal appearance and structural support of the
nose. Swelling and bruising of the nose may last for 10 days or more

Neck Injuries

Whether seemingly minor or severe, all neck injuries should be thoroughly evaluated by an otolaryngologist—head and neck surgeon. Injuries

may involve specific structures within the neck, such as the larynx (voicebox), esophagus (food passage), or major blood vessels and nerves.

Throat Injuries

The larynx is a complex organ consisting of cartilage, nerves and muscles with a mucous membrane lining all encased in a protective tissue (cartilage) framework.

The cartilages can be fractured or dislocated and may cause severe swelling, which can result in airway obstruction. Hoarseness or difficulty breathing after a blow to the neck are warning signs of a serious injury and the injured person should receive immediate medical attention.

🖙 Remember!!
Prevention

The best way to treat facial sports injuries is to prevent them. To insure a safe athletic environment, the following guidelines are suggested:

- Be sure the playing areas are large enough that players will not run into walls or other obstructions.

- Cover unremoveable goal posts and other structures with thick, protective padding.

- Carefully check equipment to be sure it is functioning properly.

- Require protective equipment—such as helmets and padding for football, bicycling and rollerblading; face masks, head and mouth guards for baseball; ear protectors for wrestlers; and eyeglass guards or goggles for racquetball and snowmobiling are just a few.

- Prepare athletes with warm-up exercises before engaging in intense team activity.

- In the case of sports involving fast-moving vehicles, for example, snowmobiles or dirt bikes—check the path of travel, making sure there are no obstructing fences, wires, or other obstacles.

- Enlist adequate adult supervision for all children's competitive sports.

Chapter 20

Neck And Spine Injuries

Neck Injuries

Neck fractures are potentially disabling. If an injured athlete complains of radiating pain with numbness in the arms, pain in the back of the neck, or paralysis below the site of injury, call for emergency medical assistance immediately and do not attempt to move the injured athlete.

Other signs of neck fracture include:

- swelling around the neck

- wryneck (muscle spasms or stiff neck)

- loss of bowel or bladder control

- tenderness around the site of injury

- difficulty breathing

- change in consciousness

- deformity around the neck in rare instances

✔ Quick Tip

Contact sports, such as football, rugby, and wrestling have been identified as being particularly high-risk activities for cervical trauma.

About This Chapter: Text in this chapter is from "Caring For The Neck And Spine," © 2003. It has been provided by the University of Pittsburgh Medical Center, Center for Sports Medicine. For more information, go to www.upmc.com. Reprinted with permission.

Other neck injuries include: neck strains or sprains such as whiplash, which is usually caused when the neck snaps back, then forward; a pinched nerve sometimes called a burner or stinger, which is characterized by a fleeting burning pain or numbness radiating down the neck and arm; or acute torticollis, otherwise known as a wryneck, characterized by muscle spasms.

✔ Quick Tip

In general, for neck injuries other than possible fractures, apply ice, and then wrap the neck in a soft cervical collar without obstructing the airway. Do not use heat on a neck injury for at least 48 hours.

Moving An Injured Athlete From The Field

All coaches and trainers should take CPR and first aid courses to learn how to treat and move athletes with potential head or neck injuries. Summon medical help if an athlete shows signs of possible neck fracture.

Remember that many head injuries have associated neck injuries. Always treat for the worst possible injury. Don't attempt to move an athlete who complains of numbness, tingling, buzzing, radiating pain, or paralysis in any part of the body. Injudiciously moving someone with an unstable spine may cause paralysis.

Obviously, athletes who have stopped breathing will need to be moved promptly to initiate resuscitation. If the head is in a position that obstructs the airway, gentle traction on the head is needed for alignment. Open the airway with the chin-lift or jaw-forward techniques without overextending or overflexing the neck during resuscitation.

There is always a chance that something could happen to jeopardize an athlete's career or life. Using the right techniques and fitted equipment are keys to preventing head and neck injuries. When injuries do occur, proper management can save lives. Coaches and trainers should prepare an emergency plan and have an ambulance service, physician, and equipment available for quick action.

Football And Neck Injuries Study

A football player who sustains a suspected neck injury during play should have his helmet left on until both the helmet and shoulder pads can be removed together in a controlled setting, say physicians at UPMC [University of Pittsburgh Medical Center] Health System.

According to a study conducted at the UPMC's Center for Sports Medicine, removing only the helmet during on-the-field medical evaluation changes the position of the cervical spine. In a football player with a potential cervical spine injury, such an alteration in neck position may create or worsen damage to the spinal cord. Immobilization with both the helmet and shoulder pads left in place will help maintain normal neck and spine alignment and minimize the risk of further spinal cord injury during transport to an appropriate medical facility.

In the study, physicians looked at the alignment of the cervical spine in 10 healthy young men with no history of neck injury while the subjects lay face up on a standard spinal immobilization backboard. Computerized tomography (CT) scans of the cervical spine were obtained in three separate settings: while the subjects wore no protective equipment; while they wore both football helmets and shoulder pads; and while they wore only shoulder pads after helmet removal.

✎ Weird Words

Acute Torticollis: Muscle spasms or a stiff neck, also known as wryneck.

Burner or Stinger: A pinched nerve in the neck that causes a burning pain or numbness that radiates down the neck or arm.

Whiplash: A strain or sprain of the neck caused by the head snapping back then forward.

Wryneck: Muscle spasms or stiff neck.

When the helmet had been removed with the shoulder pads left in place, there was a statistically significant change in overall cervical alignment compared to when no protective equipment was worn, considered to represent "normal" neck position. However, no significant change in cervical spine position was found when both the helmet and shoulder pads were left in place.

This study shows that removing only the helmet during on-the-field evaluation of a suspected neck injury could significantly alter the normal cervical alignment and cause abnormal extension of the cervical spine, potentially leading to further injury. The intent of the study was only to evaluate the cervical spine position before and after helmet removal and to make comparisons to the normal alignment found when no equipment was worn. No attempt was made to address cervical motion, which may occur with helmet and/or shoulder pad removal.

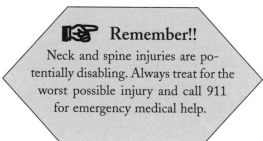

☞ Remember!!
Neck and spine injuries are potentially disabling. Always treat for the worst possible injury and call 911 for emergency medical help.

Chapter 21

Shoulder Injuries

How Common Are Shoulder Problems?

According to the American Academy of Orthopaedic Surgeons, about 4 million people in the United States seek medical care each year for shoulder sprain, strain, dislocation, or other problems. Each year, shoulder problems account for about 1.5 million visits to orthopaedic surgeons—doctors who treat disorders of the bones, muscles, and related structures.

What Are The Origin And Causes Of Shoulder Problems?

The shoulder is the most movable joint in the body. However, it is an unstable joint because of the range of motion allowed. It is easily subject to injury because the ball of the upper arm is larger than the shoulder socket that holds it. To remain stable, the shoulder must be anchored by its muscles, tendons, and ligaments. Some shoulder problems arise from the disruption of these soft tissues as a result of injury or from overuse or underuse of the shoulder. Other problems arise from a degenerative process in which tissues break down and no longer function well.

Shoulder pain may be localized or may be referred to areas around the shoulder or down the arm. Disease within the body (such as gallbladder,

About This Chapter: Text in this chapter is from "Questions and Answers about Shoulder Problems," National Institute of Arthritis and Musculoskeletal and Skin Diseases (NIAMS), May 2001.

liver, or heart disease, or disease of the cervical spine of the neck) also may generate pain that travels along nerves to the shoulder.

How Are Shoulder Problems Diagnosed?

Following are some of the ways doctors diagnose shoulder problems:

- Medical history (the patient tells the doctor about an injury or other condition that might be causing the pain).

- Physical examination to feel for injury and discover the limits of movement, location of pain, and extent of joint instability.

- Tests to confirm the diagnosis of certain conditions. Some of these tests include:

  - x-ray

  - arthrogram—Diagnostic record that can be seen on an x-ray after injection of a contrast fluid into the shoulder joint to outline structures such as the rotator cuff. In disease or injury, this contrast fluid may either leak into an area where it does not belong, indicating a tear or opening, or be blocked from entering an area where there normally is an opening.

✎ Weird Words

Arthroscopy: The doctor performs surgery through a tiny incision into which a small scope (arthroscope) is inserted to observe the inside of the joint.

Impingement Syndrome: Squeezing of the rotator cuff. Impingement syndrome may be confirmed when injection of a small amount of anesthetic (lidocaine hydrochloride) into the space under the acromion relieves pain.

Orthopaedic Surgeon: A doctor who treats disorders of the bones, muscles, and related structures.

Reduction: A procedure that puts the ball of the humerus back into the joint socket.

Rotator Cuff Injury: A strain or a tear of one or more of your rotator muscles or tendons.

Subluxation: A partial dislocation where the upper arm bone is partially in and partially out of the socket.

Tendinitis: Inflammation (redness, soreness, and swelling) of a tendon. In tendinitis of the shoulder, the rotator cuff and/or biceps tendon become inflamed, usually as a result of being pinched by surrounding structures.

- MRI (magnetic resonance imaging)—A non-invasive procedure in which a machine produces a series of cross-sectional images of the shoulder.

- Other diagnostic tests, such as injection of an anesthetic into and around the shoulder joint.

♣ **It's A Fact!!**

Shoulder injuries account for about 10% of all athletic injuries.

Source: University of Pittsburgh Medical Center/Center for Sports Medicine

Dislocation

What Is A Shoulder Dislocation?

The shoulder joint is the most frequently dislocated major joint of the body. In a typical case of a dislocated shoulder, a strong force that pulls the shoulder outward (abduction) or extreme rotation of the joint pops the ball of the humerus out of the shoulder socket. Dislocation commonly occurs when there is a backward pull on the arm that either catches the muscles unprepared to resist or overwhelms the muscles. When a shoulder dislocates frequently, the condition is referred to as shoulder instability. A partial dislocation where the upper arm bone is partially in and partially out of the socket is called a subluxation.

What Are The Signs Of A Dislocation And How Is It Diagnosed?

The shoulder can dislocate either forward, backward, or downward. Not only does the arm appear out of position when the shoulder dislocates, but the dislocation also produces pain. Muscle spasms may increase the intensity of pain. Swelling, numbness, weakness, and bruising are likely to develop. Problems seen with a dislocated shoulder are tearing of the ligaments or tendons reinforcing the joint capsule and, less commonly, nerve damage. Doctors usually diagnose a dislocation by a physical examination. X-rays may be taken to confirm the diagnosis and to rule out a related fracture.

How Is A Dislocated Shoulder Treated?

Doctors treat a dislocation by putting the ball of the humerus back into the joint socket—a procedure called a reduction. The arm is then immobilized in a sling or a device called a shoulder immobilizer for several weeks. Usually the doctor recommends resting the shoulder and applying ice three or four times a day. After pain and swelling have been controlled, the patient enters a rehabilitation program that includes exercises to restore the range of motion of the shoulder and strengthen the muscles to prevent future dislocations. These exercises may progress from simple motion to the use of weights.

After treatment and recovery, a previously dislocated shoulder may remain more susceptible to reinjury, especially in young, active individuals. Ligaments may have been stretched or torn, and the shoulder may tend to dislocate again. A shoulder that dislocates severely or often, injuring surrounding tissues or nerves, usually requires surgical repair to tighten stretched ligaments or reattach torn ones.

✔ Quick Tip

If you receive a shoulder injury, here's what you can do:

RICE = Rest, Ice, Compression, and Elevation

Rest—Reduce or stop using the injured area for 48 hours.

Ice—Put an ice pack on the injured area for 20 minutes at a time, 4 to 8 times per day. Use a cold pack, ice bag, or a plastic bag filled with crushed ice that has been wrapped in a towel.

Compression—Compression may help reduce the swelling. Compress the area with bandages, such as an elastic wrap, to help stabilize the shoulder.

Elevation—Keep the injured area elevated above the level of the heart. Use a pillow to help elevate the injury.

If pain and stiffness persist, see a doctor.

Sometimes the doctor performs surgery through a tiny incision into which a small scope (arthroscope) is inserted to observe the inside of the joint. After this procedure, called arthroscopic surgery, the shoulder is generally immobilized for about 6 weeks and full recovery takes several months. Arthroscopic techniques involving the shoulder are relatively new and many surgeons prefer to repair a recurrent dislocating shoulder by the time-tested open surgery under direct vision. There are usually fewer repeat dislocations and improved movement following open surgery, but it may take a little longer to regain motion.

Separation

What Is A Shoulder Separation?

A shoulder separation occurs where the collarbone (clavicle) meets the shoulder blade (scapula). When ligaments that hold the joint together are partially or completely torn, the outer end of the clavicle may slip out of place, preventing it from properly meeting the scapula. Most often the injury is caused by a blow to the shoulder or by falling on an outstretched hand.

What Are The Signs Of A Shoulder Separation And How Is It Diagnosed?

Shoulder pain or tenderness and, occasionally, a bump in the middle of the top of the shoulder (over the AC joint) are signs that a separation may have occurred. Sometimes the severity of a separation can be detected by taking x-rays while the patient holds a light weight that pulls on the muscles, making a separation more pronounced.

How Is A Shoulder Separation Treated?

A shoulder separation is usually treated conservatively by rest and wearing a sling. Soon after injury, an ice bag may be applied to relieve pain and swelling. After a period of rest, a therapist helps the patient perform exercises that put the shoulder through its range of motion. Most shoulder separations heal within 2 or 3 months without further intervention. However, if ligaments are severely torn, surgical repair may be required to hold the clavicle in place. A doctor may wait to see if conservative treatment works before deciding whether surgery is required.

♣ It's A Fact!!
Rotator Cuff Repair Of The Shoulder

Your Shoulder Joint

Your shoulder is made up of three bones:

- the collar bone, or clavicle (KLAV-ick-ol)
- the shoulder blade, or scapula (SKAP-you-luh)
- the bone of the upper arm, or humerus (HYOO-mer-es)

The rounded end of the humerus is called the head. The head fits into a hollow in the scapula. The hollow is called the glenoid (GLEE-noid). The head and glenoid fit together like a ball and socket and form the shoulder joint.

What Is The Rotator Cuff?

The rotator (ROW-tay-ter) cuff is made up of muscles and tendons that surround your shoulder joint. The four muscles of the rotator cuff and its tendons help to keep your shoulder steady as your arm moves.

What Is A Rotator Cuff Injury?

A rotator cuff injury is a strain or a tear of one or more of your rotator muscles or tendons. Trauma from a fall or a sports injury can cause a sudden, severe tear, which is called an acute tear. When a tear happens over time, it is called a chronic tear. Overuse, constant stress, or wear and tear from aging can cause a chronic tear.

Symptoms of an injury include:

- pain in your shoulder when you move your arm
- pain that wakes you up from a sound sleep almost every night
- weakness in your shoulder when you raise your arm
- less ability to move your shoulder and arm (called limited range of motion)

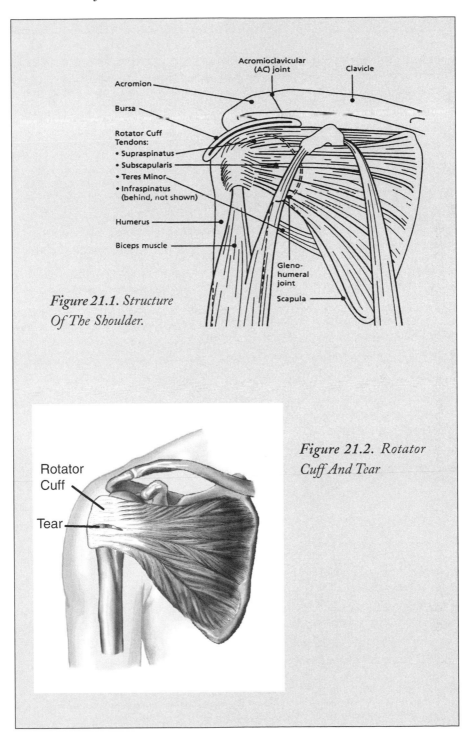

Figure 21.1. Structure Of The Shoulder.

Figure 21.2. Rotator Cuff And Tear

Why You Need Surgery

Surgery to repair the rotator cuff is necessary when you have a sudden and complete tear. Surgery may also be required if you have continuing pain and are becoming less able to move your shoulder. Surgery restores movement to your shoulder. Surgery also preserves strength of injured muscles and tendons.

During Your Surgery

During surgery, your rotator cuff is mended. First, a space is cleared. The torn muscle or tendon is shaved. Sacs between the tendons and bones act as a cushion. These sacs are called bursas (BER-suz). Sometimes a bursa has thickened, so it is removed. Bone at the tip of the shoulder blade may be shaved. Some ligaments also may be removed.

Then the edges of the tear are brought together and stitched. A sterile dressing is placed over the incision. Your affected arm is placed in a sling or in a harness called a shoulder immobilizer (im-OH-bill-EYE-zer). These devices help to keep your shoulder from moving.

After Your Surgery

The following list tells you what you need to know and do after your surgery.

Discomfort
- Your doctor will prescribe pain medicine for you.
- Your doctor may also tell you to put ice packs on your shoulder.

Care Of Your Incision
- If you have a dressing over your incision, keep the dressing clean and dry.
- If your incision is open to the air, keep the area clean and dry.
- If Steri-Strips tape covers your incision, keep the Steri-Strips clean and dry. They will peel off on their own.

- Do not put any lotion or ointment on your incision, unless your doctor says you may.

To Prevent Movement

- Your doctor will tell you how long to wear your sling or shoulder immobilizer. How long you need to wear it depends on the type of surgery you had.

- If you wear a sling, your arm should be at a 90-degree angle at the elbow. Your wrist and hand should be supported by the sling. Do not allow your wrist and hand to hang over the sling.

- If you wear a shoulder immobilizer, you may loosen the wrist strap only and straighten your lower arm at the elbow. Do not move your shoulder. Never completely remove your shoulder immobilizer until your doctor says you may.

Skin Care

- It is important to keep your underarm area clean and dry.

- Gently clean the underarm area daily with soap and water. Lean to the side, and let your affected arm hang down. Do not raise your affected arm when you clean the underarm area.

- Deodorant may be difficult to put on if you wear a shoulder immobilizer. Cream deodorants are easier to use than stick or roll-on types.

- A gauze pad placed under your arm can help absorb sweat and keep your skin from becoming irritated. Change the pad at least once a day.

Activity

- Do not move your affected arm away from your body or over your head.

- To make sleeping easier, raise your upper body on pillows. Do not lie flat.

- If you have a sling or a shoulder immobilizer, do not shower until your doctor says you may. You should take a sponge bath (not a tub bath).

- Do not lift anything with your affected arm.

- Move the fingers and wrist of your affected hand 10 times an hour while you are awake.

Rehabilitation

- Your doctor will talk to you about a program of rehabilitation and exercise.

When To Call The Doctor

If you have any of the following, call your doctor:

- fever of 101° F (38.3° C) or above

- redness, warmth, or swelling of your incision

- increase in drainage from your incision

- increase in pain

- numbness, tingling, or a bluish color in your fingers or hand

Source: "Rotator Cuff Repair of the Shoulder" is a patient information brochure from the University of Pittsburgh Medical Center. © 2003 University of Pittsburgh Medical Center. Reprinted with permission. For additional information, visit www.upmc.com, or for help in finding a doctor or health service that suits your needs, call the UPMC Referral Service at 800-533-UPMC (8762). This information is not intended to be used as a substitute for professional medical advice, diagnosis, or treatment. You should not rely entirely on this information for your health care needs. Ask you own doctor or health care provider any specific medical questions that you have.

Tendinitis, Bursitis, And Impingement Syndrome

What Are Tendinitis, Bursitis, And Impingement Syndrome Of The Shoulder?

These conditions are closely related and may occur alone or in combination. If the rotator cuff and bursa are irritated, inflamed, and swollen, they may become squeezed between the head of the humerus and the acromion. Repeated motion involving the arms, or the aging process involving shoulder motion over many years, may also irritate and wear down the tendons, muscles, and surrounding structures.

Tendinitis is inflammation (redness, soreness, and swelling) of a tendon. In tendinitis of the shoulder, the rotator cuff and/or biceps tendon become inflamed, usually as a result of being pinched by surrounding structures. The injury may vary from mild inflammation to involvement of most of the rotator cuff. When the rotator cuff tendon becomes inflamed and thickened, it may get trapped under the acromion. Squeezing of the rotator cuff is called impingement syndrome.

Tendinitis and impingement syndrome are often accompanied by inflammation of the bursa sacs that protect the shoulder. An inflamed bursa is called bursitis. Inflammation caused by a disease such as rheumatoid arthritis may cause rotator cuff tendinitis and bursitis. Sports involving overuse of the shoulder and occupations requiring frequent overhead reaching are other potential causes of irritation to the rotator cuff or bursa and may lead to inflammation and impingement.

What Are The Signs Of Tendinitis And Bursitis?

Signs of these conditions include the slow onset of discomfort and pain in the upper shoulder or upper third of the arm and/or difficulty sleeping on the shoulder. Tendinitis and bursitis also cause pain when the arm is lifted away from the body or overhead. If tendinitis involves the biceps tendon (the tendon located in front of the shoulder that helps bend the elbow and turn the forearm), pain will occur in the front or side of the shoulder and may travel down to the elbow and forearm. Pain may also occur when the arm is forcefully pushed upward overhead.

How Are These Conditions Diagnosed?

Diagnosis of tendinitis and bursitis begins with a medical history and physical examination. X-rays do not show tendons or the bursae but may be helpful in ruling out bony abnormalities or arthritis. The doctor may remove and test fluid from the inflamed area to rule out infection. Impingement syndrome may be confirmed when injection of a small amount of anesthetic (lidocaine hydrochloride) into the space under the acromion relieves pain.

How Are Tendinitis, Bursitis, And Impingement Syndrome Treated?

The first step in treating these conditions is to reduce pain and inflammation with rest, ice, and anti-inflammatory medicines such as aspirin,

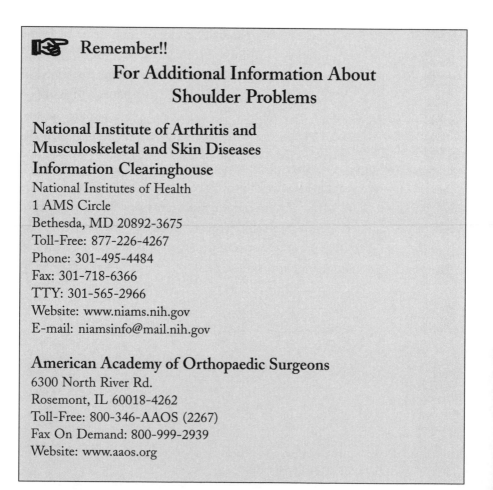

☞ Remember!!

For Additional Information About Shoulder Problems

National Institute of Arthritis and Musculoskeletal and Skin Diseases Information Clearinghouse
National Institutes of Health
1 AMS Circle
Bethesda, MD 20892-3675
Toll-Free: 877-226-4267
Phone: 301-495-4484
Fax: 301-718-6366
TTY: 301-565-2966
Website: www.niams.nih.gov
E-mail: niamsinfo@mail.nih.gov

American Academy of Orthopaedic Surgeons
6300 North River Rd.
Rosemont, IL 60018-4262
Toll-Free: 800-346-AAOS (2267)
Fax On Demand: 800-999-2939
Website: www.aaos.org

naproxen (Naprosyn*), ibuprofen (Advil, Motrin, or Nuprin), or cox-2 inhibitors (Celebrex, Vioxx, or Nobic). In some cases the doctor or therapist will use ultrasound (gentle sound-wave vibrations) to warm deep tissues and improve blood flow. Gentle stretching and strengthening exercises are added gradually. These may be preceded or followed by use of an ice pack. If there is no improvement, the doctor may inject a corticosteroid medicine into the space under the acromion. While steroid injections are a common treatment, they must be used with caution because they may lead to tendon rupture. If there is still no improvement after 6 to 12 months, the doctor may perform either arthroscopic or open surgery to repair damage and relieve pressure on the tendons and bursae.

American College of Rheumatology
1800 Century Place, Suite 250
Atlanta, GA 30345
Phone: 404-633-3777
Fax: 404-633-1870
Website: www.rheumatology.org
E-mail: acr@rheumatology.org

American Physical Therapy Association
1111 North Fairfax Street
Alexandria, VA 22314-1488
Toll-Free: 800-999-2782
Phone: 703-684-2782
Website: www.apta.org

Arthritis Foundation
1330 West Peachtree Street
Atlanta, GA 30309
Toll-Free: 800-283-7800
Phone: 404-872-7100 or call your local chapter (listed in the telephone directory)
Website: www.arthritis.org
E-mail: arthritis@finelinesolutions.com

Fracture

What Happens When The Shoulder Is Fractured?

A fracture involves a partial or total crack through a bone. The break in a bone usually occurs as a result of an impact injury, such as a fall or blow to the shoulder. A fracture usually involves the clavicle or the neck (area below the ball) of the humerus.

What Are The Signs Of A Shoulder Fracture And How Is It Diagnosed?

A shoulder fracture that occurs after a major injury is usually accompanied by severe pain. Within a short time, there may be redness and bruising around the area. Sometimes a fracture is obvious because the bones appear out of position. Both diagnosis and severity can be confirmed by x-rays.

How Is A Shoulder Fracture Treated?

When a fracture occurs, the doctor tries to bring the bones into a position that will promote healing and restore arm movement. If the clavicle is fractured, the patient must at first wear a strap and sling around the chest to keep the clavicle in place. After removing the strap and sling, the doctor will prescribe exercises to strengthen the shoulder and restore movement. Surgery is occasionally needed for certain clavicle fractures.

Fracture of the neck of the humerus is usually treated with a sling or shoulder immobilizer. If the bones are out of position, surgery may be necessary to reset them. Exercises are also part of restoring shoulder strength and motion.

Note

*Brand names included in this chapter are provided as examples only, and their inclusion does not mean that these products are endorsed by the National Institutes of Health or any other government agency. Also, if a particular brand name is not mentioned, this does not mean or imply that the product is unsatisfactory.

Chapter 22

Common Elbow Injuries In Athletes

The elbow is a hinge joint consisting of three bones that serve as the mechanical link between the upper arm and forearm. The normal range of motion of the elbow is zero degrees of extension (straightening) to 150 degrees of flexion (bending), although an arc of motion from 30 to 130 degrees is sufficient to perform most activities of daily life.

Elbow injuries are relatively common among athletes. Adolescents and older adults are most at risk—adolescents because their bones and ligaments are still growing, and older adults because their ligaments and tendons lose normal elasticity with age.

Macrotrauma

Dislocation Of The Elbow Joint

Dislocation of the elbow joint usually occurs as the result of a forceful fall onto the hand. The elbow forcibly hyperextends, causing the ligaments to rupture, and sometimes a fracture will result.

In some situations, the nerves and blood vessels around the elbow may be compressed by the displaced bones, requiring immediate reduction

About This Chapter: Text in this chapter is from "Caring for the Elbow and Shoulder" which has been provided by the University of Pittsburgh Medical Center, Center for Sports Medicine. For more information, go to www.upmc.com. © 2003 UPMC; reprinted with permission.

✎ **Weird Words**

Injuries Fall Into Two Basic Classifications

Macrotrauma: A sudden, forceful injury that results in fracture and/or dislocation.

Microtrauma: Repetitive motions—such as pitching or tennis strokes—can cause an overload to bones, ligaments, cartilage, or tendons of the elbow joint.

(repositioning) of the dislocation to relieve pressure. A physician can usually perform this procedure on the playing field or in the emergency department. Surgery is usually not necessary if there is no fracture with the dislocation.

Once the elbow dislocation is reduced, there is significant risk that the joint will become stiff. Even with torn ligaments, the elbow should rarely be immobilized in a cast, and the athlete should begin moving the elbow shortly after the injury.

Other Fractures Around The Elbow

A forceful throw or fall can cause a sudden stretching of the ligaments on the inside of the elbow and, in some cases, may pull off a piece of bone. Less frequently, the ligaments on the outside of the elbow rupture and can cause partial dislocation of the radius from the humerus. Both types of injury may require surgery.

Little League Elbow

During the acceleration phase of throwing, the inside of the elbow is subjected to a tension-type (valgus) stress. Repetitive throwing may place recurrent strain on the ligaments and tendons on the inside of the elbow, overloading them and causing tendonitis (inflammation of the tendon). In some cases, the stress may occur directly to the bones and growth plates, and this is called Little League elbow.

A typical example is the adolescent pitcher who complains of pain along the inside of the elbow after throwing for several innings. Other sports that can cause a valgus overload injury to the elbow include tennis and javelin throwing.

Treatment includes using the proper throwing technique and limiting the number of throws or pitches. If this problem develops, methods of management include rest from the offending activity, anti-inflammatory medication, alteration of throwing technique, and occasionally, bracing.

Overload Of The Lateral Elbow Joint

The same types of motion that lead to tension (valgus) strain on the inside of the elbow can result in a compression strain on the outside of the elbow joint. Repetitive overload of the joint surfaces can result in small fractures and cartilage injuries. In some cases, small pieces of cartilage may break off and become loose bodies inside the joint.

Like Little League elbow, this type of injury can be treated without surgery. When mechanical irritation of the elbow joint occurs with episodes of locking or limited motion, surgery may be necessary to remove loose bodies. Arthroscopic surgery can be performed in most cases.

Tennis Elbow

During the tennis stroke, repetitive injury and overload of the extensor tendons of the wrist may result in tendonitis at the attachment of the muscles on the outside of the elbow. This injury typically occurs in 30- to 60-year-old tennis players who use poor stroke mechanics. For example, a tennis player who performs a backhand, leading with the elbow—instead of leading with the body and shoulder—is at risk for overload of the extensor tendon origin. Such repetitive strain leads to microscopic tears, resulting in inflammation and tendonitis.

Physicians initially recommend non-operative treatment, including discontinuation of the offending activity, anti-inflammatory medication, a physical therapy program designed to increase strength and flexibility of the involved tendon and muscle groups, and application of ice and ultrasound.

Occasionally, a counterforce band applied to the forearm helps to relieve tension in this area.

If these measures fail to alleviate symptoms, a local corticosteroid injection may decrease inflammation in the affected tendon. Only one injection is recommended because repeated injections can weaken the tendon, predisposing it to possible rupture.

Approximately ten percent of patients with tennis elbow do not respond to these measures and may be candidates for surgery to decrease strain on the tendon. This surgery releases the tendon and causes blood vessels to grow in the area and to promote healing.

To minimize the risk of re-injury, tennis enthusiasts should have their stroke mechanics evaluated and make any necessary changes. Using the correct racquet also makes a difference. In general, players should choose a racquet made of light material, with a relatively large head, medium string tension, and with an appropriate grip size.

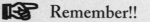

☞ Remember!!

Elbow injury in adolescent athlete is relatively common because their bones and ligaments are still growing. Proper technique in throwing and racquet sports and a reasonable training regimen will help prevent elbow injuries.

Other Injuries

Nerve Compression Syndromes

Less common injuries include nerve compression syndromes around the elbow. Compression may affect the ulnar nerve (funny bone) on the inside of the elbow or the radial nerve on the outside of the elbow. These problems typically occur in athletes who perform repetitive throwing or racquet sport motions. Vague pain develops, sometimes with a tingling sensation radiating down to the hand.

A sports medicine physician should examine athletes who complain of recurrent or persisting episodes of tingling or numbness in the elbow or hand.

Nerve injuries are usually resolved with non-surgical management consisting of rest from the offending activity. Occasionally, they require surgery to release or decompress the nerve.

Osteochondritis Dissecans

Osteochondritis dissecans, a rare condition that appears in older children, is usually caused by poor blood supply to the bone. A small area of bone and cartilage of the elbow joint may loose its blood supply, and the cartilage over the dead bone may break off into the joint as a loose body. Treatment includes avoidance of throwing activities to allow the bone to heal. Occasionally, arthroscopic or open surgery is required to remove loose fragments of cartilage or bone.

Olecranon Bursitis

The olecranon bursa is a fluid-filled sack that lubricates and decreases friction between tissues at the insertion of the triceps tendon at the back of the elbow. A fall onto the point of the elbow, or repeated microtrauma to the area, may result in inflammation of the fluid-filled sack, or bursitis. This condition appears as a swollen, tender mass on the tip of the elbow and is initially treated with ice packs and anti-inflammatory medication. Hot packs can be applied approximately 48 to 72 hours post-injury. Occasionally, the inflammation persists and there may be a possibility of infection, requiring surgical removal of the bursa.

Prevention Of Elbow Injuries

The major variable that coaches and athletes can control to prevent elbow injuries is the technique used in throwing and racquet sports. Using improper or inefficient body mechanics places athletes at greater risk for injury. Unfortunately, many athletes do not discover errors in their techniques until after injuries occur.

Another important factor is the training regimen. Overtraining causes fatigue, which in turn causes an athlete's body mechanics to deteriorate, thereby increasing the risk of injury.

Once an athlete develops an elbow injury, the risk of re-injury escalates, particularly if the athlete fails to change a faculty technique. To decrease the risk of re-injury, athletes should strengthen muscles around the elbow. Stretching muscles before throwing increases flexibility and can also provide protection against injury.

Chapter 23

Common Hand Injuries In Athletes

Hand injuries are very common in athletes. Although many are minor, others may be quite disabling if not diagnosed early and treated appropriately. Therefore, it is important to recognize common hand injuries and ensure appropriate treatment.

One of the most common injuries to an athlete's hand is an injury to the joint above the knuckle—the proximal interphalangeal (PIP) joint. Injuries to the PIP joint occur when the finger is forced into a straightened position (hyperextension) or is forced downward into a bent position (flexion). These injuries usually involve the collateral ligaments of the PIP joint. Injuries to the PIP joint also can include fractures, dislocations, and fracture-dislocations.

Collateral Ligament Sprains And Their Treatment

Injuries to the collateral ligaments of the fingers are classified by severity as first-, second-, and third-degree sprains. In a first-degree sprain, the collateral ligaments are only slightly stretched. A first-degree sprain often results in minimal swelling and slight point tenderness at the joint. Motion is usually not hindered by a first-degree sprain.

About This Chapter: "Caring for the Hand" has been provided by the University of Pittsburgh Medical Center, Center for Sports Medicine. For more information, go to www.upmc.com. © 2003 UPMC; reprinted with permission.

In a second-degree sprain, the collateral ligament is partially torn. A second-degree sprain usually results in immediate swelling, moderate to severe point tenderness at the joint, and slight abnormal joint motion.

The collateral ligament is completely torn, or avulsed (torn off the bone), in a third-degree sprain. Symptoms of a third-degree sprain include immediate swelling, severe point tenderness at the joint, and obvious deformity and instability.

An avulsion fracture at the joint may be associated with an injury to the collateral ligament. Because of the force of the injury, the collateral ligament may tear off a fragment of bone. X-rays are needed to properly diagnose an avulsion fracture.

For most collateral ligament injuries, first-aid treatment includes application of ice and protection against additional injury. Protective "buddy taping," which involves applying circular strips of ½-inch adhesive tape above and below the knuckle of the injured finger and the longer adjacent finger, should be used for two or three weeks, or until a full, pain-free motion is restored to the joint. With certain injuries, protecting the finger with an aluminum splint may be necessary for two to three weeks.

♣ **It's A Fact!!**

Tennis, gymnastics, rowing, and golf—sports that require extensive gripping—have a high incidence of hand strains.

When a dislocation of the PIP joint is suspected, it is not recommended to attempt realignment of the joint because, if done improperly, a fracture can result. The injured athlete should be taken to a hospital emergency room where a pre-reduction x-ray can determine if there is a fracture.

Common Fingertip Injuries

Fingertip (distal phalanx) injuries also are common in athletes. Most fingertip injuries are the result of direct trauma, such as jamming the finger against a hard object.

✔ **Quick Tip**

It is recommended that athletes with severe sprains—those in which there is joint instability and severe swelling and pain—consult a sports medicine specialist or hand surgeon.

Mallet, or baseball, finger is one of the most common injuries to the fingertips. This injury usually results from a blow to the tip of the out-stretched (extended) finger, causing a tearing or rupturing of the extensor tendon at the joint directly below the fingernail—the distal interphalangeal (DIP) joint. With this injury, the patient cannot straighten the fingertip. Often, this injury is treated inappropriately as a minor sprain to the collateral ligament; however, the lack of motion at the fingertip should indicate the need for treatment by a sports medicine specialist or hand surgeon.

Initial treatment for mallet finger includes ice and taping. A physician may place a special splint on the finger for two or three weeks. The splint keeps the DIP joint in hyperextension to promote healing. Surgery may be required if a dislocation or fracture also is present.

Jersey finger, the opposite of mallet finger, occurs when the fingertip is forcibly extended when, for instance, the athlete's hand is caught in an opponent's jersey. The flexor tendon, which bends the fingertip, is pulled away from the bone and the athlete cannot bend the fingertip without assistance. This injury also may require the use of a splint. It is important to recognize and treat this injury early, because delay in treatment may retard healing and necessitate surgery.

Another injury to the finger is the boutonnière deformity—a tearing of the extensor tendon of the PIP joint. This injury is usually caused by the forceful bending of the joint against an object. The classic boutonnière deformity can be recognized by hyperextension of the knuckle, the metacarpal-phalangeal (MCP) joint; flexion of the PIP joint; and hyperextension of the DIP joint. Early diagnosis of this injury is difficult because the patient's inability to straighten the finger often is attributed to pain and swelling. Therefore, an accurate diagnosis by a specialist is required. In acute injuries of this type, splinting often is required for six to eight weeks.

Common Thumb Injuries

Injuries to the ligament of the thumb at the web space—the ulnar collateral ligament—also are common in athletes. This ligament often is injured when the thumb is forcibly pulled back and away from the hand. In severe cases, the ligament is partially or completely torn. This injury commonly is called gamekeeper's thumb because it was seen in rabbit hunters who stretched the ulnar collateral ligament when twisting the rabbit's neck. Today, this injury is seen in skiers when the thumb is caught in the strap of the ski pole during a fall or when the skier falls on an outstretched hand.

Gamekeeper's thumb is sometimes treated as a minor sprain, or *stoved*, thumb. Because stability of the ulnar collateral ligament is vital to normal hand function—particularly when pinching or grasping—injuries involving

---

✎ Weird Words

Boutonnière Deformity: A tearing of the extensor tendon of the PIP joint. This injury is usually caused by the forceful bending of the joint against an object.

Boxer's Fracture: The most common fracture of the metacarpals which usually occurs when the closed fist strikes an object.

Gamekeeper's Thumb: An injury to the ligament of the thumb at the web space— the ulnar collateral ligament.

Jersey Finger: Occurs when the fingertip is forcibly extended when, for instance, the athlete's hand is caught in an opponent's jersey. The flexor tendon, which bends the fingertip, is pulled away from the bone and the athlete cannot bend the fingertip without assistance.

Mallet, Or Baseball, Finger: One of the most common injuries to the fingertips. This injury usually results from a blow to the tip of the outstretched (extended) finger, causing a tearing or rupturing of the extensor tendon at the joint directly below the fingernail

Proximal Interphalangeal (PIP) Joint: The joint above the knuckle.

the ulnar collateral ligament should be evaluated by a sports medicine specialist or hand surgeon. Partial tears of the ulnar collateral ligament require splinting and casting for four to six weeks. In some cases, surgical repair is necessary if the athlete is to recover normal function. In addition, rehabilitative exercises are required after immobilization or surgery to restore normal motion and to increase strength of the muscles in the hand and thumb.

Fractures Of The Hand

Fractures of the metacarpals and phalanges also are common in athletes. The most common fracture of the metacarpals is the boxer's fracture, which usually occurs when the closed fist strikes an object. This fracture most commonly occurs in the fifth metacarpal, right below the knuckle. With the boxer's fracture, the MCP joint is depressed, and there is tenderness and swelling over the metacarpal.

Obvious deformity and abnormal motion are the telltale signs of fractures involving the phalanges and metacarpals. Initial treatment should consist of application of ice and protection from further injury. A sports medicine specialist or hand surgeon should be consulted for further treatment.

☞ Remember!!

Learn to recognize serious hand injuries
and seek appropriate treatment.

Chapter 24

Hip And Groin Injuries

Common Hip, Thigh, And Groin Injuries

Injuries of the hip, thigh, and groin are common in athletes and dancers. Twisting, falling, trauma, and overuse are the chief culprits. Most of these maladies are soft tissue injuries that, with proper treatment, heal without problems. But injuries that are neglected or treated incorrectly may lead to serious problems.

Strains

Strains are common injuries in sports that require repetitive sprinting or sudden changes in direction. A muscle strain is an indirect injury to muscles caused by stretching or tearing of the tissues. The injury may be acute (caused by a single action, such as twisting or falling) or chronic (caused by repetitive stress). Its severity is graded from I (mild) to III (severe).

Careful sport-specific rehabilitation is needed to help prevent a strain from becoming a chronic problem. Properly treated, a Grade I strain usually will heal within seven to 10 days. More severe strains may take six weeks or longer to heal and should always be evaluated by a sports medicine specialist.

About This Chapter: "Caring for the Hip and Groin" has been provided by the University of Pittsburgh Medical Center, Center for Sports Medicine. For more information, go to www.upmc.com. © 2003 UPMC; reprinted with permission.

Signs and symptoms of Grade II and III strains include severe pain and/or swelling, ecchymosis (black and blue discoloration), limited or abnormal function, and a palpable defect in the muscle or tendon. A Grade III strain involving complete avulsion (separation) of the muscle-tendon unit may require surgery.

The best way to prevent a strain is to begin practice sessions and competitions with a proper warm-up and stretching exercises.

Quadriceps and hip flexor strains: Strains of the quadriceps and hip flexors are common in sports requiring jumping, kicking, or repetitive sprinting. Most quadriceps strains involve the rectus femoris, which is the only two-joint muscle (hip and knee) in this group; hip flexor strains may involve the rectus femoris and/or iliopsoas muscle.

> ✔ **Quick Tip**
> Muscles of the hip and thigh are responsible for hip movements. Strains and contusions are the most common athletic injuries to the hip, thigh, and groin.

With Grade I and II injuries the major concern is preventing re-injury and complete disruption (Grade III strain). Initial treatment involves ice, compression with an elastic wrap, and anti-inflammatory medications. (Certain drugs need physician approval.) Rehabilitation should be progressive and sport-specific. For example, for quadriceps strains caused by running, range-of-motion exercises and stretching should be started early and should progress to strengthening exercises, walking, pool-running, jogging, ¾-speed running, and full-speed sprints as soon as the athlete is free of pain.

Hamstring strains: Like the rectus femoris, the hamstring muscles also span two joints and are prone to strain during sprinting and kicking. Hamstring strains are common in track and field events (particularly sprinting), and in other sports requiring high-speed running. Any of the three hamstrings may be injured, but the long head of the biceps femoris is most frequently affected.

Healing of the hamstrings can be slow, and the treatment program is a delicate balance between measures designed to allow quick return and those necessary to avoid re-injury. The athletic trainer or sports medicine therapist should closely supervise rehabilitation.

Initial treatment involves ice, compression, and anti-inflammatory medications with weight bearing as tolerated. Immobilization is usually avoided. Early functional exercises include light jogging, pool-running, and stationary cycling. Initial strengthening may include prone leg curls, progressing to backward running.

Adductor (groin) strains: Adductor strains are common in sports requiring sudden sideways changes in direction, such as skating, soccer, track and field, and tennis. Most involve the adductor longus. Typically, an adductor strain is a Grade I or II strain (mild or moderate) and is characterized by groin pain when running or kicking.

A variety of other conditions that cause groin pain should be ruled out before assuming the problem is a muscular strain. These include inflammation of the pubic bone, spine pathology, hernia, prostatitis, and hip pathology.

Adductor strains are difficult to treat, and the risk of re-injury is high. As with hamstring strains, the athlete should be carefully monitored during rehabilitation. Treatment involves rest, ice, and anti-inflammatory medications, followed by adductor stretching and strengthening exercises.

Contusions

Contusions are common injuries in all contact sports but can occur in any sport. A contusion is a direct injury caused by blunt trauma, such as a blow from a knee or a football helmet.

Local swelling, pain, and tenderness are typical symptoms. The injury involves compression of the deep muscles near the bone and causes considerable pain, discoloration (caused by bleeding) and, in some cases, temporary disability (swelling, loss of motion). Acute treatment is directed toward controlling bleeding and minimizing secondary insult.

With proper treatment, minor contusions usually heal within two to three days. More severe contusions may take several weeks or months to heal and should always be evaluated by a sports medicine specialist.

The best way to prevent contusions is to supervise play carefully and to use protective equipment—correctly fitted—whenever appropriate.

Quadriceps contusions: Quadriceps contusions are common football, rugby, soccer, and basketball injuries usually caused by a direct blow to the thigh from a helmet or knee. The injury may limit motion and affect gait. The severity of the contusion is usually graded by the range of motion in the hip at the time of evaluation.

Treatment consists of immediate compression, ice, and protection from weight bearing with crutches. Ice should be applied during the first 24 to 48 hours. Oral anti-inflammatory agents may be useful in the acute phase; analgesics may be necessary. Massage is contraindicated and may in fact cause further damage (bleeding and increased pain).

Complete recovery can be expected, but painless full range of motion should be achieved before the athlete returns to his or her sport. Recovery time may last from two days to six months, depending on the severity of the injury and the development of complications, such as myositis ossificans.

♣ It's A Fact!!
An athlete with a chronic injury should be evaluated by a sports medicine specialist. The specialist may identify biomechanical problems—such as muscle imbalances or legs of different length—that predispose the athlete to injury. Strengthening and flexibility exercises or orthotics (custom-fitted shoe inserts) often can correct the problem.

Myositis ossificans is a very painful condition in which an ossifying mass (calcium deposit) may form within the muscle. In many cases, myositis ossificans is the result of recurrent trauma to a quadriceps muscle that was not properly protected after an initial injury. A history of injury should always be confirmed to rule out other causes.

A hard, painful mass in the soft tissue of the thigh and progressive loss of bending motion of the injured knee are indications of myositis ossificans. The definitive diagnosis of this condition is made by x-ray, but usually not until at least four weeks after the injury.

In the early stages, treatment consists of heat, limitation of joint motion, and rehabilitative exercises within the limits of pain. Passive stretching and vigorous exercise during the first six months after injury are discouraged. The calcium mass usually will be re-absorbed by the body; however, resorption may take three to six months. Surgical excision may be necessary if pain and limited motion persist beyond one year.

Iliac crest contusions: The iliac crest contusion, or "hip pointer," is a very painful injury caused by a direct blow to the hip. Hip pointers are common in football players who wear improperly fitting hip pads. Extreme tenderness, swelling, and ecchymosis over the iliac crest are diagnostic in cases with a history of a direct blow to the iliac crest. Treatment involves application of ice and compression followed by oral non-steroidal anti-inflammatory medications. Return to sport should be dictated by the athlete's pain level; the injured area should be padded to protect it from further injury.

Overuse Injuries

Overuse injuries are common in athletes who have focused their efforts on one sport. These injuries are caused by the cumulative effects of very low levels of stress, such as the repetitive action of running. Chronic muscle strains, stress fractures, tendinitis (overuse/overload fatigue within the tendon), snapping hip (iliopsoas tendon snapping over the head of the femur), and bursitis (inflammation and thickening of the bursa wall) are examples of overuse injuries.

An athlete with an overuse injury should rest from the sport aggravating the injury and use cross-training techniques or should take up exercises that use different parts of the body to maintain cardiovascular conditioning.

Stress fractures: Stress fractures of the pelvis occur most often in runners and dancers. Stress fractures of the femur usually occur in runners. The injured athlete may complain of chronic, ill-defined pain over the groin and thigh. Initially, many such athletes are diagnosed with a muscle strain; but if there is no history of acute injury, the correct diagnosis probably is a stress fracture. If the symptoms do not resolve with rest and rehabilitative exercise, the athlete should be examined by a sports medicine specialist. Diagnosis is performed by using x-rays and/or bone scans. Treatment of stress fractures consists of rest and non-weight bearing endurance exercises, such as running in water or swimming.

☞ Remember!!

Two weeks to six months of recovery and rehabilitation of a hip or groin injury is normal. Cross training exercises can help the athlete to stay strong and prevent reinjury.

Chapter 25

Knee Injuries: Diagnosis and Treatment

What Do The Knees Do? How Do They Work?

The knees provide stable support for the body and allow the legs to bend and straighten. Both flexibility and stability are needed for standing and for motions like walking, running, crouching, jumping, and turning.

Several kinds of supporting and moving parts, including bones, cartilage, muscles, ligaments, and tendons, help the knees do their job. Any of these parts can be involved in pain or dysfunction.

What Causes Knee Problems?

There are two general kinds of knee problems: mechanical and inflammatory.

Mechanical Knee Problems

Some knee problems result from injury, such as a direct blow or sudden movements that strain the knee beyond its normal range of movement. Other problems, such as osteoarthritis in the knee, result from wear and tear on its parts.

About This Chapter: Text in this chapter is from "Questions and Answers About Knee Problems," National Institute of Arthritis and Musculoskeletal and Skin Diseases (NIAMS), May 2001.

Inflammatory Knee Problems

Inflammation that occurs in certain rheumatic diseases, such as rheumatoid arthritis and systemic lupus erythematosus, can damage the knee.

Joint Basics

The point at which two or more bones are connected is called a joint. In all joints, the bones are kept from grinding against each other by padding called cartilage. Bones are joined to bones by strong, elastic bands of tissue called ligaments. Tendons are tough cords of tissue that connect muscle to bone. Muscles work in opposing pairs to bend and straighten joints. While muscles are not technically part of a joint, they're important because strong muscles help support and protect joints.

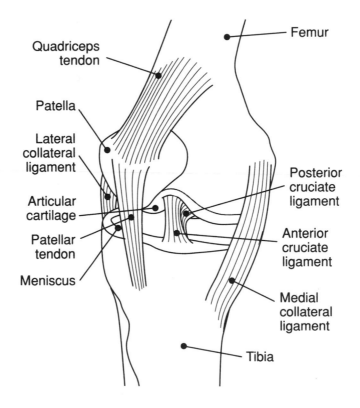

Figure 25.1. Lateral View Of The Knee

What Are The Parts Of The Knee?

Like any joint, the knee is composed of bones and cartilage, ligaments, tendons, and muscles (see Figure 25.1).

Bones And Cartilage

The knee joint is the junction of three bones: the femur (thigh bone or upper leg bone), the tibia (shin bone or larger bone of the lower leg), and the patella (knee cap). The patella is 2 to 3 inches wide and 3 to 4 inches long. It sits over the other bones at the front of the knee joint and slides when the leg moves. It protects the knee and gives leverage to muscles.

The ends of the three bones in the knee joint are covered with articular cartilage, a tough, elastic material that helps absorb shock and allows the knee joint to move smoothly. Separating the bones of the knee are pads of connective tissue. One pad is called a meniscus (muh-NISS-kus). The plural is menisci (muh-NISS-sky). The menisci are divided into two crescent-shaped discs positioned between the tibia and femur on the outer and inner sides of each knee. The two menisci in each knee act as shock absorbers, cushioning the lower part of the leg from the weight of the rest of the body as well as enhancing stability.

Muscles

There are two groups of muscles at the knee. The quadriceps muscle comprises four muscles on the front of the thigh that work to straighten the leg from a bent position. The hamstring muscles, which bend the leg at the knee, run along the back of the thigh from the hip to just below the knee. Keeping these muscles strong with exercises such as walking up stairs or riding a stationary bicycle helps support and protect the knee.

Tendons And Ligaments

The quadriceps tendon connects the quadriceps muscle to the patella and provides the power to extend the leg. Four ligaments connect the femur and tibia and give the joint strength and stability:

- The **medial collateral ligament (MCL)** provides stability to the inner (medial) part of the knee.

- The **lateral collateral ligament (LCL)** provides stability to the outer (lateral) part of the knee.

- The **anterior cruciate ligament (ACL)**, in the center of the knee, limits rotation and the forward movement of the tibia.

- The **posterior cruciate ligament (PCL)**, also in the center of the knee, limits backward movement of the tibia.

Other ligaments are part of the knee capsule, which is a protective, fiber-like structure that wraps around the knee joint. Inside the capsule, the joint is lined with a thin, soft tissue called synovium.

How Are Knee Problems Diagnosed?

Doctors use several methods to diagnose knee problems.

Medical history—The patient tells the doctor details about symptoms and about any injury, condition, or general health problem that might be causing the pain.

Physical examination—The doctor bends, straightens, rotates (turns), or presses on the knee to feel for injury and discover the limits of movement and the location of pain. The patient may be asked to stand, walk, or squat to help the doctor assess the knee's function.

Diagnostic tests—The doctor uses one or more tests to determine the nature of a knee problem.

- **X-ray (radiography)**—An x-ray beam is passed through the knee to produce a two-dimensional picture of the bones.

- **Computerized axial tomography (CAT) scan**—X-rays lasting a fraction of a second are passed through the knee at different angles, detected by a scanner, and analyzed by a computer. This produces a series of clear cross-sectional images (slices) of the knee tissues on a computer screen. CAT scan images show soft tissues such as ligaments or muscles more clearly than conventional x-rays. The computer can combine individual images to give a three-dimensional view of the knee.

- **Bone scan (radionuclide scanning)**—A very small amount of radioactive material is injected into the patient's bloodstream and detected by a scanner. This test detects blood flow to the bone and cell activity within the bone and can show abnormalities in these processes that may aid diagnosis.

- **Magnetic resonance imaging (MRI)**—Energy from a powerful magnet (rather than x-rays) stimulates knee tissue to produce signals that are detected by a scanner and analyzed by a computer. This creates a series of cross-sectional images of a specific part of the knee. An MRI is particularly useful for detecting soft tissue damage or disease. Like a CAT scan, a computer is used to produce three-dimensional views of the knee during MRI.

- **Arthroscopy**—The doctor manipulates a small, lighted optic tube (arthroscope) that has been inserted into the joint through a small incision in the knee. Images of the inside of the knee joint are projected onto a television screen. While the arthroscope is inside the knee joint, removal of loose pieces of bone or cartilage or the repair of torn ligaments and menisci is also possible.

- **Biopsy**—The doctor removes tissue to examine under a microscope.

Cartilage Injuries and Disorders

What Is Chondromalacia?

Chondromalacia (KON-dro-mah-LAY-she-ah), also called chondromalaciapatellae, refers to softening of the articular cartilage of the knee cap. This disorder occurs most often in young adults and can be caused by injury, overuse, parts out of alignment, or muscle weakness. Instead of gliding smoothly across the lower end of the thigh bone, the knee cap rubs against it, thereby roughening the cartilage underneath the knee cap. The damage may range from a slightly abnormal surface of the cartilage to a surface that has been worn away to the bone. Chondromalacia related to injury occurs when a blow to the knee cap tears off either a small piece of cartilage or a large fragment containing a piece of bone (osteochondral fracture).

Symptoms and Diagnosis

The most frequent symptom is a dull pain around or under the knee cap that worsens when walking down stairs or hills. A person may also feel pain when climbing stairs or when the knee bears weight as it straightens. The disorder is common in runners and is also seen in skiers, cyclists, and soccer players. A patient's description of symptoms and a follow-up x-ray usually help the doctor make a diagnosis. Although arthroscopy can confirm the diagnosis, it's not performed unless the condition requires extensive treatment.

Treatment

Many doctors recommend that patients with chondromalacia perform low-impact exercises that strengthen muscles, particularly the inner part of the quadriceps, without injuring joints. Swimming, riding a stationary bicycle, and using a cross-country ski machine are acceptable as long as the knee doesn't bend more than 90 degrees. Electrical stimulation may also be used to strengthen the muscles. If these treatments don't improve the condition, the doctor may perform arthroscopic surgery to smooth the surface of the cartilage and wash out the cartilage fragments that cause the joint to catch during bending and straightening. In more severe cases, surgery may be necessary to correct the angle of the knee cap and relieve friction with the cartilage or to reposition parts that are out of alignment.

> ## ✔ Quick Tip
> ## Rehabilitation Exercises
>
> These exercises are designed to build up the quadriceps and hamstring muscles and increase flexibility and strength after injury to the meniscus.
>
> - Warming up the joint by riding a stationary bicycle, then straightening and raising the leg (but not straightening it too much).
>
> - Extending the leg while sitting (a weight may be worn on the ankle for this exercise).
>
> - Raising the leg while lying on the stomach.
>
> - Exercising in a pool (walking as fast as possible in chest-deep water, performing small flutter kicks while holding onto the side of the pool, and raising each leg to 90 degrees in chest-deep water while pressing the back against the side of the pool).

Knee Arthroscopy

Knee arthroscopy (ARE-throw-skopp-ee) gives a view of the inside of your knee. This procedure allows the doctor to see if you have a knee injury or abnormality. The doctor may also use arthroscopy to correct your knee problem.

Detection

Arthroscopy can detect knee problems such as:

- tears in ligaments or tendons
- pain and swelling (inflammation)
- fractures
- loose pieces of bone or cartilage
- joint wear and tear

Treatment

Arthroscopy can treat knee problems such as:

- tears in meniscus (men-ISS-kiss) cartilage
- wear and tear of other cartilage
- tears in ligaments
- other knee problems

Arthroscopy uses only a few small incisions. Usually you have this procedure as an outpatient. You go home the same day as your surgery.

What Happens During Surgery?

First you are given anesthesia. Patients usually receive either general or spinal anesthesia. Then a very tight band is placed on the thigh of your affected leg. The band reduces the amount of bleeding in the joint and gives the doctor a better view. This band is called a tourniquet.

Two or three small incisions are made in the knee. The doctor can insert instruments through the incisions. First your knee is filled with

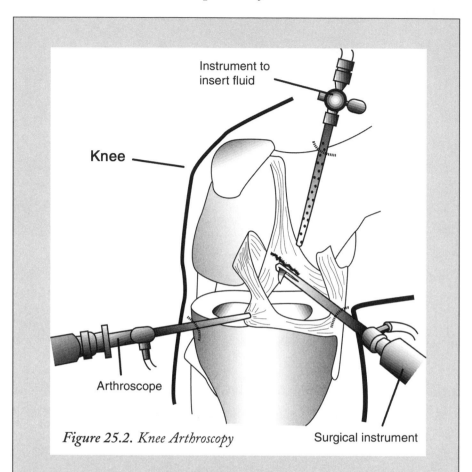

Figure 25.2. Knee Arthroscopy

sterile fluid. The fluid expands the knee joint to make more room inside for the doctor to see and work.

Next, a tube that has a small light and camera is inserted in the knee. The tube is called an arthroscope (ARE-throw-scope). The camera sends an image of your knee to a TV monitor. The doctor can view the inside of your knee on the monitor.

When possible, the doctor uses special surgical instruments to correct the injury or abnormality. Then the joint is washed out with a stream of fluid, and the instruments are removed. The incisions are closed with stitches, staples, or Steri-Strips. Last, a dressing is put on the incisions.

After Your Surgery

Dressing Care

It is important to keep the outer dressing clean and dry after surgery. The doctor will let you know when to remove this outer dressing. Underneath the outer dressing, you will find a smaller dressing over the incision. This may be a clear plastic dressing, called Opsite. You also may find several Band-Aids or Steri-Strips on the incision. Keep this smaller dressing in place until your follow-up visit, unless your doctor tells you otherwise. The Steri-Strips will peel off themselves.

For Pain And Swelling

It is important to keep your leg raised when you are not walking. Keep your ankle higher than your knee, and your knee higher than your hip. This will help reduce swelling and relieve pain.

Ice packs also can help with swelling and pain. For the first 48 hours, you may use ice packs for 20 to 30 minutes at a time, several times a day.

Your doctor may prescribe pain medicine to use at home. Take your pain medicine as prescribed.

To Prevent Movement

You may need to wear a special brace or immobilizer (im-OH-bill-eye-zer) on your knee. These devices provide support and comfort.

Physical Therapy

Your doctor or therapist may tell you to do special exercises after surgery. These will help restore movement and strength to your knee. You may be given crutches. Crutches help control the amount of weight you place on your leg. Your doctor or therapist will tell you how to use the crutches and when you can stop using them.

When To Call The Doctor

If you have any of the following, call your doctor:

- chills or a fever of 101° F (38.3° C) or above
- new or unusual drainage on your dressing
- redness, swelling, or drainage from your incisions
- swelling or pain in the calf of your affected leg
- chest pain or shortness of breath
- pain not relieved by taking prescribed pain medicine, raising your leg, or applying ice
- discoloration, numbness, or tingling in the affected leg or toes of the affected leg

Follow-Up Appointment

Keep your follow-up appointments with your doctor. It is important for your doctor to monitor your progress. Your doctor will check for any problems that may develop after surgery.

Call your doctor's office for a follow-up appointment:

Date: _____ Doctor's name: _____

Doctor's phone number: _____

If You Have Questions

If you any questions or concerns, call your doctor or nurse.

Source: "Knee Arthroscopy" is a patient information brochure from the University of Pittsburgh Medical Center. © 2003 University of Pittsburgh Medical Center. Reprinted with permission. For additional information, visit www.upmc.com, or for help in finding a doctor or health service that suits your needs, call the UPMC Referral Service at 800-533-UPMC (8762). This information is not intended to be used as a substitute for professional medical advice, diagnosis, or treatment. You should not rely entirely on this information for your health care needs. Ask your won doctor or health care provider any specific medical questions that you have.

Injuries To The Meniscus

What Causes Injuries To The Meniscus?

The meniscus is easily injured by the force of rotating the knee while bearing weight. A partial or total tear may occur when a person quickly twists or rotates the upper leg while the foot stays still (for example, when dribbling a basketball around an opponent or turning to hit a tennis ball). If the tear is tiny, the meniscus stays connected to the front and back of the knee; if the tear is large, the meniscus may be left hanging by a thread of cartilage. The seriousness of a tear depends on its location and extent.

Symptoms

Generally, when people injure a meniscus, they feel some pain, particularly when the knee is straightened. If the pain is mild, the person may continue moving. Severe pain may occur if a fragment of the meniscus catches between the femur and the tibia. Swelling may occur soon after injury if blood vessels are disrupted, or swelling may occur several hours later if the joint fills with fluid produced by the joint lining (synovium) as a result of inflammation. If the synovium is injured, it may become inflamed and produce fluid to protect itself. This makes the knee swell. Sometimes, an injury that occurred in the past but was not treated becomes painful months or years later, particularly if the knee is injured a second time. After any injury, the knee may click, lock, or feel weak. Although symptoms of meniscal injury may disappear on their own, they frequently persist or return and require treatment.

Diagnosis

In addition to listening to the patient's description of the onset of pain and swelling, the doctor may perform a physical examination and take x-rays of the knee. The examination may include a test in which the doctor bends the leg, then rotates the leg outward and inward while extending it. Pain or an audible click suggests a meniscal tear. An MRI may be recommended to confirm the diagnosis. Occasionally, the doctor may use arthroscopy to help diagnose and treat a meniscal tear.

Treatment

If the tear is minor and the pain and other symptoms go away, the doctor may recommend a muscle-strengthening program. Exercises for meniscal problems are best started with guidance from a doctor and physical therapist or exercise therapist. The therapist will make sure that the patient does the exercises properly and without risking new or repeat injury.

If the tear is more extensive, the doctor may perform arthroscopic or open surgery to see the extent of injury and to repair the tear. The doctor can sew the meniscus back in place if the patient is relatively young, if the injury is in an area with a good blood supply, and if the ligaments are intact. Most young athletes are able to return to active sports after meniscus repair.

If the patient is elderly or the tear is in an area with a poor blood supply, the doctor may cut off a small portion of the meniscus to even the surface. In some cases, the doctor removes the entire meniscus. However, osteoarthritis is more likely to develop in the knee if the meniscus is removed. Medical researchers are investigating a procedure called an allograft, in which the surgeon replaces the meniscus with one from a cadaver. A grafted meniscus is fragile and will shrink and tear easily. Researchers have also attempted to replace a meniscus with an artificial one, but this procedure is even less successful than an allograft.

Recovery after surgical repair takes several weeks, and postoperative activity is slightly more restricted than when the meniscus is removed. Nevertheless, putting weight on the joint actually fosters recovery. Regardless of the form of surgery, rehabilitation usually includes walking, bending the legs, and doing exercises that stretch and build up leg muscles. The best results of treatment for meniscal injury are obtained in people who do not show articular cartilage changes and who have an intact ACL.

Ligament Injuries

What Are The Causes Of Anterior And Posterior Cruciate Ligament Injuries?

Injury to the cruciate ligaments is sometimes referred to as a sprain. The anterior cruciate ligament (ACL) is most often stretched or torn (or both) by a sudden twisting motion (for example, when the feet are planted one way and the knees are turned another).

The posterior cruciate ligament (PCL) is most often injured by a direct impact, such as in an automobile accident or football tackle.

Symptoms And Diagnosis

Injury to a cruciate ligament may not cause pain. Rather, the person may hear a popping sound, and the leg may buckle when he or she tries to stand on it. The doctor may perform several tests to see whether the parts of the knee stay in proper position when pressure is applied in different directions. A thorough examination is essential. An MRI is very accurate in detecting a complete tear, but arthroscopy may be the only reliable means of detecting a partial one.

Treatment

For an incomplete tear, the doctor may recommend that the patient begin an exercise program to strengthen surrounding muscles. The doctor may also prescribe a brace to protect the knee during activity. For a completely torn ACL in an active athlete and motivated person, the doctor is likely to recommend surgery. The surgeon may reattach the torn ends of the ligament or reconstruct the torn ligament by using a piece (graft) of healthy ligament from the patient (autograft) or from a cadaver (allograft). Although synthetic ligaments have been tried in experiments, the results have not been as good as with human tissue. One of the most important elements in a patient's successful recovery after cruciate ligament surgery is a 4- to 6-month exercise and rehabilitation program that may involve using special exercise equipment at a rehabilitation or sports center. Successful surgery and rehabilitation will allow the patient to return to a normal lifestyle.

What Is The Most Common Cause Of Medial And Lateral Collateral Ligament Injuries?

The MCL is more easily injured than the LCL. The cause is most often a blow to the outer side of the knee that stretches and tears the ligament on the inner side of the knee. Such blows frequently occur in contact sports like football or hockey.

Symptoms And Diagnosis

When injury to the MCL occurs, a person may feel a pop and the knee may buckle sideways. Pain and swelling are common. A thorough examination is needed to determine the kind and extent of the injury. To diagnose a collateral ligament injury, the doctor exerts pressure on the side of the knee to determine the degree of pain and the looseness of the joint. An MRI is helpful in diagnosing injuries to these ligaments.

Treatment

Most sprains of the collateral ligaments will heal if the patient follows a prescribed exercise program. In addition to exercise, the doctor may recommend ice packs to reduce pain and swelling and a small sleeve-type brace to protect and stabilize the knee. A sprain may take 2 to 4 weeks to heal. A severely sprained or torn collateral ligament may be accompanied by a torn ACL, which usually requires surgical repair.

Tendon Injuries And Disorders

What Causes Tendinitis And Ruptured Tendons?

Knee tendon injuries range from tendinitis (inflammation of a tendon) to a ruptured (torn) tendon. If a person overuses a tendon during certain activities such as dancing, cycling, or running, the tendon stretches like a worn-out rubber band and becomes inflamed. Also, trying to break a fall may cause the quadriceps muscles to contract and tear the quadriceps tendon above the patella or the patellar tendon below the patella. This type of injury is most likely to happen in older people whose tendons tend to be weaker. Tendinitis of the patellar tendon is sometimes called jumper's knee because in sports that require jumping, such as basketball, the muscle contraction and force of hitting the ground after a jump strain the tendon. After repeated stress, the tendon may become inflamed or tear.

Symptoms And Diagnosis

People with tendinitis often have tenderness at the point where the patellar tendon meets the bone. In addition, they may feel pain during running, hurried walking, or jumping. A complete rupture of the quadriceps or patellar tendon is not only painful, but also makes it difficult for a person to bend, extend, or lift the leg against gravity. If there is not much swelling, the doctor will be able to feel a defect in the tendon near the tear during a physical examination. An x-ray will show that the patella is lower than normal in a quadriceps tendon tear and higher than normal in a patellar tendon tear. The doctor may use an MRI to confirm a partial or total tear.

Treatment

Initially, the doctor may ask a patient with tendinitis to rest, elevate, and apply ice to the knee and to take medicines such as aspirin or ibuprofen to relieve pain and decrease inflammation and swelling. If the quadriceps or patellar tendon is completely ruptured, a surgeon will reattach the ends. After surgery, the patient will wear a cast for 3 to 6 weeks and use crutches. For a partial tear, the doctor might apply a cast without performing surgery.

Rehabilitating a partial or complete tear of a tendon requires an exercise program that is similar to but less vigorous than that prescribed for ligament injuries. The goals of exercise are to restore the ability to bend and straighten the knee and to strengthen the leg to prevent repeat injury. A rehabilitation program may last 6 months, although the patient can return to many activities before then.

What Causes Osgood-Schlatter Disease?

Osgood-Schlatter disease is caused by repetitive stress or tension on part of the growth area of the upper tibia (the apophysis). It is characterized by inflammation of the patellar tendon and surrounding soft tissues at the point where the tendon attaches to the tibia. The disease may also be associated with an injury in which the tendon is stretched so much that it tears away from the tibia and takes a fragment of bone with it. The disease most commonly affects active young people, particularly boys between the ages of 10 and 15, who play games or sports that include frequent running and jumping.

Symptoms And Diagnosis

People with this disease experience pain just below the knee joint that usually worsens with activity and is relieved by rest. A bony bump that is particularly painful when pressed may appear on the upper edge of the tibia (below the knee cap). Usually, the motion of the knee is not affected. Pain may last a few months and may recur until the child's growth is completed.

Osgood-Schlatter disease is most often diagnosed by the symptoms. An x-ray may be normal, or show an injury, or, more typically, show that the growth area is in fragments.

Treatment

Usually, the disease resolves without treatment. Applying ice to the knee when pain begins helps relieve inflammation and is sometimes used along with stretching and strengthening exercises. The doctor may advise the patient to limit participation in vigorous sports. Children who wish to continue moderate or less stressful sports activities may need to wear knee pads for protection and apply ice to the knee after activity. If there is a great deal of pain, sports activities may be limited until discomfort becomes tolerable.

What Causes Iliotibial Band Syndrome?

This is an overuse condition in which inflammation results when a band of a tendon rubs over the outer bone (lateral condyle) of the knee. Although iliotibial band syndrome may be caused by direct injury to the knee, it is most often caused by the stress of long-term overuse, such as sometimes occurs in sports training.

Symptoms And Diagnosis

A person with this syndrome feels an ache or burning sensation at the side of the knee during activity. Pain may be localized at the side of the knee or radiate up the side of the thigh. A person may also feel a snap when the knee is bent and then straightened. Swelling is usually absent and knee motion is normal. The diagnosis of this disorder is typically based on the symptoms, such as pain at the outer bone, and exclusion of other conditions with similar symptoms.

Treatment

Usually, iliotibial band syndrome disappears if the person reduces activity and performs stretching exercises followed by muscle-strengthening exercises.

In rare cases when the syndrome doesn't disappear, surgery may be necessary to split the tendon so it isn't stretched too tightly over the bone.

Other Knee Injuries

What Is Osteochondritis Dissecans?

Osteochondritis dissecans results from a loss of the blood supply to an area of bone underneath a joint surface and usually involves the knee. The affected bone and its covering of cartilage gradually loosen and cause pain. This problem usually arises spontaneously in an active adolescent or young adult. It may be due to a slight blockage of a small artery or to an unrecognized injury or tiny fracture that damages the overlying cartilage. A person with this condition may eventually develop osteoarthritis.

Lack of a blood supply can cause bone to break down (avascular necrosis). The involvement of several joints or the appearance of osteochondritis dissecans in several family members may indicate that the disorder is inherited.

Symptoms And Diagnosis

If normal healing doesn't occur, cartilage separates from the diseased bone and a fragment breaks loose into the knee joint, causing weakness, sharp pain, and locking of the joint. An x-ray, MRI, or arthroscopy can determine the condition of the cartilage and can be used to diagnose osteochondritis dissecans.

Treatment

If cartilage fragments have not broken loose, a surgeon may fix them in place with pins or screws that are sunk into the cartilage to stimulate a new blood supply.

If fragments are loose, the surgeon may scrape down the cavity to reach fresh bone and add a bone graft and fix the fragments in position. Fragments that cannot be mended are removed, and the cavity is drilled or scraped to stimulate new cartilage growth. Research is being done to assess the use of cartilage cell and other tissue transplants to treat this disorder.

☞ **Remember!!**

For more information about knee problems contact:

National Institute of Arthritis and Musculoskeletal and Skin Diseases Information Clearinghouse
National Institutes of Health
1 AMS Circle
Bethesda, MD 20892-3675
Toll-Free: 877-22-NIAMS (226-4267)
Phone: 301-495-4484; Fax: 301-718-6366; TTY: 301-565-2966
Website: www.niams.nih.gov; E-mail: niamsinfo@mail.nih.gov

American Academy of Orthopaedic Surgeons
6300 North River Rd.
Rosemont, IL 60018-4262
Toll-Free: 800-346-AAOS (2267); Fax On Demand: 800-999-2939
Phone: 847-823-7186
Website: www.aaos.org

American College of Rheumatology
1800 Century Place, Suite 250
Atlanta, GA 30345
Phone: 404-633-3777; Fax: 404-633-1870
Website: www.rheumatology.org; E-mail: acr@rheumatology.org;

American Physical Therapy Association
1111 N. Fairfax Street
Alexandria, VA 22314
Toll-Free: 800-999-APTA (2782)
Fax: 703-684-7343
Website: www.apta.org

Arthritis Foundation
1330 West Peachtree Street
Atlanta, GA 30309
Toll-Free: 800-283-7800
Phone: 404-872-7100 or call your local chapter (listed in the local telephone directory)
Website: www.arthritis.org; E-mail: arthritis@finelinesolutions.com

What Is Plica Syndrome?

Plica (PLI-kah) syndrome occurs when plicae (bands of synovial tissue) are irritated by overuse or injury. Synovial plicae are the remains of tissue pouches found in the early stages of fetal development.

As the fetus develops, these pouches normally combine to form one large synovial cavity. If this process is incomplete, plicae remain as four folds or bands of synovial tissue within the knee. Injury, chronic overuse, or inflammatory conditions are associated with this syndrome.

Symptoms And Diagnosis

People with this syndrome are likely to experience pain and swelling, a clicking sensation, and locking and weakness of the knee. Because the symptoms are similar to those of some other knee problems, plica syndrome is often misdiagnosed. Diagnosis usually depends on excluding other conditions that cause similar symptoms.

Treatment

The goal of treatment is to reduce inflammation of the synovium and thickening of the plicae. The doctor usually prescribes medicine such as ibuprofen to reduce inflammation. The patient is also advised to reduce activity, apply ice and an elastic bandage to the knee, and do strengthening exercises. A cortisone injection into the plica folds helps about half of those treated. If treatment fails to relieve symptoms within 3 months, the doctor may recommend arthroscopic or open surgery to remove the plicae.

What Kinds Of Doctors Treat Knee Problems?

Extensive injuries and diseases of the knees are usually treated by an orthopaedic surgeon, a doctor who has been trained in the nonsurgical and surgical treatment of bones, joints, and soft tissues such as ligaments, tendons, and muscles. Patients seeking nonsurgical treatment of arthritis of the knee may also consult a rheumatologist (a doctor specializing in the diagnosis and treatment of arthritis and related disorders).

How Can People Prevent Knee Problems?

Some knee problems, such as those resulting from an accident, can't be foreseen or prevented. However, a person can prevent many knee problems by following these suggestions:

- Before exercising or participating in sports, warm up by walking or riding a stationary bicycle, then do stretches. Stretching the muscles in the front of the thigh (quadriceps) and back of the thigh (hamstrings) reduces tension on the tendons and relieves pressure on the knee during activity.

- Strengthen the leg muscles by doing specific exercises (for example, by walking up stairs or hills, or by riding a stationary bicycle). A supervised workout with weights is another way to strengthen the leg muscles that support the knee.

- Avoid sudden changes in the intensity of exercise. Increase the force or duration of activity gradually.

- Wear shoes that both fit properly and are in good condition to help maintain balance and leg alignment when walking or running. Knee problems can be caused by flat feet or overpronated feet (feet that roll inward). People can often reduce some of these problems by wearing special shoe inserts (orthotics). Maintain a healthy weight to reduce stress on the knee. Obesity increases the risk of degenerative (wearing) conditions such as osteoarthritis of the knee.

Chapter 26

Foot And Ankle Injuries

Making Contact

For many sports enthusiasts, making contact is what real competition is all about. Youth football is an integral part of American culture, and the Super Bowl is the most watched annual event on television.

Soccer, which fills huge stadiums the world over, is among the most popular youth sports in the United States. Other contact sports like lacrosse, from Native American tradition, and British rugby have become popular as well.

All these sports require miles of running—with quick stops and starts—per game. Competition is usually on grass fields, which give so players may change direction quickly. It also provides a soft landing surface on which to crash.

Injuries are inevitable in contact sports. The lower extremities—an athlete's steering, accelerator, and braking systems—are particularly susceptible. But with proper conditioning, equipment, and technique, competitors in contact sports have successful, healthy playing seasons.

About This Chapter: Text in this chapter is reprinted with permission from "Your Podiatric Physician Talks About Contact Sports and Your Feet," a brochure produced by the American Podiatric Medical Association, www.apma.org. © 1999 APMA. Reprinted by permission.

Podiatric physicians, specialists in care of the lower extremity, not only treat injuries athletes and get them back into competition as soon as safely possible, but also help athletes get into a condition that minimizes their risk of injury to the foot and ankle.

Preventing Overuse Injuries

The time a football, soccer, or lacrosse player spends in an actual game represents only a tiny fraction of time spent in practice conditioning for competition. Practice involves hours of running, repetitive drills, and scrimmages every day.

While conditioning exercises in practice will strengthen and improve flexibility in the lower extremity, the repeated stress of practice may bring on chronic, or overuse injuries. These injuries can nag at a player and hamper, if not end, a season of competition.

Overuse injuries also come from faulty biomechanics of the feet—how the lower extremity physically adjusts to the ground. If an athlete has flat feet, which tend to pronate (out-toe) or excessively high arches, which often supinate (in-toe), extensive running and cutting can produce chronically strained ankles.

Before taking the practice field, it's wise to be examined by a podiatric physician specializing in sports medicine, who will identify any biomechanical abnormalities that increase the chance of injury. The podiatrist may recommend specific exercises to strengthen and improve flexibility of the foot and ankle, or recommend taping or padding of the foot or ankle before practice and competition. A podiatrist may also prescribe orthoses, customized shoe inserts that correct biomechanical problems by redistributing the body's weight.

Podiatric physicians say proper stretching and warm-up before and after home workouts, practice, and before games go far to prevent overuse injuries to the supporting structures of the lower extremity. Warm-up and cool-down exercises should take 5–10 minutes and should be conducted in a stretch/hold/relax pattern, without any bouncing or pulling. When muscles are properly warmed up, the strain on muscles, tendons, and joints is reduced.

✔ Quick Tip
Immediate Treatment Of Foot And Ankle Emergencies

Foot and ankle emergencies happen every day. Broken bones, dislocations, sprains, contusions, infections, and other serious injuries can occur at any time. Early attention is vitally important. Whenever you sustain a foot or ankle injury, you should seek immediate treatment from a podiatric physician.

That advice is universal, even though there are lots of myths about foot and ankle injuries. Some of them follow.

Myths

1. **"It can't be broken, because I can move it."** False; this widespread idea has kept many fractures from receiving proper treatment. The truth is that often you can walk with certain kinds of fractures. Some common examples: breaks of the thinner of the two leg bones; small chip fractures of either foot or ankle bones; and the frequently neglected fracture of a toe.

2. **"If you break a toe, immediate care isn't necessary."** False; a toe fracture needs prompt attention. If x-rays reveal it to be a simple, displaced fracture, care by your podiatrist usually can produce rapid relief. However, x-rays might identify a displaced or angulated break. In such cases, prompt realignment of the fracture by your podiatric physician will help prevent improper or incomplete healing. Many patients develop post-fracture deformity of a toe, which in turn results in formation of a painfully deformed toe with a most painful corn. A good general rule is: Seek prompt treatment for injury to foot bones.

3. **"If you have a foot or ankle injury, soak it in hot water immediately."** False; don't use heat or hot water if you suspect a fracture, sprain, or dislocation. Heat promotes blood flow, causing greater swelling. More swelling means greater pressure on the nerves, which causes more pain. An ice bag wrapped in a towel has a contracting effect on blood vessels,

produces a numbing effect, and prevents swelling and pain. After seeing a podiatric physician, warm compresses and soaks may be used.

4. **"Applying an elastic bandage to a severely sprained ankle is adequate treatment."** False; ankle sprains often mean torn or severely over-stretched ligaments, and they should receive immediate care. X-ray examination, immobilization by casting or splinting, and physiotherapy to insure a normal recovery all may be indicated. Surgery may even be necessary.

5. **"The terms fracture, break, and crack are all different."** False; all of those words are proper in describing a broken bone.

Before Seeing The Podiatrist

If an injury or accident does occur, the steps you can take to help yourself until you can reach your podiatric physician are easy to remember if you can recall the word *rice*.

1. Rest. Cut back on your activity, and get off your feet if you can.

2. Ice. Gently place a plastic bag of ice, or ice wrapped in a towel, on the injured area in a 20-minute-on, 40-minute-off cycle.

3. Compression. Lightly wrap an Ace bandage around the area, taking care not to pull it too tight.

4. Elevation. Sit in a position that you can elevate the foot higher than the waist, to reduce swelling and pain.

5. Switch to a soft shoe or slipper, preferably one that your podiatrist can cut up in the office if it needs to be altered to accommodate a bulky dressing.

6. For bleeding cuts, cleanse well, apply pressure with gauze or a towel, and cover with a clean dressing. It's best not to use any medication on the cut before you see the doctor.

7. Leave blisters unopened if they are not painful or swollen.

8. Foreign materials in the skin, such as slivers, splinters, and sand, can be removed carefully with a sterile instrument. A deep foreign object, such as broken glass or a needle, must be removed professionally.

9. Treatment for an abrasion is similar to that of a burn, since raw skin is exposed to the air and can easily become infected. Cleansing is important to remove all foreign particles. Sterile bandages should be applied, along with an antibiotic cream or ointment.

Prevention

1. Wear the correct shoes for any event. Good walking shoes provide more comfort and better balance.

2. Wear hiking shoes or boots in rough terrain.

3. Different sports activities call for specific footwear to protect feet and ankles. Use the correct shoes for each sport. Don't wear any sports shoe beyond its useful life.

4. Wear safety shoes if you're in an occupation which threatens foot safety. There are specific safety shoes for a variety of on-the-job conditions. Be certain they are fitted properly.

5. Always wear hard-top shoes when operating a lawn mower or other grass-cutting equipment.

6. Don't walk barefoot on paved streets or sidewalks.

7. Watch out for slippery floors at home and at work. Clean up obviously dangerous spills immediately.

8. If you get up during the night, turn on a light. Many fractured toes and other foot injuries occur while attempting to find your way in the dark.

Source: Reprinted with permission from, "Your Podiatric Physician Talks About Foot and Ankle Injuries," a brochure produced by the American Podiatric Medical Association. www.apma.org © 1999 APMA. Reprinted with permission.

Crashes, Bumps, And Bruises

Football players, who today more than ever combine size with speed, experience high-impact collision on virtually every play. Lacrosse players check much like hockey players, but wear thin pads on the arms and shoulders. Rugby players wear no padding at all. Though technically soccer is not a contact sport, players of any age will tell you that high speed collisions, kicks in the shin, and body contact happen all the time.

The foot and ankle bear the brunt of the crashes, bumps, and bruises of contacts sports. Feet get stepped on, kicked, jammed, twisted, and cut. Quick changes in direction and hard tackling can lead to sprains and fractures of the ankle.

Impact, or trauma injuries are more serious than overuse injuries, and require recovery time away from the practice and game field. Immediate treatment should include the RICE formula: Rest, Ice, Compression, and Elevation.

Trauma injuries should always be treated by a medical professional such as a podiatrist, and be fully healed before returning to the field. Players who lie about how an injury feels, or take pain-killers to play through a trauma injury, are not helping their team by doing so, but rather putting themselves in danger of aggravated or permanent injury.

Footwear

Cleats are the footwear of choice for all contacts sports down to the youth leagues. Cleats are generally safe for young ankles, say podiatrists. Cleats should be light and flexible, and always fit properly. Uppers should be supple (no hand-me-downs, please), and there should be, and at least a finger's width should separate the tip of the big toe and the end of the shoe. Laces should be tight.

When shopping for cleats, wear the same style of socks you intend to wear in competition. Shop in the afternoon, when the feet are naturally slightly swollen. Investing in proper footwear for a young athlete is much less expensive than medical treatment later.

Artificial Turf

Contact sports are sometimes played on artificial turf, which presents a new set of concerns for an athlete. Some surfaces simulate the texture of grass, and others are little more than carpet. All forms of artificial surface are harder than grass, and make for speeded-up competition. Cross-training shoes or sneakers are the footwear of choice on artificial turf.

Because the surfaces do not give like grass, playing on them may be more hazardous to the lower extremity. Players should be well-familiarized with the dynamics of running and changing direction on turf before competing on that surface.

Trainers and physicians frequently tape the feet and ankles of their players for added stability, especially on artificial turf. Proper taping can help prevent injuries from occurring, and keep a minor injury from becoming a major one.

Injuries And Treatments

Keeping the lower extremity healthy is so important to an athlete that most all professional football and soccer teams have a team podiatrists, who treats minor problems like corns, calluses, and blisters, to major injuries like fractures and dislocations. These are the most common injuries suffered in contact sports:

Turf Toe. Turf toe is a painful jam or hyperextension of the big toe. The condition is more common on artificial turf, but can happen on grass as well. Immediate treatment includes the RICE regimen, and wearing a stiffer shoe prevents aggravation of the injury. Splinting the toe or special orthoses can also help.

Ankle Sprains. Making contact on a firmly planted ankle can forcibly invert the joint and damage ligaments, resulting in a sprain. Immediate treatment using the RICE formula to reduce swelling is important to quick healing. Any sprain that doesn't show improvement in three days should be checked by a podiatric or family physician.

Stress Fractures. There are two distinct kinds of fractures that require vastly different treatment. Stress fractures are incomplete cracks in bone caused by overuse. Stress fractures heal with complete rest. Extra padding in shoes helps prevent stress fractures.

Fractures. Fractures are more serious injuries that require immediate medical attention. Casting and sometimes surgery is required to immobilize fractures and set breaks. Requiring 10-12 weeks for rehabilitation, a fracture or a break essentially ends a season of competition in any contact sport.

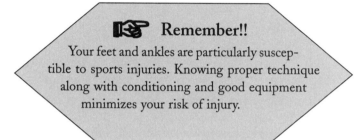

☞ Remember!!
Your feet and ankles are particularly susceptible to sports injuries. Knowing proper technique
along with conditioning and good equipment
minimizes your risk of injury.

Chapter 27

Female Athlete Triad: Disordered Eating, Amenorrhea, and Osteoporosis

With dreams of Olympic trials and college scholarships in her mind, Hannah joined the track team her freshman year and trained hard to become a lean, strong sprinter. When her coach told her losing a few pounds would improve her performance, she didn't hesitate to start counting calories and increasing the duration of her workouts. She was too busy with practices and meets to notice that her period had stopped—she was more worried about that stress fracture in her ankle slowing her down.

♣ **It's A Fact!!**

The condition female athlete triad was first recognized by the American College of Sports Medicine in 1992. Before then, doctors considered disordered eating separately from a girl's athletic participation, but health pros now know that athletic participation and the disordered eating in girls with female athlete triad are interrelated.

About This Chapter: Text in this chapter is from "Female Athlete Triad." This information was provided by KidsHealth, one of the largest resources online for medically reviewed health information written for parents, kids, and teens. For more articles like this one, visit www.KidsHealth.org, or www.TeensHealth.org. © 2001 The Nemours Center for Children's Health Media, a division of The Nemours Foundation. Reprinted with permission.

Although Hannah thinks her intense training and disciplined diet are helping her performance, they may actually be hurting her—and her health.

What Is Female Athlete Triad?

"The benefits of sports and exercise far outweigh the risks of female athlete triad, and exercise should always be part of a balanced life," says Angela Smith, MD, president of the American College of Sports Medicine and an orthopedic surgeon. The good news is that girls who play sports are healthier; get better grades; are less likely to experience depression; and use alcohol, cigarettes, and drugs less frequently. But for some girls, not balancing the needs of their bodies and their sports can have major consequences.

✎ Weird Word

Female Athlete Triad: A combination of three conditions: disordered eating, amenorrhea (pronounced: ay-meh-nuh-ree-uh, loss of a girl's period), and osteoporosis (a weakening of the bones). A female athlete can have one, two, or all three parts of the triad.

Girls who have disordered eating often have many of the signs and symptoms of anorexia nervosa or bulimia nervosa, such as low body weight for height and age and episodes of binge eating and purging, but they try to lose weight primarily to improve their athletic performance. Sometimes the disordered eating that accompanies the female athlete triad is "not really an eating disorder—many girls with the female athlete triad are trying to meet the needs of their sports," Dr. Smith says, although, like teens with eating disorders, girls with female athlete triad may use behaviors such as calorie restriction, purging, and exercise to lose weight.

Dr. Smith emphasizes that female athletes must balance their energy intake with the need for strong muscles and strong bones. "If you're not taking in enough energy, you're tearing down muscle mass, tearing down bone, putting yourself at risk for stress fractures, and you may actually have more body fat than when you started limiting your energy intake," she says.

Because a girl with female athlete triad is simultaneously exercising intensely and reducing her weight, she may experience decreases in estrogen, the hormone that helps to regulate the menstrual cycle. As a result, a girl's periods may become irregular or stop altogether. (It's important to remember, though, that in many cases, a missed period indicates another medical condition—pregnancy. If you have missed a period and you are sexually active, you should talk to your doctor.) Some girls may never even get their first period because they've been training so hard—this is called primary amenorrhea. Other girls may have had periods, but once they increase their training and change their eating habits, their periods may stop—this is called secondary amenorrhea.

Low estrogen levels and poor nutrition can also lead to osteoporosis, the third aspect of the triad. Osteoporosis is a weakening of the bones due to the loss of bone density and improper bone formation, and "unfortunately, the osteoporosis that results from female athlete triad may not be reversible," Dr. Smith says. This condition can ruin a female athlete's career because it may lead to stress fractures and other injuries due to weakened bones. Because of poor nutrition, a girl's body may not be able to repair the injuries efficiently. Usually, the teen years are a time when girls should be building up their bone mass to their highest levels—called peak bone mass. Female athlete triad can lead to a lower level of peak bone mass and a lot of time on the sidelines. After she becomes an adult, a girl may also develop health problems related to osteoporosis at an earlier age than she would have otherwise.

Who Gets This Disorder?

Most girls have concerns about the size and shape of their bodies, but girls who develop female athlete triad have certain risk factors that set them apart. Being a highly competitive athlete and participating in a sport that requires you to train hard is a risk factor. Girls with female athlete triad often care so much about their sport that they would do almost anything to improve their performance. Martial arts and rowing are examples of sports that classify athletes by weight class, so focusing on weight becomes an important part of your training program and can put you at risk for disordered eating.

Participation in sports where a thin appearance is valued can also put a girl at risk for female athlete triad. Sports such as gymnastics, figure skating, diving, and ballet are examples of sports that value a thin, lean body shape. Some girls may even be told by coaches or judges that losing weight would improve their scores.

Even in sports where body size and shape aren't as important for judging purposes, such as distance running and cross-country skiing, girls may be pressured by teammates, parents, partners, and coaches who mistakenly believe that losing just a few pounds would improve their performance. "Girls who are starving themselves limit their energy intake, and as soon as they eat, their bodies pack on the calories as fat instead of muscle," Dr. Smith says. So losing those few pounds generally doesn't improve performance at all—and it interferes with a girl's healthy body processes such as menstruation and bone development.

> ♣ **It's A Fact!!**
> How common is female athlete triad? Some studies have found between 15% to 62% of female college athletes have disordered eating, one component of the triad. Other surveys have indicated that as many as 66% of female athletes have amenorrhea.

For some competitive female athletes, low self-esteem, a tendency toward perfectionism, and family problems place them at risk for disordered eating.

What Do Doctors Do?

"There's a lot of secrecy surrounding the problems of female athlete triad," Dr. Smith says. It's easy for girls to hide information about their periods and any damage done to bones usually isn't visible to friends and family. And lots of girls become very skilled at hiding their disordered eating habits.

A doctor may recognize components of the triad during a regular exam. An extensive physical examination is a crucial part of diagnosing the triad. A doctor who suspects a girl has female athlete triad will ask many questions about her periods, her nutrition and exercise habits, any medications she takes, and her feelings about her body. Because inadequate nutrition can

✔ Quick Tip

What Are The Signs And Symptoms?

If you have risk factors for female athlete triad, you may already be experiencing some symptoms and signs of the disorder, such as:

- weight loss

- absent or irregular periods

- fatigue and decreased ability to concentrate

- stress fractures (fractures that occur unrelated to significant trauma or injury)

- muscle injuries

Because disordered eating is a component of female athlete triad, signs and symptoms of eating disorders such as anorexia nervosa and bulimia nervosa are also commonly present, such as:

- eating alone

- preoccupation with food and weight

- continuous drinking of water and diet soda

- frequent trips to the bathroom during and after meals

- using laxatives

- presence of lanugo hair (fine, soft hair that grows on the body)

- eroded (worn away) tooth enamel (from frequent vomiting)

- anemia (fewer red blood cells in the blood than normal)

- sensitivity to cold

- heart irregularities and chest pain

affect the body in many ways, a doctor might also test for anemia and mineral imbalances. Because osteoporosis can put a girl at higher risk for bone fractures, tests to measure bone density may also be performed if female athlete triad is suspected.

Doctors don't work alone to help a girl with female athlete triad—coaches, parents, physical therapists, pediatricians and adolescent medicine specialists, internists, nutritionists and dietitians, and psychologists and psychiatrists all work together to treat the physical and emotional problems that a girl with female athlete triad experiences.

It might be tempting for a girl with female athlete triad to shrug off several months of missed periods, but getting help promptly is crucial. In the short term, a girl with female athlete triad may have muscle weakness, stress fractures, improper bone development, and reduced physical performance. In the long term, a girl with female athlete triad may suffer from bone weakness, damage to her reproductive system, and heart problems.

A girl who is recovering from female athlete triad may work with a dietitian to help get to and maintain a healthy weight and ensure she's eating enough nutrients for health and good athletic performance. Depending on how much the girl is exercising, she may have to reduce the length of her

---

☞ Remember!!

Tips For Female Athletes

Here are a few tips to help teen athletes stay on top of their physical condition:

- **Keep track of your periods.** It's easy to forget when you had your last visit from Aunt Flo, so keep a little calendar in your gym bag and mark down when your period starts and stops and if the bleeding was particularly heavy or light. That way, if you start missing periods, you'll know right away and you'll have accurate information to give to your doctor.

- **Don't skip meals or snacks.** You're constantly on the go between school, practice, and competitions, so it may be tempting to skip meals and snacks to save time. But eating now will improve your performance later, so stock your locker or bag with quick and easy favorites such as bagels, string cheese, unsalted nuts and seeds, raw vegetables, energy bars, and fruit.

- **Visit a dietitian or nutritionist who works with teen athletes.** He or she can help you get your dietary game plan into gear and can help you determine if you're getting enough key nutrients such as iron, calcium, and protein. And, if you need supplements, a nutritionist can recommend the best choices.

- **Do it for you.** Pressure from teammates, parents, or coaches can turn an activity you took up for fun into a nightmare. If you're not enjoying your sport, make a change. Remember: it's your body and your life—and any damage you do to your body now, you'll have to live with later.

workouts. Talking to a psychologist or therapist can help a girl deal with depression, pressure from coaches or family members, or low self-esteem and can help her find ways to deal with her problems other than controlling her food intake or exercising excessively.

In some girls, hormone replacement therapy will be needed in addition to other treatments to help supply them with the estrogen their bodies should be producing so they can get their periods started again and protect the health of their bones. In such cases, birth control pills are often used to regulate a girl's menstrual cycle. Calcium and vitamin D supplementation is also common for a girl who has suffered bone loss as the result of female athlete triad.

What If I Think Someone I Know Has Female Athlete Triad?

A girl with female athlete triad can't just ignore the disorder and hope it goes away—she needs to get help from a doctor and other health professionals. If your friend, sister, or teammate has signs and symptoms of female athlete triad, discuss your concerns with her and encourage her to seek treatment. If she refuses to seek treatment, you may need to mention your concern to her parent, coach, teacher, or school nurse.

Looking for ways to be supportive to your friend with female athlete triad? You may worry about being nosy, but don't: your concern is a sign that you're a caring friend. Lending an ear may be just what your friend needs.

Chapter 28

A Guy's Guide To Testicular Injuries

It's your nightmare if you're a guy. You're at sports practice, working hard to get ready for the next game. Just as you realize you forgot to put on your athletic cup, you take a hit to the testicles and drop to your knees in pain.

Ouch—you might be flinching just imagining it. No guy wants to experience testicular trauma, but you can prepare yourself by knowing the warning signs of a serious problem and when to call the doctor. Keep reading so you'll be ready if you're caught without a cup.

What Are Testicular Trauma and Torsion?

Because the testicles hang in a sac outside the body, they are not protected by bones and muscles like the rest of the reproductive system. The location of the testicles makes it easier for them to be injured or hit, a painful sensation most guys have experienced at some time. Generally, because the testicles are loosely attached to the body and are made of a spongy material, they are able to absorb the shock of impact without permanent damage.

About This Chapter: Text in this chapter is from "A Guy's Guide to Testicular Injuries." This information was provided by KidsHealth, one of the largest resources online for medically reviewed health information written for parents, kids, and teens. For more articles like this one, visit www.KidsHealth.org, or www.TeensHealth.org, © 2001 The Nemours Center for Children's Health Media, a division of The Nemours Foundation. Reprinted with permission.

Another common type of testicular problem that occurs suddenly is called testicular torsion, and it occurs frequently in guys between the ages of 12 and 18. Within the scrotum, the testicles are secured at either end. Sometimes, a testicle can become twisted, cutting off the blood vessels that supply blood to the testicle. Testicular torsion might occur as the result of trauma to the testicles, strenuous activity, or it might develop while a guy is sleeping. In the United States, testicular torsion occurs in one out of 4,000 guys younger than 25.

An extremely rare type of testicular trauma is called testicular rupture. This condition may occur when the testicle receives a direct blow or when the testicle is crushed by some object. The testicle is compressed against the pubic bone, crushing the testicle against the bone and the object, causing blood to leak into the scrotum.

What Are The Signs And Symptoms?

If you are kicked or struck in the genital area, you may experience nausea, lightheadedness, dizziness, and sweating in addition to pain. For minor testicular injuries, the pain should gradually subside in less than an hour and the other symptoms should go away.

The signs and symptoms of testicular torsion are more severe and usually affect only one testicle, usually the left testicle. A guy with testicular torsion might experience rapid swelling and extreme pain in the scrotum that does not go away, nausea, vomiting, and abdominal pain.

Testicular rupture also causes extreme pain and swelling in the scrotum, nausea, and vomiting.

What Do Doctors Do?

If you are experiencing pain in your testicles that has lasted an hour or longer, extreme swelling, discoloration, or if your testicle was punctured, you need to seek medical treatment immediately, either by going to the emergency room or telling your parent, doctor, coach, or physical trainer.

The first thing a doctor will do is look at how you're acting—he or she can often assess the severity of your pain by observing whether you're writhing in pain or lying comfortably, whether you can talk to friends and family, and whether you're able to walk around without extreme discomfort.

The doctor may examine your abdominal and groin area to rule out a hernia. In addition, the doctor will look at your scrotum for swelling, color, and thickening of the skin. Because it's important how long you've been experiencing symptoms, the doctor may ask you questions like, "How long have you had pain?" "Have you had any blows or kicks to your testicles?" and "Do you play any sports?" In addition, the doctor will examine the testicle itself to check for tenderness and swelling.

♣ It's A Fact!!

It's common for guys to experience testicular trauma, which is when the testicles are struck, hit, kicked, or crushed. Almost all testicular injuries occur during sports.

To check for testicular torsion, your doctor may check a reflex in your genital area. The doctor will stroke or gently pinch the skin of the upper thigh while watching the muscles of your scrotum. If you don't have this reflex, it may tell the doctor that you have testicular torsion.

Because infections caused by bacteria can also cause extreme testicular pain, your doctor may give you a urine test to rule out a urinary tract infection. Ultrasounds are another tool doctors may use to look at your scrotum, however, because testicular torsion and rupture often require immediate surgery, your doctor may not do an ultrasound to save time and get you to the operating room.

Depending on the situation, the doctor may try to fix a twisted testicle by manually rotating the testicle. In most cases, though, surgery is the treatment for testicular torsion. A urologist (pronounced: you-rah-leh-jist), a doctor who specializes in urinary and genital problems, will make a small incision in your scrotum. He or she will check to see if the testicle is healthy, untwist it, and surgically anchor it so twisting can't occur in the future.

In the case of testicular rupture, surgery by a urologist is also necessary to drain and repair the ruptured testicle.

Dealing With And Preventing Testicular Injuries

If you've suffered a testicular injury, there are a few things you can do to feel better. Lie down, gently support the testicles with supportive underwear, and apply ice packs to relieve swelling and pain.

If you have had surgery for testicular torsion or rupture, your recovery time will be a little longer. According to T. Ernesto Figueroa, MD, a urologist who works with teens in Wilmington, Delaware, it can take weeks to months until a guy recovers from testicular surgery and can resume normal sports activities. Even then, Dr. Figueroa says, in teens "the genital area is more sensitive and prone to injury." Your doctor or urologist will give you specific instructions on pain relief and how to care for yourself after testicular surgery.

Do you have to worry that your sexuality or sperm production will be affected if you have a testicular injury? Your testicles, although sensitive, can bounce back pretty quickly and minor injuries rarely have long-term effects.

> ### ♣ It's A Fact!!
>
> With treatment within 6 hours from the time pain starts, 80% to 100% of guys with testicular torsion do not have to have the testicle removed. However, after 6 hours, there is a much greater possibility that infertility and loss of the testicle could result, so that's why it's so important to get treatment immediately. If a testicle does have to be removed, a guy will still be able to have normal sexual function. And because both testicles produce sperm, a guy will probably still be able to have children someday, even if one testicle has been removed.

Reading this chapter probably has you wondering how you can keep these injuries from happening to you. Try these tips to keep testicular trauma away:

- Always wear an athletic cup and supporter when you are playing sports or doing strenuous activity. This is the single most important thing you can do to protect yourself from genital injury.

- Check your fit. Make sure the athletic supporter and cup you wear are the right size—safety equipment that is too small or too large won't protect you as effectively from injury.

- Keep your doctor informed. If you play sports, you probably have regular physical exams by a doctor. If you experience testicular pain even occasionally, talk to your doctor about it because you might be prone to genital injury.

- Be aware of the risks of your sport. Dr. Figueroa says that lacrosse and baseball are the sports that have the highest incidence of testicular injury. Horseback riding may also put you at risk. If you play a sport with a higher risk for injury, talk to your coach or doctor about additional protective gear.

☞ Remember!!

Sports are a great way to stay fit and relieve stress. Make sure that using protective gear is part of your pre-practice and pre-game routine and you'll be able to play hard without fear of testicular injury.

Chapter 29

Repetitive Stress Injuries

Michael takes as many English courses as his schedule allows and writes science fiction stories in his spare time. He spends many hours writing and researching on the computer at school and at home. Lately he's had numbness and tingling in his hand, but he figures it's a normal result of spending so much time clicking the mouse.

Michael doesn't realize he has the first symptoms of carpal tunnel syndrome, a repetitive stress injury. Repetitive stress injuries are an increasing health problem among teens.

What Are Repetitive Stress Injuries?

RSIs are the most common work-related injuries that people get and often affect people who work on computer keyboards a lot.

RSIs are more common in adults, although they are becoming more prevalent in kids and teens because they spend more time than ever using computers. Playing sports like tennis that involve repetitive motions can also

About This Chapter: Text in this chapter is from "Repetitive Stress Injuries." This information was provided by KidsHealth, one of the largest resources online for medically reviewed health information written for parents, kids, and teens. Fore more articles like this one, visit www.KidsHealth.org. or www.TeensHealth.org. © 2003 The Nemours Center for Children's Health Media, a division of The Nemours Foundation. Reprinted with permission.

lead to RSIs. You may hear sports-related RSIs referred to as overuse injuries. Teens who spend a lot of time playing musical instruments or video games are also at risk for RSIs.

In general, RSIs include more than 100 different kinds of injuries and illnesses resulting from repetitive wear and tear on the body. These injuries vary from person to person in type and severity.

In teens, overuse injuries most often occur at growth plates (areas at the ends of bones where bone cells multiply rapidly, making bones longer as someone grows). Areas most affected by RSIs are the elbows, shoulders, knees, and heels.

> **✎ Weird Word**
>
> Repetitive Stress Injuries (RSIs): A group of injuries that happen when too much stress is placed on a part of the body, resulting in inflammation (pain and swelling), muscle strain, or tissue damage. This stress generally occurs from repeating the same movements over and over again.

What Causes Repetitive Stress Injuries?

Most RSI conditions found in teens are linked to the stress of repetitive motions at the computer or in sports. When stress occurs repeatedly over time, the body's joints don't have the chance to recover, and the joints and surrounding tendons and muscles become irritated and inflamed.

Certain jobs that involve repetitive tasks such as scanning items as a supermarket checker or carrying heavy trays over your head as a waiter can lead to certain RSIs. Rarely, playing musical instruments can cause problems from overuse of certain hand or arm movements.

Using improper equipment while playing sports or using a computer is another important factor involved in RSIs. For example, running in athletic shoes that don't provide enough support can lead to shin splits and foot and ankle problems. Improperly fitted tennis rackets can contribute to tennis elbow.

Teens may be susceptible to RSIs because of the significant physical growth that occurs in the teen years. Growth spurts (rapid growth periods during puberty) can create extra tightness and tension in muscles and tendons, making teens more prone to injury.

Nutritional factors also come into play in RSIs. Proper nutrition is essential for developing and maintaining strong muscles and bones—and to keep up the energy levels needed to play sports and perform other physical activities well.

What Kinds Of Repetitive Stress Injuries Can Teens Get?

RSIs that can develop in teens include:

Bursitis—Inflammation of the bursa, which are fluid-filled sacs that act as cushions for the joints, is known as bursitis. Signs of bursitis include pain and swelling. It is associated with frequent overhead reaching, carrying overloaded backpacks, and overusing certain joints during sports such as the knee or shoulder.

Carpal tunnel syndrome—In carpal tunnel syndrome, swelling occurs inside a narrow tunnel formed by bone and ligament in the wrist. This tunnel surrounds nerves that conduct sensory and motor impulses to and from the hand, causing pain, tingling, and numbness. Carpal tunnel syndrome is caused by excessive up-and-down motions of the wrist from typing, playing video games (using joysticks), and other activities. It is rare in teens and is more common in adults, especially those in computer-related jobs.

Epicondylitis (pronounced: ep-ih-kon-dih-lie-tis)—This condition is characterized by pain and swelling at the point where the bones join at the elbow. It's nicknamed tennis elbow because it frequently shows up in tennis players who repeatedly straighten their elbows and extend their wrists.

Osgood-Schlatter disease—This is a common cause of knee pain in teens, especially teen athletes who are undergoing a growth spurt. Frequent use and physical stress (such as running long distances) can cause an inflammation at the area where the tendon from the kneecap attaches below the shinbone.

Patellar femoral syndrome—This is a softening or breaking down of kneecap cartilage. Squatting, kneeling, and climbing stairs and hills can aggravate pain around the knee.

Shin splints—This term refers to pain along the shin or front of the lower leg. Shin splints are commonly found in runners and are usually harmless, although they can be quite painful.

Stress fractures—Stress fractures are tiny cracks in the bone's surface caused by rhythmic, repetitive overloading. These injuries can occur when a bone comes under repeated stress from running, marching, or other activities or from stress on the body like when a person changes running surfaces too quickly.

Tendonitis—In tendonitis, tearing and inflammation occur in the tendons, rope-like bands of tissue that connect muscles to bones. Tendonitis is associated with repetitive overstretching and overuse of certain muscles.

Preventing Sports-Related Repetitive Stress Injuries

- You should always begin any sports season with a full physical exam from your doctor so that any problems or concerns can be addressed before you begin workouts and competitions.

- Always warm-up and cool-down with appropriate stretching exercises before and after playing.

♣ It's A Fact!!
What Happens When Teens Have Repetitive Stress Injuries?

Symptoms of RSIs include:

- tingling, numbness, or pain in the affected area

- stiffness or soreness in the neck or back most of the time

- feelings of weakness or fatigue in the hands or arms that doesn't seem to get better with rest

- frequent headaches

If you notice any of these warning signs of RSIs, make an appointment to see your doctor. Even if your symptoms seem to come and go, don't ignore them or they may lead to more serious problems.

Without treatment, RSIs can become more severe and prevent you from doing simple everyday tasks and participating in sports, music, and other favorite activities.

- Wear the proper clothing and equipment for your sport. For example, tennis players should be fitted for rackets that allow for a good grip on the handle. Wear appropriate safety gear for your sport such as knee pads and waist supports.

- Drink plenty of water before, during, and after your workouts. Listen to your body and rest when you feel tired.

- If you are experiencing symptoms such as pain, swelling, numbness, or stiffness while playing your sport, stop playing right away and see your doctor as soon as possible.

What Do Doctors Do?

The sooner an RSI is diagnosed, the sooner your body can heal, so be sure to see your doctor if you have symptoms.

The doctor will ask you about your medical history and give you a physical examination. He or she will try to assess how the injury occurred and

---

☞ **Remember!!**

Taking Care Of Yourself

Prevention is the best medicine when it comes to RSIs. Here are some general guidelines that can help you to prevent RSIs:

- Avoid overuse. Be sensible about the amount of time you spend doing any repeated motions.

- Remember warm-ups! It's important to stretch and do warm-up exercises before any vigorous activities or sports.

- Exercise regularly and stay active. Overall flexibility and strength can help to prevent RSIs.

- Take breaks. Remember to give yourself periodic breaks, about every 30 minutes, from an activity. Take a short walk or do some stretches.

- Vary your day-to-day activities. Alternate distance running with bicycling or swimming, for example.

what motions cause pain. Your doctor may perform x-rays, blood tests, or other tests to make sure there are no other health problems.

If you are diagnosed with an RSI, resting the affected area is the key to getting better. Your doctor may recommend that you take anti-inflammatory medication (such as Motrin) for a period of time. Moist heat treatments are sometimes also recommended to reduce pain and swelling.

After the swelling and pain have gone away, your doctor may suggest a rehabilitation program with a physical therapist to exercise your muscles slowly and to prevent loss of joint movement.

Part Four

Rehabilitation And Physical Therapy

Chapter 30

Going To A Physical Therapist

It was the last minute of the big soccer game. Kelly was running toward the goal line hoping to kick the winning point when she crashed into another player. Ouch! When she tried to stand up, Kelly's leg really hurt. Her parents took her to the emergency room. There, a doctor told Kelly she had broken her right leg.

Kelly would have to use crutches and wear a cast for 6 weeks. She was worried. What would happen when her leg was healed? Would it ever be strong enough for soccer or softball again? Several days after the accident, Kelly's parents took her to a physical therapist. "Don't worry," he said. "I'll have you running and kicking in no time."

What Is Physical Therapy?

A physical therapist can treat different conditions in many ways, including massage, heat and cold treatments, or electric stimulation. They might also help a person use exercise equipment like a treadmill, step or stair climber, or stationary bicycle. More than 90,000 physical therapists treat nearly 1 million people every day.

About This Book: Text in this chapter is from "Going to a Physical Therapist." This information was provided by KidsHealth, one of the largest resources online for medically reviewed health information written for parents, kids, and teens. For more articles like this one, visit www.KidsHealth.org, or www.TeensHealth.org. © 2001 The Nemours Center for Children's Health Media, a division of The Nemours Foundation. Reprinted with permission.

Who Needs It?

Physical therapists work with people of all ages and in a variety of places. Some work in schools with children who have physical disabilities. Many physical therapists work in hospitals or clinics. They may work with children who are recovering from injuries like a broken arm or a sprained ankle. Other kids who have medical conditions like cerebral palsy or juvenile rheumatoid arthritis or kids who were born without a leg or arm may be helped with physical therapy.

Some physical therapists work with athletes. They design fitness training programs and help athletes like Kelly recover from injuries. Physical therapy can also help relieve pain and prevent complications from developing after an operation or illness.

> **✔ Quick Tip**
>
> Physical therapists use other treatments, as well. Most help to reduce inflammation and pain in the area being treated, and may include:
>
> • massage
>
> • heat packs
>
> • ultrasound (vibrations with frequencies above the range that humans can hear)
>
> • whirlpool bath (a bath that uses whirling currents of warm water)

Visiting The Physical Therapist

A visit to the physical therapist is easy and can even be fun! During the first visit, the physical therapist will evaluate your condition. He or she will figure out how flexible or strong your body is, how well you are able to do things like get in and out of bed, and whether you can walk on your own or need to use a cane or wheelchair.

> **✎ Weird Word**
>
> Physical Therapy: The use of exercises and other special treatments to help people make their bodies healthier and stronger.

Then the therapist creates a treatment plan just for you. Kelly learned how to walk and go up steps with her crutches as well as several exercises she could do at home. The exercises made sure her muscles didn't get weak while she couldn't walk.

As soon as Kelly's cast was removed, the real work began. She learned how to stretch her leg muscles. She also rode a stationary bicycle and walked on a treadmill. Her therapist applied ice packs to the leg afterward to reduce pain and swelling. Sometimes, he used a machine that sent a mild electrical current to the muscles in her leg through pads applied to the skin. The electrical stimulation also reduced pain and swelling and helped relieve stiffness. Some days Kelly got to work out in a heated swimming pool. Using the water to support her body made it easier to move.

How Long Will My Treatment Last?

Most physical therapy sessions last 45 to 60 minutes. Kids with a minor injury are usually completely healed within 6 weeks. Children who use physical therapy to increase their independence may visit a physical therapist once a week for many years.

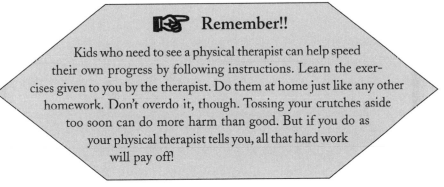

☞ Remember!!

Kids who need to see a physical therapist can help speed their own progress by following instructions. Learn the exercises given to you by the therapist. Do them at home just like any other homework. Don't overdo it, though. Tossing your crutches aside too soon can do more harm than good. But if you do as your physical therapist tells you, all that hard work will pay off!

Chapter 31

Rehabilitation Methods

Rehabilitation is the restoration of the ability to function in a normal or near-normal manner following an illness or injury. In sports medicine, rehabilitation usually involves reducing pain and swelling, restoring range of motion, and increasing strength. Rehabilitation for sports-related injuries is usually performed on an outpatient basis.

Rehabilitation Methods

Rehabilitation methods differ among patients based on the type and severity of their injuries and the level of physical wellness prior to injury.

♣ **It's A Fact!!**
Rehabilitation programs reduce recovery time and speed the return to work and sports activity.

Electrostimulation provides pain relief by preventing nerve cells from transmitting pain impulses to the brain. Electrostimulation also is used to make a muscle contract, which helps prevent muscle atrophy and maintain or increase muscle strength.

Heat is applied to soft tissue injuries and causes the blood vessels to dilate, increasing the blood flow to the injury site. Increased blood flow aids

About This Chapter: Text in this chapter is from "Rehabilitation," © 2000 The American Orthopaedic Society for Sports Medicine, reprinted with permission. For more information, visit www.sportsmed.org.

the healing process by removing dead tissues and substances that cause swelling and pain. Heat is generally used 48 hours after the injury occurs.

Ice is generally used within the first 48 hours after an injury. Icing an injury causes blood vessels to constrict and limits blood flow to the injury. Ice is primarily used to reduce swelling but it also reduces pain by numbing injured tissue.

Nonsteroidal anti-inflammatory drugs (NSAIDs) such as aspirin, ibuprofen, and naproxen sodium can help reduce inflammation, swelling, and pain.

Physical therapy is used to increase the range of motion and strength after an injury. Physical therapy includes various exercise and physical fitness programs that can be customized to meet each patient's needs.

Rest is the cessation of physical activity. Limiting activity can help stabilize an injury, which allows the body to heal itself more rapidly.

Ultrasound uses the vibrations from sound waves to stimulate blood flow to soft tissue such as muscles and ligaments. Stimulation of blood flow helps reduce swelling and aids healing.

Whirlpools operate similarly to heat and ultrasound. Whirlpools can increase circulation and blood flow to an injury to facilitate healing.

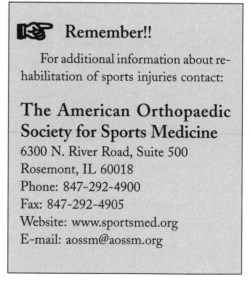

☞ Remember!!

For additional information about rehabilitation of sports injuries contact:

The American Orthopaedic Society for Sports Medicine
6300 N. River Road, Suite 500
Rosemont, IL 60018
Phone: 847-292-4900
Fax: 847-292-4905
Website: www.sportsmed.org
E-mail: aossm@aossm.org

Chapter 32

Returning To Play

What Does Return To Play Mean?

This refers to the point in recovery from an injury when a person is able to go back to playing their sport or participating in an activity at a level close to that which they participated at before.

No one likes to be sidelined with an injury. One of the goals of sports medicine is to try to get an athlete back into action as soon as possible. Returning too soon, before adequate healing or recovery, can put you at risk for re-injury and possibly an even longer down time.

A Lesson From The Pros

Why does it seem that professional athletes return to play so much faster? Professional athletes are usually in tremendous physical condition at the time of their injury. This fitness level helps them in many ways because studies have shown that good conditioning can not only prevent injuries, but can also lessen the severity of an injury and speed recovery.

About This Chapter: Text in this chapter is from "Sports Tips: Return to Play," © 1997 The American Orthopaedic Society for Sports Medicine, reprinted with permission. For more information, visit www.sportsmed.org. Reviewed in June 2003 by Dr. David A. Cooke, MD, Diplomate, American Board of Internal Medicine.

Professional athletes also get prompt treatment when an injury occurs and this lessens the acute phase of the injury. Early treatment means that there is less swelling, stiffness, and loss of muscle tone. In addition, they work extremely hard with a physical therapist and/or certified athletic trainer during their recovery.

In addition, they bring to their recovery what they bring to their sport—a positive attitude. While you may not have access to many things professional athletes have, you can harness the power of a positive attitude for your own benefit during recovery.

♣ **It's A Fact!!**
With the right game plan for sports injuries, from early diagnosis and treatment to full functional rehabilitation, you can often safely accelerate your return to play.

Your Recovery Plan

Recovery from an injury involves a series of logical steps from the time of the injury until you are able to be back on the field or court. Each step should be outlined and monitored by your physician and physical therapist.

During the acute phase, the focus should be on minimizing swelling. This involves the RICE formula: Rest, Ice, Compression, and Elevation, along with a limitation of activities. Depending on the type and severity of your injury, treatment may also involve surgery, bracing, or even casting.

During this period, it is very important to maintain overall conditioning while the injury heals. Creative techniques can be used to safely work around the injury. For example, a runner with a leg injury can often run in water or use a stationary bicycle to maintain conditioning. Even if one leg is in a cast, the rest of the body can be exercised by performing strength training exercises. Do not wait until your injury is healed to get back into shape.

In the next phase of recovery, you should work on regaining full motion and strength of the injured limb or joint. An exact plan should be outlined by your physician, therapist, or certified athletic trainer. For most injuries, gentle protective range of motion exercises can be started almost immediately. Muscle tone can be maintained with the use of electrical stimulation or simple strengthening exercises.

When strength returns to normal, functional drills can be started. This may include brisk walking, jumping rope, hopping, or light jogging for lower extremity injuries and light throwing or easy ground strokes for upper extremity injuries. Specific balance and agility exercises can bring back coordination that may have been lost in the injury.

Once you have progressed with motion, strength, endurance, and agility, and are tolerating functional drills, you can try higher levels of functional tests and drills that incorporate sport specific movement patterns on the field or court. This is monitored by your physical therapist or certified athletic trainer. You may find that tape, braces, or supports help during this transition time.

Only when you are practicing hard without significant difficulty and the healing has progressed to the point where the likelihood of injury or harm is low, are you ready to return to play. During these final phases of recovery, you should be closely monitored and special attention should be given to adequate warm-up before and icing after activity.

✔ Quick Tip

Tips From The Pros To Speed Your Recovery

- Maintain year round balanced physical conditioning.

- Make sure that injuries are recognized early and treated promptly.

- Participate in a full functional rehabilitation program.

- Stay fit while injured.

- Keep a positive, upbeat attitude.

A Word Of Caution

Following the rational progression of recovery not only lessens the chance of re-injury but assures that you will be able to perform at your best when you return to play. All too often, athletes think they are ready to return as soon as the limp or the swelling subsides. They may feel good, but they are probably only 70 to 75% recovered. This invites re-injury.

Sports medicine experts are working on ways to help athletes get as close to 100% recovery from injuries as possible, as quickly as safety allows. There is often tremendous pressure to get the athlete back as soon as possible, but the athlete's health and safety must be placed above all other concerns.

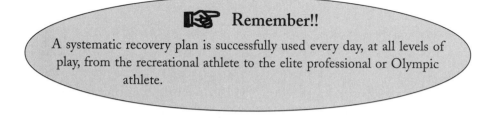

Remember!!

A systematic recovery plan is successfully used every day, at all levels of play, from the recreational athlete to the elite professional or Olympic athlete.

Part Five

Preventing Sports Injuries In Teens

Chapter 33

Minimizing The Risk Of Injury In High School Athletics

Introduction

Athletics are an important part of the high school experience for many students. Sports can provide a positive learning environment that will help student athletes in many aspects of their lives. And like pep rallies, Friday night football, and cross-town rivalries—injuries are an inevitable part of high school athletics regardless of the preventive measures taken. Students can, however, reduce their risk of injury by following several basic steps. One of the most important is proper overall conditioning, which can also enhance rehabilitation and shorten the down time of athletes.

The following guidelines have been developed based on interviews with a number of certified athletic trainers around the country. This listing is not all-inclusive, but is designed to provide guidance.

In addition to these general guidelines, the National Athletic Trainers' Association encourages all athletes to develop the specific skills involved in their sport and to be aware of the rules governing their athletic endeavors.

About This Chapter: Text in this chapter is excerpted with permission from "Minimizing the Risk of Injury in High School Athletics," a brochure from the National Athletic Trainers' Association (NATA), © 2003 NATA.

It is essential to remember that medical, legal, financial, and professional standards, limitations and requirements change continually and vary from place to place, person to person, and setting to setting. These guidelines must not, therefore, be taken to represent uniformly applicable national standards.

General Guidelines

- Every student athlete should receive a pre-participation physical exam, including a general exam and an orthopedic exam. The general exam should include checks on height, weight, blood pressure, pulse, respiration, eye, ear, nose, chest, and abdomen. The orthopedic exam should focus on joint flexibility, joint range of motion, and a re-examination of past bone and joint injuries.

- Athletes should work with athletic trainers and coaches year-round to ensure they maintain their condition with appropriate exercises and nutrition. In addition, athletes should engage in appropriate conditioning programs for a minimum of six weeks before the start of daily practice.

- Athletes should focus on developing muscular strength and endurance, cardiovascular fitness, and flexibility.

- Good nutritional practices incorporate the basic food groups: grains, fruits and vegetables, dairy, and meat/poultry/fish. Athletes' diets should be high in complex carbohydrates while also including essential proteins and fats.

- Athletes practicing or playing in warmer climates should become acclimatized to high levels of activity in hot weather. Practice should be held early in the morning or late in the afternoon.

- Limit workouts and practices to no more than two hours.

- The night before an event, athletes should hydrate with electrolyte fluids to reduce the risk of dehydration.

- Fluid breaks should be offered at least every 45 minutes, and athletes should be entitled to unrestricted amounts of fluids to help prevent dehydration and other forms of heat-related illness.

- All athletes should use appropriate equipment that fits properly. This equipment should be checked before and after each use to ensure that it is in proper working condition, and replaced or repaired immediately if any problems are noted.

- Appropriate protective equipment should be worn in all practices as well as during competitions.

- Shoes should fit appropriately and provide the necessary support for each individual sport.

- Foot diseases, such as athlete's foot, should be treated immediately and fully to avoid more extensive problems.

- Mouth guards should be used in all collision sports, including ice hockey, football, and rugby; and recommended for all sports where contact could occur, including basketball, baseball, lacrosse, soccer, etc. Not only do they help to prevent dental injuries, but they can also absorb shocks from blows to the jaw or head and reduce the severity of these blows.

- Players should stretch properly before and after workouts of any kind.

- A minimum 15-minute warm-up period before any game or practice, and an appropriate cool-down period afterward, is recommended. Athletes should also warm-up for five minutes during any prolonged breaks in activity (including half time, between periods, etc.).

- Ice should be available on the sidelines of every game and practice to apply to appropriate injuries.

- Injuries involving bones or joints should be examined by a licensed physician.

- All injuries should be evaluated immediately. Parents should be aware of who is responsible for injury care at their child's school.

- Parents should ask if this person is qualified to handle all injuries and provide proper instruction and rehabilitation, as well as whether he or she is available for both practice and games.

- Every school with an athletic program should have a written emergency plan which is reviewed regularly and addresses every level of medical care for injured athletes.

- Every school should be encouraged to develop an Injury Protection Manual, which answers any questions a parent may have about the way an injury is to be handled and who will be primarily responsible. The school should distribute this manual to all athletes' parents.

- The athletic department should be encouraged to have an Emergency Medical Authorization Card on file for every athlete. This card gives parental permission for emergency medical care if it is required. The card should include name, address, parents' home and work phone numbers, etc.

- The athletic department should be encouraged to have parents sign a waiver that indicates they are aware of the inherent risk of injury to their children.

- Coaches should be certified in first aid and CPR and, where possible, earn a state- or nationally-approved certificate to coach specific sports.

- All individuals involved in the athletes' health and safety—including athletic trainers, coaches, physicians, emergency medical personnel (paramedics and EMTs), school administrators, and parents—should be encouraged to maintain cooperative liaisons.

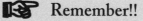 **Remember!!**

For additional safety information for specific sports review the sport-specific guidelines available in *Part VII: Sport Safety Guidelines For Active Teens.*

Chapter 34

Pre-Participation Physical Examinations

Past Medical History

History of any of the following should be made available to the healthcare provider:

- allergy
- birth defects
- eating disorders
- heart problems
- hernia
- measles
- mental disorders
- rheumatic fever
- tuberculosis

- allergies to medications
- chicken pox
- glasses/contacts
- heat problems
- high blood pressure
- medications
- mononucleosis
- seizures

- asthma
- diabetes
- heart murmur
- hepatitis
- kidney disease
- menstrual history
- pneumonia
- sickle cell trait or disease

Sport-Specific History

- Orthopedic injuries (sprains, fractures, dislocations) or surgeries

About This Book: Text in this chapter is reprinted with permission of the American College of Sports Medicine, *Pre-participation Physical Exam* Brochure, © 2002.

- Back or neck injuries

- Dental trauma

- Chest pain with exercise

- Feeling faint or having passed out with exercise

- Excessive shortness of breath or fatigue with exercise

- "Burners" or "Stingers"— caused by contact that produces burning pain that moves into the extremity.

- Withheld from participating in a sport for medical reason

Family History

- Heart disease or high blood pressure

- Diabetes

- Unexpected death before the age of 50

Physical Exam

The physical exam will usually consist of the following:

- Pulse rate

- Blood pressure rate

- Height

- Weight

- Vision screening

- Hearing screening

  Exam by health-care provider:

- Head—eyes, ears, throat, teeth, neck

✔ Quick Tip

After a thorough history and physical exam, the healthcare provider will make a participation decision by answering the following questions:

- Is there a problem that places the athlete at increased risk of injury?

- Is any other participant at risk of injury because of this problem?

- Can the athlete safely participate with treatment of the problem?

- Can limited participation be allowed while treatment is initiated?

- If clearance is denied for certain activities, in what activities can athlete safely participate?

- Is consultation with another healthcare provider necessary to answer the above questions?

- Thorax—heart, lungs, chest wall

- Abdomen—liver, spleen, kidney, intestines

- Genitalia—sexual maturity, testicles, hernias

- Neurological—reflexes, strength, coordination

- Orthopedic—joints, spine, ligaments, tendons, bones (pain, range of motion, strength)

Other exams (laboratory, electrocardiogram, x-rays) may be done at the discretion of the health care provider.

Restriction from participation must be made based upon the best medically objective evidence, and should be determined with the musculoskeletal, cardiac, and aerobic demands of the proposed activity in mind. An understanding of how strenuous the activity is in relation to the physical limitations is crucial. If clearance is denied, recommendations for correction prior to participation should be communicated, and a follow-up evaluation should be scheduled. If acute illnesses or correctable conditions are resolved, clearance should be given.

Each case should be evaluated individually. Understanding the value of participation should guide the practitioner in determining a suitable approach for clearance. Although the PPE may identify health problems or needs not associated with exercise, it should not be used to replace ongoing medical care or routine check-ups with primary care physicians.

The pre-participation physical exam (PPE) is an important step toward safe participation in organized sports. It is important to understand that the purpose of the PPE is not to disqualify or exclude an athlete from competition, but to help maintain the health and safety of the athlete in training and competition. The PPE has the following goals:

- Identify medical and orthopedic problems of sufficient severity to place the athlete at risk for injury or illness.

- Identify correctable problems that may impair the athlete's ability to perform.

- Help maintain the health and safety of the athlete.

- Assess fitness level for specific sports.

- Educate athletes and parents concerning sports, exercise, injuries, and other health-related issues.

- Meet legal and insurance requirements.

Although there is some disagreement among health professionals as to the frequency and timing of the exam, the PPE is generally a formal requirement prior to participation in junior high, high school, college, or professional sports, with interim exams done annually if required or indicated. The qualifications of the health-care professional who performs the PPE is based on practitioner availability, clinical expertise, and individual state laws.

The PPE is best done in a medical setting to insure proper equipment and appropriate privacy. However, the large number of athletes involved, limited time for the exam, and deadlines for participation often require the PPE to be done in a format of multiple stations, with several health-care providers each focusing on their areas of expertise.

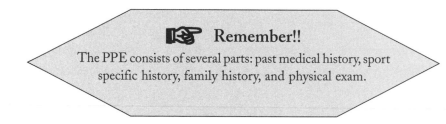

☞ **Remember!!**
The PPE consists of several parts: past medical history, sport specific history, family history, and physical exam.

Chapter 35

Fitness: A Key To Injury Prevention

Why Get Fit?

You've probably heard about how fitness can help you live longer and prevent diseases like heart disease in your future. But what can physical fitness do for you right now? A whole lot! Most of all, getting fit can and should be fun.

Increased Strength

When you are fit, you are more able to generate force with your body—whether that force is needed to lift weights or your book bag or your little brother. Being strong is useful for all sports as well as for life in general. Life is full of effort. Being strong all around makes everything a little easier, and it is a critical component of team and individual exercise activities.

Increased Stamina And More Energy Overall

Physical fitness training increases your stamina—your ability to keep going during moderate or strenuous activity. Stamina is also known as endurance. Your heart and lungs are able to work longer the more fit you are. You can

About This Chapter: Text in this chapter is from "Fit for Life: Why Get Fit?" from the National Women's Health Information Center, updated July 2002.

run farther, dance longer, and keep on playing well past sundown when you have good stamina. Exercise gives you more energy in general to do things you want to do.

Increased Flexibility

Flexibility refers to your range of motion around a joint. Touching your toes, reaching a high shelf, and arching your back gracefully are all examples of flexibility. Flexibility is very important to daily life, as well as to mastering the techniques of most sports activities. Many adults lose their flexibility as they grow older. Being flexible when you are young and maintaining it through the years can help you prevent that decline.

Psychological Benefits, Including Better Sleep

Exercise is a fabulous way to feel better any day of the week. Is family or school stressing you out? A moderate workout can ease the tension and leave you with an all-over good feeling. That's because exercise releases endorphins, special chemicals in the brain that make you feel peaceful and relaxed. When you are fit, you are generally better able to handle life's ups and downs too. You feel more self-confident and strong on the inside when you are strong on the outside. Regular exercise also helps you sleep better, which can really brighten your whole outlook each day.

Social Benefits

Participating in sports clubs, group exercise classes, or team sports can be a great way to meet new people and make friends with people with similar interests. If you're fit, your self-confidence will make you less shy.

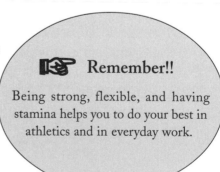

☞ **Remember!!**

Being strong, flexible, and having stamina helps you to do your best in athletics and in everyday work.

Body Fat Management

Regular, moderate exercise is one of the healthiest ways to keep your muscle-to-fat ratio where it should be. While each person has their own unique shape and size, everyone benefits from having a good balance of muscle and fat. It is important to remember that too little fat and too much fat can be a serious problem, so it is important to maintain a moderate exercise program and a healthy diet to ensure you get all of the nutrients, vitamins, minerals, and fat that you need.

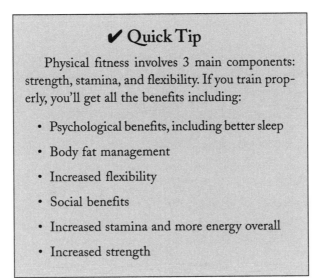

✔ **Quick Tip**

Physical fitness involves 3 main components: strength, stamina, and flexibility. If you train properly, you'll get all the benefits including:

- Psychological benefits, including better sleep
- Body fat management
- Increased flexibility
- Social benefits
- Increased stamina and more energy overall
- Increased strength

Chapter 36

Sports And Exercise Safety

Scene #1—Liz practices golf every day after school as well as on weekends. She feels persistent pain in her elbow, but she doesn't want to be off the golf team, so she doesn't say anything to her coach. A little while later, she is diagnosed with tendinitis.

Scene #2—Kevin, playing guard in a game of pick-up basketball, wants the ball so he can shoot it. Without looking to see where other players are, he fakes and spins before stepping awkwardly and spraining his ankle.

Scene #3—Marcel falls onto an opponent's skate blade during a hockey game. Because he's not wearing a face mask, he loses an eye.

Although injuries like these from sports and recreational activities are common, getting hurt doesn't have to happen. For teens, the best way to ensure a long and injury-free athletic career is to play it safe from the start. Sports injury prevention keeps everyone on the court or playing field—you and your teammates. Read on to learn the basics of sports and exercise safety.

About This Chapter: Text in this chapter is from "Sports and Exercise Safety." This information was provided by KidsHealth, one of the largest resources online for medically reviewed health information written for parents, kids, and teens. For more articles like this one, visit www.KidsHealth.org or www.TeensHealth.org. © 2002 The Nemours Center for Children's Health Media, a division of The Nemours Foundation. Reprinted with permission.

Essential Equipment

Did you know that playing tennis with a badly strung (too loose or too tight) racquet while wearing worn-out shoes can be just as dangerous as playing football with an out-of-place shoulder pad? Using the wrong—or improperly fitted—equipment is a major reason why teens are injured.

> ✔ **Quick Tip**
>
> Even if you don't belong to a team, you can use regular workouts and practices to enhance your performance and lessen the chance of injuries. Remember, if a tool isn't used, it gets rusty, so keep yourself in top shape with regular practice. For instance, try doing tennis drills or practicing your serve before starting a set. Shoot some baskets or play a quick game of one-on-one with a friend. Practice gets your brain and body to work together while improving your performance.

The equipment you wear while participating in sports and other activities is an important factor in keeping yourself injury-free. Whether you are playing league baseball or street hockey, you need to wear safety gear such as kneepads, goggles, wrist pads, shin guards, mouth guards, helmets, elbow pads, ankle supports, waist supports, shoulder pads, and proper footwear.

Not only is the right kind of equipment important—so is the right fit. If you don't know if your equipment fits properly, check with a parent, coach, or gym teacher to make sure you have the right size and that you are wearing it correctly. The bottom line: wearing the right equipment with the right fit dramatically decreases your chances of getting hurt.

Warm Up To Keep Your Game Up

Don't rush into any sport or exercise without warming up first—muscles that haven't been properly prepared tend to be injured more easily. Start out with some light cardiovascular activities, such as easy jogging, jumping jacks, or brisk walking, just to get your muscles warmed.

Follow your brief warm-up with some stretches. "Stretching is important after warm-ups because your tissues will be more elastic [flexible] due to the increase in heat and blood flow to the muscles," explains Michael Stanwood, a sports medicine specialist in Wilmington, Delaware.

In addition to warm-ups and stretches, practice sessions are also an excellent preparation for most sports or activities. If you belong to a team, attend as many team practices and games as possible. This will put you in top physical condition and help you and your teammates work together—and knowing how your teammates play will help prevent injuries.

Although you should practice regularly, don't overdo it. Sudden increases in training frequency, duration, or intensity might produce better performance in the short run but almost certainly will lead to injuries later. Your doctor or coach can help you develop a training and conditioning program that is appropriate for your age and level of development.

Staying Off The Court When You're Hurt

If you're injured and you try to come back too soon, the already weakened area is at increased risk for re-injury. Your doctor, coach, or team trainer will give you specific advice on when you should return to your sport or activity. Don't let anyone—including yourself, your parents, your friends, or even your coach—pressure you into playing before your body is fully healed.

In addition, seek medical treatment whenever you experience:

- moderate to severe pain

- pain that interferes with daily activity or sleep

- swelling of the injured area

- an inability to perform normal activities

The same advice goes for a cold or flu virus—don't play if you're sick. You won't be able to concentrate if your head is stuffed up and

♣ It's A Fact!!

Instead of seeking treatment, many teen athletes use pain relievers to avoid pain. If you feel persistent pain, don't use pain relievers to mask it. Taking large amounts of pain relievers can be dangerous and if you have a lot of pain, you need to seek treatment from a medical professional.

your nose is running faster than you are, and your lack of concentration can put you at risk for injury. It's better to wait until you feel better, so you can have a safe season.

The Rules Of The Game

Rules and regulations usually exist for a good reason—to keep your and your teammates in the game and away from injuries. Do yourself a favor and learn the rules thoroughly—and then follow them. Rules aren't restrictions—they are designed to promote safety so that everyone can enjoy the game. Sometimes rules may not be directly related to a sport or activity but need to be followed anyway. For instance, in-line skating, skateboarding, or bike riding teens should pay strict attention to all traffic laws.

Other sports use proper techniques, instead of rules, to promote safety. For example, when two tennis players rush the net, a nicely angled volley is the correct shot—not a hard smash socked directly at an opponent's face. "Good players trained by proper coaching seldom show poor form," Stanwood says, "Proper coaching, and the techniques that go with it, usually prevent unsafe play."

Another example of a safe technique occurs in weight lifting. Weight lifters should take a breath between each repetition. "On any pushing phase of a lift, you want to exhale. So if you're doing a bench press, let the bar come down to your chest, and if you're pushing up, breathe out," Stanwood says. And if you hold your breath? "It really raises your blood pressure, and pressing a lot of weight can lead to a blackout or fainting spell."

☞ **Remember!!**

So whether you're following rules, regulations, or proper techniques, remember that they aren't there to restrict you—they are there to keep you safe and injury-free.

Chapter 37

Handling Sports Pressure And Competition

"Winning is not a sometime thing: it's an all-the-time thing. You don't win once in a while; you don't do the right things once in a while; you do them right all the time. Winning is a habit. Unfortunately, so is losing."

That quote is from Vince Lombardi, the Green Bay Packers coach who led his team to five NFL championships in the 1960s.

Who could disagree? Competitive sports are all about winning, right?

Winning is certainly a goal of competitive sports, but sometimes players feel more than just the thrill of the game.

✎ Weird Words

<u>Distress</u>: A bad type of stress, a stress overload.

<u>Eustress</u>: A good type of stress that energizes you.

Being in an environment that stresses winning at all costs can make you totally stressed out. Read on to find out how to handle sports pressure and competition.

About This Chapter: Text in this chapter is from "Handling Sports Pressure and Competition." This information was provided by KidsHealth, one of the largest resources online for medically reviewed health information written for parents, kids, and teens. For more articles like this one, visit www.KidsHealth.org or www.TeensHealth.org. © 2001 The Nemours Center for Children's Health Media, a division of The Nemours Foundation. Reprinted with permission.

Why Do I Feel Stress When Competing?

Stress is your body's response to a physical or mental challenge. The gnawing feeling you get in your stomach before taking a test, the clammy palms you get on the day you have to give an oral report, and the feeling you get while sitting in your dentist's waiting room are all results of stressors (factors or situations that cause stress).

Stressors trigger your body's "fight or flight" response, an internal alarm system. When you perceive a threat, your adrenal glands secrete the hormone epinephrine (commonly called adrenaline) into the bloodstream. Your muscles tense, your heart races, your blood pressure rises, you breathe faster, and you start to sweat. Your body literally prepares to fight or flee.

Distress is a bad type of stress that arises when you must adapt to too many negative demands. Suppose you had a fight with a close friend last night, you forgot your homework this morning, and you're playing in a tennis match this afternoon. You try to get psyched for the game but can't. You've hit stress overload! Continuous struggling with too much stress can exhaust your energy and drive.

However, some stress is necessary, even helpful. Eustress is a good type of stress that stems from the challenge of a pleasant activity, such as a training run, tackling a tricky hobby, or rehearsing for a performance. Eustress pumps you up, providing a healthy spark for any task you undertake.

For example, champion golfer Tiger Woods can be tense on the golf course. His father wondered aloud why Tiger wouldn't just relax. Tiger told him, "That's how I enjoy myself, by shooting low scores."

What seemed like distress to his father was eustress to Tiger. Only Tiger could make the distinction. And only you can determine when stress is bad for you.

What Can I Do To Ease Pressure?

When the demands of competition start to get to you, try these relaxation techniques:

- **Deep breathing**—Find a quiet place to sit down. Inhale slowly through your nose, drawing air deep into your lungs. Hold your breath for about 5 seconds, then release it slowly. Repeat the exercise five times.

- **Muscle relaxation**—Contract (flex) a group of muscles tightly. Keep them tensed for about 5 seconds, then release. Repeat the exercise five times, selecting different muscle groups.

- **Visualization**—Close your eyes and picture a peaceful place or an event from your past. Recall the beautiful sights and the happy sounds. Imagine stress flowing away from your body.

- **Mindfulness**—Watch out for negative thoughts. Whether you're preparing for a competition or coping with a defeat, repeat to yourself: "I learn from my mistakes!" "I am in control of my feelings!" "I can do this!"

Christy Smith, guard for the WNBA's Charlotte Stings, offers this advice when sports get too stressful: "Get away from the pressure. Go to a movie, or hang out with friends."

Christy prepares for competition by lying in bed at night prior to a game, imagining herself completing one crucial shot after another. On game day, she recalls her stored images to help calm her nerves and boost her self-confidence.

Keeping Stress In Check

If sports make you so nervous that you get headaches, become nauseated, or can't concentrate on other things, you're experiencing symptoms of unhealthy, potentially chronic (which means long-lasting and continuous) stress. Don't keep such stress bottled up inside you; suppressing your emotions might mean bigger health troubles for you later on.

Talk about your concerns with a friend. Simply sharing your feelings can ease your anxiety.

Sometimes it may take an adult perspective to help resolve your conflict. A logical starting point is with your coach or physical fitness instructor.

It's possible that your anxiety stems only from uncertainty. Meet privately with your coach or instructor; ask for clarification if his or her expectations seem vague or inconsistent. Although most instructors do a good job of fostering athletes' physical and mental development, you may need to be the one who opens the lines of communication. You may also want to talk with your parents or another adult family member.

Recognizing when you need guidance to steer yourself out of a stressful situation doesn't represent weakness; it's a sign of courage and wisdom. Don't stop looking for support until you've found it.

Enjoying The Game

Winning is exhilarating! But losing and some amount of stress are part of almost any sports program. Sports are about enhancing self-esteem, building social skills, and developing a sense of community.

☞ Remember!!
Remember that above all, sports are about having fun

Chapter 38

Connecting With Your Coach

Your day was rotten from the minute you rolled out of bed half an hour late. You stepped in a lake of mud with your new shoes, forgot your lunch money, bombed a pop history quiz, had a fight with your best friend, and lost your keys. It's time for track practice, but after a day like that you just don't feel like going. What's the big deal about skipping out, right?

Well, aside from letting your teammates down and missing a chance to develop your athletic skills, you could jeopardize your relationship with an important person in your life: the coach. Keep reading to find out how you can keep this relationship a positive one.

What Your Coach Can Do For You

Even though athletics are an extra activity, they teach you about team-work, dedication, responsibility, and lots of other qualities you'll rely on throughout your life. And a good relationship with your coach helps you get the most out of your chosen sport.

Obviously, your coach can give you pointers on your performance. After all, he or she has probably been part of the sport longer than you have. You can draw on your coach's expertise to improve how you play, how you psych yourself up before a game or meet, or how you deal with a big loss or setback, and your coach can help keep you injury-free. Not only have coaches dealt with lots of players, and have seen which techniques work and which don't, but many of them have played the sport themselves and can share their personal experiences.

You also need a good relationship with your coach if you're going to put in those long hours and tough practices. The coach is the one setting the schedule, and if you plan to drag yourself to swim practice at 5:30 A.M. or do lay-ups for 2 hours, you have to like the person who's making you break a sweat. If you don't respect your coach, you're more likely to resent all the hard work instead of appreciating how it can help you in the long run.

Off the playing field, coaches can be good mentors and advisers, offering an adult perspective on nonsports problems or questions. (Many Olympic and professional athletes have had strong relationships with their coaches outside the game.)

✔ Quick Tip

Types Of Coaches

Figuring out how the coach manages the team will also help you develop your relationship. There are essentially two types of coaches: those who run their teams based on obedience and those who rely on responsibility, according to Stephen Mosher, PhD, an associate professor of sports studies in New York. **Obedience coaches** basically say, "I'm the one in charge, and I'm going to make the rules." To develop a good relationship with this type of coach, you have to follow the rules and respect his or her authority.

By contrast, **responsibility coaches** allow the players to have more input in setting team policies, like deciding which reasons for missing practice are valid or how to reprimand someone who's always late. You should show respect for this type of coach as well, but his or her approach to running the team is not as rigid. (If you think a team rule is unfair, for example, the coach might be open to revising it.)

Relationships with your coach can be different from relationships you have with your parents or boss. Those relationships follow a more established structure, whereas a coach is usually closer to your level, working with you toward a goal. When you're on more of an equal footing with someone, you might feel more comfortable opening up to him or her. For instance, if you're having a problem at home, talking things over with your coach might help you see the situation in a different light.

Getting Close To Your Coach

Ideally, a relationship between a coach and an athlete is based on mutual respect and trust. You can make a good impression by showing up for practice on time, abiding by team rules, and always putting a lot of effort into your performance, whether it's a workout or a game, meet, or match.

But to truly build respect, you have to do more than go through the motions. You have to recognize that the coach is an authority figure within the sports setting, based on his or her expertise. So even if you sometimes don't agree with your coach's opinion, your coach has a lot more experience than you do. After all, you would respect the opinion of a fellow player who had more experience than you—just think of the coach as a player who has been around for a while. But you shouldn't be afraid of your coach or unwilling to talk to him or her. Communication is crucial so both athlete and coach know what the other wants to achieve.

You also have to make sure you don't tell the coach you can do something you know you can't just to impress him. Failing to follow through on a promise will only erode the trust between you.

Common Coach Problems

Unfortunately, you might not have a great relationship with every coach you meet. Teens and their coaches often disagree about the amount of time team members get to play or favoritism the coach shows to certain players. Some athletes also complain that their coaches are too bossy and take all the fun out of the sport.

But one of the easiest ways for a relationship with a coach to go bad is for the coach to focus on winning instead of striving to improve. When a team feels too much pressure to win, the athletes can feel underappreciated, and that damages the trust between the coach and the team.

What Should You Do If You Don't Get Along?

If you do get off to a bad start with your coach, you can take steps to repair the damage. It's best not to involve your parents in minor issues like how much playing time you're getting. Instead, find a time to sit down with the coach and discuss what's bothering you—don't go up to him or her during practice or a game, however; try to schedule a time when it's less hectic.

When you talk, try not to complain. Instead, ask for help in fixing the problem. Listen carefully to the coach's response and try to understand where he or she is coming from; your coach might not have realized he or she had been giving you less playing time, or he or she might not have known you wanted a bigger role on the team. Usually, once you express yourself, the two of you will understand each other better and can work on building a stronger relationship. If the situation doesn't improve, though, you will have to decide if you can live with the way the coach runs the team.

What Should You Do If A Coach Harms You?

Unlike a simple disagreement over playing time, some situations call for immediate action. If a coach is verbally abusing you or driving you so hard that you risk injuring yourself, talk to your parents and set up a meeting with the coach's supervisor. There's usually someone above your coach's authority, like an athletic director or a principal.

If a coach assaults you physically or sexually, don't go back to practice. Never let something like that just happen without taking action. No one has the right to treat you that way. Tell your parents and the coach's supervisor, as well as the police if the situation warrants it. Sports may be an important part of your life, but it's far more important to protect your health and well-being.

☞ Remember!!

Connect with your coach through respectful communication, adherence to rules, and doing your best at practice and in competition.

Chapter 39

Helmets Prevent Sports-Related Injuries

One family's leisurely bike ride on a Sunday afternoon ended in the emergency room. "A cyclist came up from behind and didn't see the littlest rider. It was like a chain reaction. They all went down—hard," says Chris Hartzell, an emergency room nurse at Canonsburg Hospital outside of Pittsburgh, Pennsylvania. Mom, Dad, and three young children went to the emergency room by ambulance with head injuries. The youngest girl, who was knocked unconscious, was flown to a trauma center. Thankfully, everyone recovered. But according to Hartzell, this mishap could have been avoided if they had all worn helmets.

Statistics Hit Home

Many summer sports that people enjoy require the use of helmets for safety. Yet while helmet usage is on the rise, many people still neglect to strap one on before climbing aboard a bike, lacing up skates, or hitting the trails on horseback.

The bottom line: Leaving the helmet behind is dangerous—and potentially deadly.

About This Chapter: Text in this chapter is reprinted with permission from "Choose the Right Helmet for Your Favorite Summer Sport," *Family Safety and Health*, Summer 2000. Permission to reprint granted by the National Safety Council, a membership organization dedicated to protecting life and promoting health. For more information, visit the website of the National Safety Council at www.nsc.org.

Cushion Your Head Correctly

Regardless of the sport, helmets cushion the blow of a fall, hit, or other impact on the head. Nearly all helmets are made with expanded polystyrene, the same material found in picnic coolers.

Style and construction vary by sport, and you need to use the helmet appropriately. "However," says Randy Swart, director of the Bicycle Helmet Safety Institute in Arlington, Virginia, "wearing a helmet not designed for your sport is better than a bare head. It's just not ideal."

Here is some guidance on finding the proper helmet for your favorite sport.

♣ It's A Fact!!

Head injuries cause three-quarters of about 800 bicycle deaths each year, according to the Bicycle Helmet Safety Institute, a helmet advocacy program of the Washington, DC-area Bicyclist Association.

Another 82,000 people suffer brain injuries each year while playing sports, according to the Brain Injury Association in Alexandria, Virginia.

Biking And In-Line Skating

Wearing a helmet is regulated more for biking than other sports since, in recent years, many city and county governments have adopted helmet laws.

Although one helmet will work for both biking and in-line skating, serious skaters should consider using a helmet that offers better protection for the back of the head—the most likely area to hit the ground.

Wear either helmet low on your forehead, about two finger widths above your eyebrows. Sit the helmet evenly between your ears and flat on your head. Adjust the straps and pads so the helmet is snug and secure and doesn't move up and down or side to side when the strap is tightened.

Make certain any attached mirrors can break away during a fall. Remove visors that can shatter and cut your face.

More than 60 percent of childhood bicycle-related fatalities occur on small neighborhood roads, according to the U.S. Consumer Product Safety Commission. The CPSC estimates that about half of all bikers wear a helmet. "Fifty percent is good, but it means 50 percent are not wearing one," says Ken Giles, a CPSC spokesman.

♣ It's A Fact!!

Serious in-line skaters are more likely to experience an injury to the back of the head.

Skateboarding

Unlike bike helmets, most skateboarding helmets are designed to withstand multiple blows. "Helmets for this sport are different because crashes are more frequent and less severe," says Swart.

Look for proper fit and a sturdy chin strap. Padding should not restrict circulation and should not be so loose that the helmet can fall off. Also, notice whether the helmet blocks your vision and hearing.

Baseball/Softball

The head is involved in more baseball injuries than any other body part, according to the Brain Injury Association.

As in other sports, a baseball or softball batting helmet should fit squarely and snugly on the head, covering the forehead and not rocking side to side or forward and backward. These helmets should also include ear protectors. Players should consider eye protection as well.

Horseback Riding

Equestrian riding helmets are worn at a slight angle. The brim should rise about 10 degrees above the back of the helmet, according to the American Association for Horseman Safety.

Use Your Head For A Safe Start

Follow these helmet tips before venturing out.

- **Find a good fit.** Adjust straps so the helmet sits comfortably on your head, snugly touching all around but not squeezing. You should not be able to pull the helmet off or move it in any direction. Wear the helmet on top of your head, not tilted in any direction.

- **Know when to replace your helmet.** Some helmets need to be replaced after you've been in a collision. Others, such as for skateboarding, are designed for multiple knocks. Read your helmet's instruction manual.

  "Even though it may not show a crack, you never know what may have happened to the integrity of the helmet," says Patricia Gleason, president of the Safety Equipment Institute in McLean, Va. "You can't ensure that the helmet will protect the way it did before the fall."

- **Establish a helmet habit.** Children are more likely to wear helmets if their parents do and if they're introduced to them early. Always wear a helmet when participating in an activity that can cause injury to your head.

- **Remember these four S's:**

  Size: The Snell Memorial Foundation, a not-for-profit organization that tests and develops helmet safety standards, advises sports enthusiasts to try on several different helmets before purchasing. The best way to gauge comfort level and fit is through comparison.

  Strap: Make sure the chin strap fits under your chin snuggly and the V in the straps meets under the ear. Expect to spend 15 minutes on this, says Randy Swart of the Bicycle Helmet Safety Institute.

  Straight: Wear a helmet low on the forehead, about two finger widths above your eyebrows.

  Sticker: Look for a manufacturer's sticker citing the U.S. Consumer Product Safety Commission standard. You can also look for independent certification by Snell or the Safety Equipment Institute.

The helmet should fit equally around your head without exposing the forehead or obscuring your vision. Rock the helmet up and down and back and forth. If the scalp moves but the helmet is still comfortable, it fits. After wearing the helmet for about 5 minutes, take it off and look for marks on your forehead. If there are marks, try a larger size. Secure long hair at the nape of the neck rather than on top of the head.

Advice varies about whether to replace or repair this helmet after each fall. A safe rule of thumb is to have the helmet inspected any time it touches the ground in a fall.

Sports For The Rest Of The Year

After the highly publicized skiing deaths of Michael Kennedy in 1997 and Sonny Bono in 1998, the CPSC began urging skiers and snowboarders to wear helmets.

In 1998, more than 16,000 skiers and snowboarders suffered head injuries on the slopes. The CPSC estimates that more than 7,000 of those could have been prevented or reduced in severity with a helmet.

Athletes should also wear helmets for football and ice hockey. Helmets for these sports protect the ears and can withstand multiple blows.

For Additional Information About Helmets

National Safety Council
1121 Spring Lake Drive
Itasca, IL 60143-3201
Phone: 630-285-1121
Fax: 630-285-1315
Website: www.nsc.org; E-mail: info@nsc.org

Bicycle Helmet Safety Institute
4611 Seventh Street South
Arlington, VA 22204-1419
Phone: 703-486-0100
Website: www.helmets.org; E-mail: info@helmets.org

Safety Equipment Institute
1307 Dolley Madison Blvd., Suite 3A
McClean, VA 22101
Phone: 703-442-5732
Fax: 703-442-5756
Website: www.SEInet.org; E-mail: info@SEInet.org

U.S. Consumer Product Safety Commission
4330 East-West Highway
Bethesda, MD 20814-4408
Toll-Free: 800-638-2772
Phone: 301-504-6816
Fax: 301-504-0124 and 301-504-0025
Website: www.cpsc.gov; E-mail: info@cpsc.gov

The Snell Memorial Foundation
3628 Madison Avenue, Suite 11
North Highlands, CA 95660
Toll-Free: 888-SNELL99 (763-5599)
Phone: 916-331-5073
Fax: 916-331-0359
Website: www.smf.org; E-mail: info@smf.org

The Brain Injury Association of America
105 North Alfred St.
Alexandria, VA 22314
Toll-Free: 800-444-6443
Phone: 703-236-6000
Website: www.biausa.org; E-mail: familyhelpline@biausa.org

☞ Remember!!
Children, teens, and adults should wear the appropriate helmet when participating in sports or recreational activities where head injuries are a risk.

Chapter 40

The Right Shoe Can Prevent Injuries

The athletic shoe industry continues to offer new features and technologies, but the basic criteria for choosing athletic shoes remain the same as ever—comfort and safety. New developments such as unique designs for women and new lacing systems have improved shoe fit. Beyond the fit, knowledge of foot types and of the demands of each sport helps physicians guide patients toward shoes that will help them avoid injuries.

The abundant marketing glitz and hoopla may suggest that athletic shoes have undergone a revolution in recent years. They haven't. Rather, the trend has been a steady evolution in design and materials as manufacturers have sought to improve safety and performance.

"Even if [the shoe industry] had something that was earth-shattering, it would be evolved into place, not thrown into place," says Tom Brunick, director of the Athlete's Foot Stores Research and Development Center in Naperville, Illinois, and footwear editor of *Walking* magazine.

What's New?

Improvements within the last 4 or 5 years cover a broad range of design details, from the shape of the shoe to new lacing systems.

About This Chapter: Text in this chapter is reprinted with permission from Martin, DR: How to steer patients toward the right sport shoe. *Physician and Sportsmedicine* 1997, 25 (9), 138-144. © 1997. The McGraw-Hill Companies. All Rights Reserved. Reviewed in June 2003 by Dr. David A. Cooke, MD, Diplomate, American Board of Internal Medicine.

Options for women. Perhaps the most significant recent advance in athletic footwear is the acknowledgment that women's feet are usually anatomically different from men's and that they therefore benefit from specially designed shoes. A woman's foot is typically narrower than a man's and has a narrower heel relative to the forefoot.

"There are more and more women's shoes that aren't based on downsized or graded men's shoes," says Carol Frey, MD, director of the Orthopedic Foot and Ankle Center in Manhattan Beach, California. "More of them are now being developed based on the shape and function of a female foot. Companies are developing entire female divisions, developing [women's] lasts, the form over which a shoe is made." Shoes built from women's lasts reduce the heel slippage that can occur in downsized men's shoes.

> ✔ **Quick Tip**
> Companies that have used women's lasts [the form over which a shoe is made], according to Frey, include Nike, Asics, and Reebok.

More women than men now buy athletic footwear, and their demands have influenced the athletic shoe market. Though general fitness footwear remains important, competitive female athletes want performance shoes, just like their male counterparts. For example, Nike offers a line of basketball shoes designed specifically for women—11 different styles. Adidas has seven different women's soccer shoes. Brunick says, "You wouldn't have had that 4 years ago."

Midsole changes. The cushioning midsole of athletic shoes has been the Achilles heel of shoe design; the ethyl vinyl acetate (EVA) or polyurethane foam used in them breaks down relatively quickly. To improve durability, shoe manufacturers have devised midsoles that encapsulate air or gel; some running shoe midsoles are cushioned entirely with air. Though midsoles with encapsulated air or gel have never been wear tested, Frey says they do improve durability. "A good guess would be 25% to 50%," she says.

Another recent improvement is better support at the midsole; many companies are inserting support devices, according to *Runner's World* magazine.[1]

Older split-sole shoe designs tended to flex incorrectly at the midfoot rather than the forefoot, contributing to problems such as plantar fasciitis.

Laces and loops. Round laceroni shoelaces—similar to those used in hiking boots—are starting to show up in athletic shoes. Though the new laces untie more readily during use (without double-knotting or lace locks), when used with the new loop or web eyelets, they slide more easily through a shoe's loops and distribute the pressure across the top of the foot more evenly than flat laces.

Glenn Pfeffer, MD, an orthopedic surgeon and assistant clinical professor at the University of California, San Francisco, says the new laces allow a better fit than flat laces do. "They don't kink, they don't cause pressure points, and they glide easily," he says.

Neoprene sleeves. New shoe technology usually appears first in running shoes, and the latest development is the neoprene sleeve—an elasticized, padded cuff around the opening of the shoe. Neoprene sleeves "keep the shoe from pistoning up and down as you run," says Frey. "It gives you a better fit and grips the foot."

Thinner midsoles. In court shoes, the trend is to bring athletes closer to the court by reducing the thickness of the midsole, yet still provide good cushioning. Thinner midsoles lower the athlete's center of gravity and reduce side-to-side ankle motion.

Good Fit, Bad Fit

If female-specific shoes, laceroni, and neoprene sleeves were merely marketing gambits, they would merit little notice. However, they are providing active people and athletes with improvements that augment the fit and therefore the safety of athletic footwear. Poorly fitted shoes, after all, can cause many difficulties that don't happen when shoes fit well.

"Even the smallest [fit] problem can prevent athletes from performing to the best of their capabilities," writes Tom Clanton, MD, chair of the department of orthopedic surgery at the University of Texas Medical School at Houston.[2] Medical conditions that can arise from improper shoe fit, according to Clanton, include new-onset bunion pain (from narrow shoes or those with rigid material covering the forefoot), metatarsalgia or Morton's neuroma (shoes that are too tight across the forefoot), and black toe (a shallow toe box). Toe deformities such as hammer toe, claw toe, and overlapping fifth toe may become symptomatic in athletes whose shoes have toe boxes that are either too narrow or too shallow. Though calluses and blisters are more or less expected in many sports, they are more common with a shoe that rubs the skin excessively or allows the foot to move or slide around.

Physicians and other health professionals can help point patients who ask about shoes in the right direction. The physician can start by showing the patient the type of arch he or she has: high (pes cavus), medium, or low (pes valgus).

About 25% of the population needs some type of specialized shoe, says Pfeffer: patients who are flat-footed, are pronators, or have very high arches. "What should come to the doctor's mind are the two Cs—cushioning or control," says Pfeffer. "Patients who have very high-arched feet have very stiff feet, and they need cushioning. Patients who have flat feet and are prone to a lot of motion need a shoe that can control that motion," he says.

The average foot needs a middle style of shoe—one that's not too hard or too soft, says Michael Lowe, DPM, a podiatrist in Salt Lake City and president of the American Academy of Podiatric Sports Medicine. "That midrange is going to give you a nice, stable, functional kind of shoe," he says.

A patient's arch determines which type of last, or shape, the shoe should have. Patients who have low arches do best in a shoe that has a straight shape and a board last; those who have high arches require a shoe with a curved shape and slip-lasted construction; and

> **✔ Quick Tip**
>
> Patients should be reminded to consider their past foot problems when selecting new athletic shoes, says Pierce Scranton, MD, an associate clinical professor at the University of Washington. For example, if the patient has a history of repeated ankle sprains, perhaps he or she should select high-topped rather than low-topped aerobic shoes or cross-trainers.

those who have a medium arch benefit from one that has a semi-curved shape with a combination last.

Obviously, active people are wise to try a shoe on before buying it. That usually means buying at a retail store rather than by mail order or on the Internet. Physicians can help pick a good store. Clanton, for example, recommends that physicians develop a relationship with a local shoe store. "I've gone to several different shoe stores and tried on shoes myself and talked with some of the salesmen," he says. "I've gotten an idea of stores where I feel like my patients could benefit from the knowledge of the people there. That's where I make referrals."

Also, to help patients select correctly sized shoes, Clanton provides them with shoe-fit cards. He traces the patient's foot on a piece of paper, cuts an index card to match the tracing of the widest part of the foot, and then cuts out a half-inch notch where the card is the widest. The patient can place the card against the ball area of shoes being considered. Shoes narrower than the card may cause problems; shoes narrower than the notched width are almost certain to.

A Role In Injury Prevention

Besides comfort, injury prevention is what athletic shoes are all about. Shoes for running and other foot-strike activities are designed to prevent stress fractures, and shoes for court sports are designed to prevent ankle sprains.

"If you look at overall injuries and problems created by shoes, fit is the number one consideration," says Clanton. However, he says researchers focus not on how well shoes fit, but on how cushioning and control features prevent injuries. One study[3] put Israeli military recruits into modified basketball shoes, substantially reducing the incidence of metatarsal stress fractures that related to regular military boots. Other research has produced similar findings.[4] It's also been suggested that inadequate cushioning in shoes can cause injuries to runners.[5]

Shoe traction plays a role in preventing knee injuries such as noncontact anterior cruciate ligament ruptures. Traction is a particular issue with court

✔ Quick Tip

Replacing Basketball Shoes
Frequently Can Decrease Overuse Injuries

The average high school basketball player can greatly decrease his incidence of overuse injury by simply replacing his basketball shoes frequently, said Michael Lowe, DPM, past president of the American Academy of Podiatric Sports Medicine and team podiatrist of the Utah Jazz National Basketball Association team for over 18 years.

Dr. Lowe presented a study which showed that the average high school basketball player will utilize only one pair of new basketball shoes per season. The average runner will replace their running shoes every 350-500 miles (or equivalent to 66 hours running). The average high school or college player will easily work out 72 hours per month. The shoes are made of equivalent materials, i.e. sole, and "eva" midsole material which has a deformation fatigue factor that when exceeded, greatly increases stress to the foot, leg, and related soft tissue and bone structures. In time, the stress to a certain soft tissue or bone structure will create a fatigue injury which then renders the player unable to participate in his or her sport.

Dr. Lowe recommended that the basketball shoe be changed monthly during the season in practice and during games. This has been found to greatly decrease the rate of injury to professional players, to the point that they will often replace shoe gear every two to three days or games.

—Michael Lowe, DPM, past president of the AAPSM.

Source: Reprinted with permission from the American Academy of Podiatric Sports Medicine (AAPSM). © 2000 AAPSM. For additional information, visit www.aapsm.org.

☞ Remember!!

The right sport shoe will be comfortable and will help you to avoid injury.

and cleated sports shoes in regards to their interface with the playing surface. Frey explains that proper traction depends on the specific sport; too little traction may impair athletic performance, while too much traction increases the risk of injury.

Clanton says that while collegiate and professional athletes are apt to take the risk of higher-traction footwear for performance's sake, it makes little sense for people at the high school or less competitive levels to chance serious knee injuries.

Shorter cleats on football shoes or use of soccer shoes, for example, have been shown to reduce knee and ankle injuries in high school football players.[6,7] Clanton recommends that cleats on a shoe for younger people be no longer than one-half inch.

Scranton, team physician for the Seattle Seahawks of the National Football League, recalls a football shoe that was designed for play on snow and ice that could generate incredible torque. "My concern is that some star-struck kid, on a hot summer day, remembers seeing the Green Bay Packers slug it out on an ice-covered field wearing [this shoe]," he says, "and he goes down to the store and orders them."

Traction concerns can also apply to court shoes, since the friction produced by the outer sole depends on the material used and its interaction with the playing surface. "Different surfaces have different characteristics related to the shoes, and while the human body can adapt to a great degree, there are different exposure rates to injury based on traction," Scranton says.

Clanton says understanding of the shoe-surface interface hasn't advanced enough to warrant specific recommendations to athletes. "But it has become clear that friction is a critical factor in injury rates," he says. One study[8] has suggested that shoe manufacturers provide indications and suggested playing surface conditions for their shoes.

Scranton says that what's needed is "the development of a shoe that has good frictional characteristics but that will not 'Velcro' to a surface—whether it be a cleated shoe getting stuck in natural grass or a turf shoe getting stuck on a dry, hot field on a summer day."

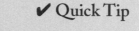

Athletic Shoes

Proper-fitting sports shoes can enhance performance and prevent injuries. Follow these specially-designed fitting facts when purchasing a new pair of athletic shoes.

- Try on athletic shoes after a workout or run and at the end of the day. Your feet will be at their largest.

- Wear the same type of sock that you will wear for that sport.

- When the shoe is on your foot, you should be able to freely wiggle all of your toes.

- The shoes should be comfortable as soon as you try them on. There is no break-in period.

- Walk or run a few steps in your shoes. They should be comfortable.

- Always relace the shoes you are trying on. You should begin at the farthest eyelets and apply even pressure as you a crisscross lacing pattern to the top of the shoe.

- There should be a firm grip of the shoe to your heel. Your heel should not slip as you walk or run.

- If you participate in a sport three or more times a week, you need a sports specific shoe.

It can be hard to choose from the many different types of athletic shoes available. There are differences in design and variations in material and weight. These differences have been developed to protect the areas of the feet that encounter the most stress in a particular athletic activity.

Athletic shoes are grouped into seven categories:

- **Running, training, and walking.** Includes shoes for hiking, jogging, and exercise walking. Look for a good walking shoe to have a comfortable soft upper, good shock absorption, smooth tread, and a rocker sole design that encourages the natural roll of the foot during the walking motion. The features of a good jogging shoe include cushioning, flexibility, control and stability in the heel counter area, lightness, and good traction.

- **Court sports.** Includes shoes for tennis, basketball, and volleyball. Most court sports require the body to move forward, backward, and side-to-side. As a result, most athletic shoes used for court sports are subjected to heavy abuse. The key to finding a good court shoe is its sole. Ask a coach or shoes salesman to help you select the best type of sole for the sport you plan on participating in.

- **Field sports.** Includes shoes for soccer, football, and baseball. These shoes are cleated, studded, or spiked. The spike and stud formations vary from sport to sport, but generally are replaceable or detachable cleats, spikes, or studs affixed into nylon soles.

- **Winter sports.** Includes footwear for figure skating, ice hockey, alpine skiing, and cross-country skiing. The key to a good winter sports shoe is its ability to provide ample ankle support.

- **Track and field sport shoes.** Because of the specific needs of individual runners, athletic shoe companies produce many models for various foot types, gait patterns, and training styles. It is always best to ask your coach about the type of shoe that should be selected for the event you are participating in.

- **Specialty sports.** Includes shoes for golf, aerobic dancing, and bicycling.

- **Outdoor sports.** Includes shoes used for recreational activities such as hunting, fishing, and boating.

Source: Reprinted with permission from "Athletic Shoes," a patient information fact sheet co-developed by the American Orthopaedic Foot & Ankle Society (AOFAS) and the American Academy of Orthopaedic Surgeons (AAOS) © 2001. For additional information, visit www.aofas.org or http://orthoinfo.aaos.org.

Pairing Shoes With Sports

In general, patients who participate in a certain sport or type of exercise three or more times a week should wear shoes designed for that activity. This will avoid problems such as the higher midsoles that cushion running shoes creating instability during the lateral movements of aerobics and court sports like tennis or basketball, and court shoes lacking the cushioning that running requires.

Cross-training shoes combine some elements of both running and court shoes, says Lowe. "For low mileage in either activity they're moderately successful, and they function well as a walking shoe," he says "We're very comfortable placing our couch-potato patients in a cross-training shoe and letting them do multiple activities."

Patients whose main activity is walking should be advised to consider a shoe designed for walking, says Pfeffer. "It has a much more cushioned heel and a stiffer midsole [than joggers], and more spring in the toe to encourage the follow-through when toeing off."

Health And Comfort

The human foot is a remarkable structure that comes in many shapes and sizes. It's asked to bear extraordinary loads and strain. A 200-lb. man, for example, lands with up to 600 lb. of force on each foot several thousand times in a few miles of running. But with appropriate footwear, athletes and duffers alike can help keep pain and injuries at bay and enjoy the physical activities they choose.

"I would bet that if we were allowed to wear athletic shoes to work we could save the healthcare system in excess of a billion dollars a year," says Pfeffer. "These shoes are comfortable, and what's comfortable is probably what's healthy."

References

1. Wischina B, Brunick T: Spring 1997 shoe buyer's guide. *Runner's World* 1997;32(4):50.

2. Clanton TO: Sport shoes, insoles, and orthoses, in DeLee J, Drez D, Stanitski CL (eds), *Orthopaedic Sports Medicine: Principles and Practice.* Philadelphia, WB Saunders, 1994, pp 1982-2021.

3. Milgrom C, Giladi M, Kashtan H, et al: A prospective study of the effect of a shock-absorbing orthotic device on the incidence of stress fractures in military recruits. *Foot Ankle* 1985;6(2):101-104.

4. Frey C: Footwear and stress structures. *Clin Sports Med* 1997;16(2):249-256.

5. Gardner LI Jr, Dziados JE, Jones BH, et al; Prevention of lower extremity stress fracture: a controlled trial of a shock absorbent insole. *Am J Public Health* 1988;78(12):1563-1567.

6. Torg JS, Quedenfeld T: Knee and ankle injuries traced to shoes and cleats. *Phys Sportsmed* 1973;1(2):39-43.

7. Torg JS, Quedenfeld TC, Landau S: Football shoes and playing surfaces: from safe to unsafe. *Phys Sportsmed* 1973;1(3):51-54.

8. Heidt RS Jr, Dormer SG, Cawley PW, et al: Differences in friction and torsional resistance in athletic shoe-turf surface interfaces. *Am J Sports Med* 1996;24(6):834-842.

Special Issues Guide Hiking Boot Choice

Hiking boots are perhaps the most costly off-the-shelf sport footwear, with $250 price tags not uncommon for high-end models. But for serious hikers and backpackers, there's no more vital piece of gear. The wrong boot can lead to a sprained ankle or broken leg miles from help. It can even mean the difference between life and death.

Hiking boot selection is guided by the wearer's hiking level, says Steven Zell, MD, associate professor of medicine at the University of Nevada School of Medicine in Reno and an experienced back-country hiker. He co-wrote the chapter on medical equipment and supplies in *Wilderness Medicine: Management of Wilderness and Environmental Emergencies.*[9]

Zell says an ideal hiking boot for serious hikers should support an adult and a pack of up to 100 lb. with a high center of gravity. The upper should be full-grain leather reaching above the ankle, and the boot should have a shank running through a thick sole for torsional rigidity. For good breathability, patients should seek a good quality boot made from leather at critical support areas and a breathable waterproof material such as Gore-Tex.

A casual hiker probably won't be carrying much more than a small day pack or fanny pack. His or her center of gravity is lower, so there's less torsion on the ankle. In case of a misstep, the day hiker can more easily maintain an upright posture. Such a hiker, says Zell, can wear a day boot that's light and breathable. Michael Lowe, DPM, a podiatrist in Salt Lake City and past president of the American Academy of Podiatric Sports Medicine, suggests at least a three-quarter top for day boots.

Patients should be aware that some shoes on the market look like hiking boots, but lack a steel, carbon resin, or fiberboard shank that provides the necessary support and torsional stability. Lowe teaches patients to grab the heel and forefoot and bend the boot or shoe upward. "The boot they buy should bend across the toes, not across the midfoot," he says.

Socks are also an important part of the hiking boot equation, says Lowe. Acrylic socks are preferred because they don't compress and they wick moisture away from the foot. "They're warmer in the winter, cooler in the summer, and virtually don't wear out," he says. "We significantly decrease blister formation with them."

In no other athletic shoe is break-in more important than in hiking boots, since they're so much stiffer. Break-in allows hikers to know what to expect on the trail, says Tom Clanton, MD, chair of the department of orthopedic surgery at the University of Texas Medical School at Houston. To break in the boots, patients should wear them at home for a couple weeks and during a few short day hikes. Clayton says, "The fit and relationship of the boot to the foot is probably more critical than in just about any other situation."

Reference

9. Zell S, Goodman P: Wilderness equipment and medical supplies, in Auerbach PS: *Wilderness Medicine: Management of Wilderness and Environmental Emergencies*, ed 3. St Louis, CV Mosby, 1995, pp 413-445.

—D.R. Martin

D.R. Martin is a medical journalist and copywriter in Minneapolis.

Chapter 41

Guard Against Facial Injuries

Mouthguards

Despite the new innovations in mouth and face guard technology, many athletes still subject themselves to needless sports-related injuries to the mouth and face.

Members of the American Association of Oral and Maxillofacial Surgeons would like to see helmets, face masks, and mouth guards—every kind of safety gear that reduces the risk of injury— become standard pieces of athletic equipment.

Guard Against Injuries

Oral and maxillofacial surgeons are the specialists called in to treat the broken jaws, splint the loosened teeth, and replant the knocked-out tooth. Every day they treat the painful results of needless sports-related injuries. That's why oral and maxillofacial surgeons support the mandatory use of safety equipment. As always, prevention is the best policy.

About This Chapter: Text from this chapter is from "Sports Safety," reprinted with permission from the American Association of Oral and Maxillofacial Surgeons, © 1999. For additional information, visit www.aaoms.org. Also, "Frequently Asked Questions: Mouth Protectors/Mouthguards," reprinted with permission of the American Dental Association, © 2003. For additional information, visit www.ada.org.

Protection Is The Best Prevention

Elaborate protective equipment is available for sports that involve contact and present a greater probability of injury. Among these sports are:

Football. Helmets with face guards and mouth guards should be worn. Many of the helmets manufactured for younger players have plastic face guards that can be bent back into the face and cause injury. These should be replaced by carbon steel wire guards.

Baseball. A catcher should always wear a mask. Batting helmets with a clear molded plastic face guard are now available; these can also be worn while fielding.

Ice Hockey. Many ice hockey players are beginning to wear cage-like face guards attached to the helmet. These are superior to the hard plastic face masks worn by some goalies as the face guard and the helmet take the pressure of a blow instead of the face. For extra protection both face and mouth guards—including external mouth guards made of hard plastic and secured with straps—can be worn.

Wrestling. More and more high school athletic associations require wrestlers to wear head gear. A strap with a chin cup holds the gear in place and helps to steady the jaw. Recently, face masks have been developed for wrestlers who have suffered facial injuries. Mouth guards should also be worn by wrestlers.

Boxing. Mouth guards are mandatory in this sport. A new pacifier-like mouth guard for pugilists has been designed with a thicker front, including air holes to aid breathing.

> ✔ **Quick Tip**
>
> There are five criteria to use when being fitted for a mouth protector. The device should:
>
> • cover the upper and/or lower teeth and gums;
>
> • be fitted so that it does not misalign the jaw and throw off the bite;
>
> • be light;
>
> • be strong; and
>
> • be easy to clean.

Lacrosse. Hard plastic helmets resembling baseball batting helmets, with wire cage face masks, are manufactured for this sport.

Field Hockey. Oral and maxillofacial surgeons recommend that athletes participating in this sport wear mouth guards. Goalies can receive extra protection by wearing Lacrosse helmets.

Soccer. Soccer players should wear mouth guards for protection. Oral and maxillofacial surgeons advise goalies to also wear helmets.

By encouraging athletes to wear mouth guards and other protective equipment, oral surgeons hope to help change the *face* of sports.

In the event that a facial or mouth injury occurs which requires a trip to the emergency room, the injured athlete, his parent, or coach should be sure to ask that an oral and maxillofacial surgeon is called for consultation. With their background and training, oral and maxillofacial surgeons are the specialists most qualified to deal with these types of injuries. In some cases, they may even detect a hidden injury that might otherwise go unnoticed.

Changing The Face Of Sports

From their experience with athletes—ranging from NFL All-Pros to Olympians to the kid playing sandlot ball—oral and maxillofacial surgeons recommend that athletes participating in such sports as basketball, soccer, water polo, handball, rugby, karate, judo, gymnastics, and horseback riding, be fitted with mouth guards.

New synthetic materials and advances in engineering and design have resulted in mouth guards that are sturdier yet lightweight enough to allow ease of breathing. Mouth guards can vary from very inexpensive boil and bite models to custom-fabricated guards made by dentists, which can be adapted to the sport and are generally more comfortable.

A mouth protector should be evaluated from the standpoint of retention, comfort, ability to speak and breathe, tear resistance, and protection provided to the teeth, gums, and lips.

✔ Quick Tip

Tips For Buying Sports Eye Protectors

In 2001 nearly 40,000 people were treated at U.S. hospital emergency room for eye injuries related to sports activities. Using the right kind of eye protection while playing sports can help prevent serious eye injuries and even blindness. In reality, the number of sports injuries may be two to three times greater, as many injuries are treated at outpatient clinics and doctors' offices.

Prevent Blindness America recommends that athletes wear sports eyeguards when participating in sports. Prescription glasses, sunglasses, and even occupational safety glasses do not provide adequate protection.

Sports eyeguards come in a variety of shapes and sizes. Eyeguards designed for use in racquet sports are now commonly used for basketball and soccer and in combination with helmets in football, hockey, and baseball. The eyeguards you choose should fit securely and comfortably and allow the use of a helmet if necessary.

Expect to spend between $20 and $40 for a pair of regular eyeguards and $60 or more for eyeguards with prescription lenses.

Guidelines For Buying The Right Sports Eyeguards For You

- If you wear prescription glasses, ask your eye doctor to fit you for prescription eyeguards. If you're a monocular athlete (a person with only one eye that sees well), ask you eye doctor what sports you can play safely. Monocular athletes should always wear sports eyeguards.

- Buy eyeguards at sports specialty stores or optical stores. At the sports store, ask for a sales representative who's familiar with eye protectors to help you.

- Don't buy sports eyeguards without lenses in them. Only protectors with lenses are recommended for sports use. Make sure the lenses either stay in place or pop outward in the event of an accident. Lenses that pop in against your eyes can be very dangerous.

- Fogging of the lenses can be a problem when you're active. Some eyeguards are available with anti-fog coating and others have side vents for additional ventilation. Try on different types to determine which is most comfortable for you.

- Polycarbonate eyeguards are the most impact resistant. For sports use, polycarbonate lenses must be used with protectors that meet or exceed the requirements of the American Society for Testing and Materials (ASTM). Each sport has a specific ASTM code, so check the package to make sure the right ASTM label for the sport is on the product, before buying it.

- Sports eyeguards should be padded or cushioned along the brow and bridge of the nose. Padding will prevent the eyeguards from cutting your skin.

- Try on the eye protector to determine if it's the right size. Adjust the strap and make sure it's not too tight or too loose. If you bought your eyeguards at an optical store, an optical salesperson can help you adjust the eye protector for a comfortable fit.

Until you get used to wearing a pair of eyeguards, it may feel strange, but bear with it! It's a lot better than suffering an eye injury—an injury that could possible lead to the loss of vision!

Recommended Sports Eye Protectors

Baseball

Type of eye protection:

- Faceguard (attached to helmet) made of polycarbonate material
- Sports eyeguards

Eye injuries prevented:

- Scratches on the cornea
- Inflamed iris
- Blood spilling into the eye's anterior chamber
- Traumatic cataract
- Swollen retina

Basketball

Type of eye protection:

• Sports eyeguards

Eye injuries prevented:

• Fracture of the eye socket
• Scratches on the cornea
• Inflamed iris
• Blood spilling into the eye's anterior chamber
• Swollen retina

Soccer

Type of eye protection:

• Sports eyeguards

Eye injuries prevented:

• Inflamed iris
• Blood spilling into the eye's anterior chamber
• Swollen retina

Football

Type of eye protection:

• Polycarbonate shield attached to a faceguard
• Sports eyeguards

Eye injuries prevented:

• Scratches on the cornea
• Inflamed iris
• Blood spilling into the eye's anterior chamber
• Swollen retina

Hockey

Type of eye protection:

• Wire or polycarbonate mask
• Sports eyeguards

Eye injuries prevented:

• Scratches on the cornea
• Inflamed iris
• Blood spilling into the eye's anterior chamber
• Swollen retina

Frequently Asked Questions: Mouth Protectors/ Mouthguards

I don't play football or hockey. Do I need a mouth protector?

Anyone who participates in a sport that carries a significant risk of injury should wear a mouth protector. This includes a wide range of sports like basketball, baseball, gymnastics, and volleyball.

Mouth protectors, which typically cover the upper teeth, can cushion a blow to the face, minimizing the risk of broken teeth and injuries to the soft tissues of the mouth. If you wear braces or another fixed dental appliance on your lower jaw, your dentist may suggest a mouth protector for these teeth as well.

What are the advantages of using a mouth protector?

Accidents can happen during any physical activity. A mouth protector can help cushion a blow to the face that otherwise might result in an injury to the mouth. A misdirected elbow in a one-on-one basketball game or a spill off a bicycle can leave you with chipped or broken teeth, nerve damage to a tooth, or even tooth loss. A mouth protector can limit the risk of such injuries as well as protect the soft tissues of your tongue, lips, and cheek lining.

A properly fitted mouth protector will stay in place while you are wearing it, making it easy for you to talk and breathe.

Are there different types of mouth protectors?

There are three types of mouth protectors:

- stock;
- boil and bite;
- custom-fitted.

✔ Quick Tip
If you have a retainer or other removable appliance, do not wear it during any contact sports.

Stock mouth protectors are inexpensive and come pre-formed, ready to wear. Unfortunately, they often don't fit very well. They can be bulky and can make breathing and talking difficult.

Boil and bite mouth protectors also can be bought at many sporting goods stores and may offer a better fit than stock mouth protectors. They should be softened in water, then inserted and allowed to adapt to the shape of your mouth. If you don't follow the directions carefully you can wind up with a poor-fitting mouth protector.

Custom-fitted mouth protectors are made by your dentist for you personally. They are more expensive than the other versions, but because they are customized they can offer a better fit than anything you can buy off the shelf.

I wear braces. Can I use a mouth protector?

A properly fitted mouth protector may be especially important for people who wear braces or have fixed bridge work. A blow to the face could damage the brackets or other fixed orthodontic appliances. A mouth protector also provides a barrier between the braces and your cheek or lips, limiting the risk of soft tissue injuries.

Talk to your dentist or orthodontist about selecting a mouth protector that will provide the best protection. Although mouth protectors typically only cover the upper teeth, your dentist or orthodontist may suggest that you use a mouth protector on the lower teeth if you have braces on these teeth too.

Additional Information About Preventing Facial Injuries

Prevent Blindness America
500 East Remington Road
Schaumburg, IL 60173
Toll-Free: 800-331-2020
Fax: 847-843-8458
Website: www.preventblindness.org

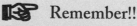 **Remember!!**

Using mouth guards and eye protection can prevent serious injuries that could cause permanent disability.

American Association of Oral and Maxillofacial Surgeons
9700 W. Bryn Mawr Avenue
Rosemont, IL 60018-5701
Phone: 847-678-6200; Fax: 847-678-6286
Website: www.aaoms.org

Chapter 42

Beat The Heat Before It Beats You

Keeping Cool When The Weather Is Hot

It's summertime and you head out for a run. Before you even finish the first mile, your body feels as though it might ignite from the heat. It's not your imagination. Fifteen minutes into your run and your body temperature could be as high as 5° F above normal. If you were to continue at this pace, fatigue and heat illness would no doubt take over.

Strategies To Protect Yourself From Heat Illness

The above scenario doesn't have to happen. Drinking enough fluid, whether it be water or a sports drink, is imperative for exercising in hot or humid weather. Maintenance of body fluids is essential to maintaining proper body temperature. Sweat dispels heat through your skin. If you let your body become dehydrated, you'll find it much more difficult to perform even the lightest of workouts. But don't wait until you're thirsty to start replenishing those fluids. Chances are, by the time you actually feel thirsty, your body is well on its way to becoming severely dehydrated.

The following strategies will help you protect yourself from the onset of heat illness.

About This Chapter: Text in this chapter is from "Fit Facts: Beat The Heat Before It Beats You," © 2001. Reprinted with permission from the American Council on Exercise®, www.acefitnes.org.

✦ It's A Fact!!

Table 42.1. Heat Stress Index

Relative Humidity	Air Temperature ° F					
	70°	80°	90°	100°	110°	120°
	Heat Stress Index					
0%	64°	73°	83°	91°	99°	107°
10%	65°	75°	85°	95°	105°	116°
20%	66°	77°	87°	99°	112°	130°
30%	67°	78°	90°	104°	123°	148°
40%	68°	79°	93°	110°	137°	
50%	69°	81°	96°	120°	150°	
60%	70°	82°	100°	132°		
70%	70°	85°	106°	144°		
80%	71°	86°	113°			
90%	71°	88°	122°			
100%	72°	91°				

Table 42.2. Heat Sensation Risk of Heat Injury

Air Temperature ° F	Possible Heat Injury
90°-105°	Possibility of heat cramps
105°-130°	Heat cramps or heat exhaustion likely. Heat stroke possible.
130°+	Heat stroke a definite risk.

Hydration

Fluid replenishment before, during, and after exercise is essential to avoid progressive dehydration. Always consume more fluids than you think you need before and after exercise, and strive to drink six to eight ounces of fluid every 15 to 20 minutes during exercise.

✣ **It's A Fact!!**

In hot weather you can become dehydrated before you feel thirsty.

Exercise Intensity

You should probably reduce the intensity of your workout, particularly the first few times you are exposed to higher temperatures.

Temperature

Use the heat stress index table to determine the risk of exercising at various combinations of temperature and humidity. While a 90° F outdoor temp is relatively safe at 10 percent humidity, the heat stress of 90° F at 50 percent humidity is the equivalent of 96° F. When the heat stress index rises above 90° F, you may want to consider postponing your exercise session until later in the day. Or, plan ahead, and beat the day's heat by working out early in the morning.

Fitness

Physical training and heat acclimation can increase your blood volume, helping to regulate body temperature more effectively.

✎ Weird Words

Dehydration: A loss of fluid in the body caused by illness or environmental factors such as hot weather.

Hydration: Drinking enough fluid to maintain body temperature.

Interestingly, the acclimatization process can be completed in 7 to 14 days of repeated heat exposure. However, you must always continue to drink fluids before, during, and after exercise.

Clothing

Wear minimal clothing to provide greater skin surface area for heat dissipation. Your clothing should be lightweight, loose fitting, light colored to reflect the sun's rays, and of a material that absorbs water, such as cotton.

Rest

Know when to say no to exercise. Using common sense is your best bet for preventing heat stress when Mother Nature turns up the heat.

☞ Remember!!
Stay hydrated when exercising on hot, humid days.

Chapter 43

Lack Of Sleep May Pose Risks For Athletes

It's your choice—10 teenagers have been at your house all night for a sleep over. The problem is most of the youth did everything but sleep. They watched movies, ate junk food, played videogames, and talked all night. There were two teenagers who did sleep because before arriving at your house they had been drinking alcohol and wanted to sleep. Early the next morning the teenagers who slept, got up, went to their car and downed six more beers that were left over from the night before. It's now 7:00 AM and according to your assessment you have two groups of young people—group one is moderately intoxicated and the other group is significantly sleep deprived. Which of the two parties should you be most concerned about as you contemplate their drive home?

Australian researcher Dr. Drew Dawson wanted to answer this specific question in a recent study. Several teenagers were randomly divided into two groups. The first group was given an alcoholic beverage to consume every 30 minutes until their blood alcohol level reached 1.0. The legal maximum blood alcohol in most states is .08 for driving a vehicle. The second group of youth were not permitted to sleep during their regular sleep cycle. Measurements of driving impairment, using a driving simulator, were measured for all subjects throughout the experiment. What Dawson discovered was that sleep deprived subjects who stayed up until three o'clock in the morning had a driving impairment equal to subjects with blood alcohol concentration of .05. By seven o'clock in the morning the sleep deprived subjects exhibited impairments equal to subjects who have a blood alcohol concentration of 1.0. In other words, teenagers who were kept up until seven o'clock in the morning were at greater risk of an automobile accident than subjects who would be legally intoxicated.

♣ It's A Fact!!
Sleep deprivation compromises a young athlete's emotional, mental, and physical ability.

Most adults underestimate the level of impairment youth experience while driving under the influence of sleep deprivation. Likewise, parents and coaches can be naïve to the risks young athletes are exposed to when chronic sleep loss occurs. Not only does this reduce performance, it exposes an athlete to a host of potential hazards. The purpose of this chapter is to list the symptoms of sleep deprivation and discuss how it contributes to sports injuries. In addition, two simple solutions will be presented to young people who suffer from sleep loss.

Effects of Sleep Deprivation on Youth

The first symptom associated with sleep deprivation is a reduced ability to deal with emotions. With even minimal sleep loss a child's threshold for containing anger is lowered. Several studies demonstrate that sleep deprived youth consistently exhibit increased levels of stress, anxiety, worry, and frustration. One study examined the level of perceived exertion in a cardiovascular fitness test between athletes who were fully rested as opposed to athletes moderately sleep deprived. Athletes who were sleep deprived reported significantly higher levels of perceived exertion (they rated the task more difficult) than the rested subjects even though the workload was the same for both groups.

Competition is filled with obstacles, challenges, mistakes, successes, and defeats. Sporting events, which are generally open to public view, create some of the most powerful emotional feelings children experience. Coaches and parents eager to teach emotional maturity must realize that sleep loss places an additional burden on young athletes who are already emotionally challenged by competition.

Mental function is compromised when sleep loss occurs. According to James Mass, Ph.D., of Cornell University, one of the primary activities of the brain during sleep is to organize acquired information. Each day we receive a plethora of data via our senses. During sleep, the receptors of external stimuli are largely turned off and the brain sorts, prioritizes, and files information. Without sleep, our brains function like an enormous disorganized library where books are not found on shelves but rather strewn recklessly all over the floor.

Scientific studies suggest that sleep deprived athletes take more time to discover, process, and integrate information during practice than if they had been fully rested. During competition, sleep researchers report that sleep loss reduces an individual's ability to reason logically, maintain visual and auditory vigilance, and make decisions effectively. Mental awareness is critical in sports like diving, gymnastics, football, and ice skating where there is a high potential for serious injury if an athlete fails to maintain a strong mental focus.

♣ It's A Fact!!

Did You Know?

- 80% of your growth hormone is released during sleep.

- Reaction time is directly connected to getting adequate sleep.

- Mental awareness and decision-making slows down if you haven't slept enough.

Physical growth and restoration suffer as a result of sleep loss. Although the body is continually in a process of revitalization, this process accelerates during sleep. Two physiological events cause this effect. First, metabolic activity is at its lowest point, and second the endocrine system increases the secretion of growth hormone via the pituitary gland during sleep. Simply put, during sleep all bodily activity is curtailed so that physical restoration and growth can be maximized. One example of this accelerated rate of production is epithelial (skin) tissue. Skin cells double their rate of production during sleep.

Probably the most severe physical by-product of chronic sleep deprivation among children is stunted growth. Over 80% of our body's natural growth hormone is released during sleep. If during the developmental years the production of growth hormone via the endocrine system is significantly reduced, growth cannot take place normally. Fortunately, sleep deprivation of sufficient duration and intensity to impair growth is rare. However, there are physiological changes that do occur with moderate amounts of sleep loss.

One of the most common physical impairments caused by sleep deprivation is a slowing of reaction time. David Dinges, Center for Sleep & Respiratory Neurobiology at the University of Pennsylvania School of Medicine examined the effects of sleep deprivation on reaction time. Data on reaction time to a stimulus presented to subjects every four seconds over a ten-minute period showed that not only is the perception/reaction response slower initially, the difference increases over time. In a more recent study, sleep deprived subjects averaged a 20% decline in reaction time.

Some sports measure time in 1/100th of a second intervals. Delayed reactions can easily mean the difference between 1st and 3rd place. Not only can reaction time separate winners and losers, it can mean the difference between stepping aside and getting hit by a fastball or avoiding a head-on collision in football.

♣ It's A Fact!!

Table 43.1. Age Appropriate Sleep Recommendations

Age	Sleep Needs of Children
2 year old	16-18 hours at night, including a single after lunch nap that lasts one to two hours
3 year old	12-12.5 total hours
4 year old	11.5-12 total hours
5 year old	11 hours
6 year old	10.75-11 hours
7 year old	10.5-11 hours
8 year old	10.25-10.5 hours
9 year old	10-10.3 hours
10 years to puberty	9.75-10 hours
Teens	9.25 hours

Sleep Solutions

Fortunately the cure for most sleep problems among children involves two lifestyle changes. The first step it to identify how much sleep a child needs.

It is important to realize that children's individual sleep needs may vary from suggested amounts. Sleep is very much like a shoe size. Some children have unusually small feet while others are larger than the norm. The same is true for sleep. Your child should wake up naturally, without the aid of an alarm clock in the morning and feel fully rested.

Having established how much sleep a child needs is critical to use that knowledge in developing a consistent sleep schedule. A consistent bedtime and rise time followed seven days a week is one of the most important keys to quality sleep according to many experts. The reason for this is that following a specific schedule gets our body in sink with our circadian rhythm. Practically all-living things (people, animal, and plants) have a circadian or daily rhythm. This internal clock determines, among other things, when we feel sleepy and alert. The circadian rhythm needs consistency to perform efficiently. Dr. Martin Moore-Ede, sleep specialist at the Harvard Medical School, says that changing one's schedule for more than two days or sleeping more than one hour longer on weekends disrupts the biological clock.

—Peter Hudson Walters,
PhD., CSCS

Dr. Peter Hudson Walters
Kinesiology Department
Wheaton College
501 E. College Avenue
Wheaton, IL 60187
Phone: 630-752-5000
Website: www.wheaton.edu

 Remember!!

Whether driving an automobile or participating in sports, young people who fail to get the sleep they need are exposed to increased risk of injury. Emotional instability, mental fatigue, and physical unreadiness all contribute to a higher potential of peril. This danger can largely be avoided simply by getting the proper amount of sleep seven days a week.

Chapter 44

How To Begin A Weight Training Program

What Is Weight Training?

Weight training means adding resistance to the body's natural movements in order to make those movements more difficult, and encourage the muscles to become stronger.

Why Weight Train?

Weight training increases fitness by:

- Increasing muscle strength and endurance
- Enhancing the cardiovascular system
- Increasing flexibility
- Maintaining the body's fat within acceptable limits

Weight training can be an important component of your fitness program, regardless of your age or gender.

About This Chapter: Text in this chapter is from "How To Begin A Weight Training Program," ©1997 American Orthopaedic Society for Sports Medicine, reprinted with permission. For additional information, visit www.sportsmed.org. Reviewed in June 2003 by Dr. David A. Cooke, MD, Diplomate, American Board of Internal Medicine.

What Equipment Is Needed To Weight Train?

Weight training programs can be done with free weights or with weight machines. Free weights are less expensive than weight machines and are more easily adapted to smaller and larger body types. Machines are safer than most free weights because the weight is more controlled.

With multiple purpose machines, like the Universal™ gym, several individuals can exercise simultaneously on the same piece of equipment within a small space. If you use free weights, select a set of barbells or dumbbells and a weight bench for the upper extremities and barbells for the lower extremities.

For all lifting, use a weight belt. Some people feel that weight gloves give them better grip strength, but they are not necessary. Good athletic shoes that provide firm floor traction are a must.

How Do I Start A Weight Training Program?

First, you should establish goals for your program. Decide if you want to exercise to obtain good muscular tone and cardiovascular endurance, to build muscle strength in a particular muscle group to improve sports performance, or to rehabilitate an injured muscle.

If you want to improve muscle tone and cardiovascular performance, design your program along the lines of a circuit program. In such a program, exercises are done at least four times a week for approximately 20 to 30 minutes a session, and very short rest periods

---

☞ **Remember!!**

Precautions

To avoid injury when weight training, you should:

- Wear appropriate clothing
- Keep the weight training area clean and free of debris
- Stay well hydrated while lifting.
- Get adequate rest.
- Eat sensibly.
- Stretch after warming up but before lifting.
- Always use a spotter when doing bench presses and squats.
- Lift with a buddy, whenever possible.

(30 seconds or less) are allowed between exercises. This program would generally consist of 15 to 20 repetitions of an exercise for each major muscle group.

If you want to build strength, you should exercise the muscle group you are strengthening to fatigue. This program incorporates fewer repetitions than circuit training. For example, you would do three sets of repetitions, but only 8 to 10 repetitions per set, with a longer rest period of 60 to 90 seconds between each exercise. This may be done every other day, but not as frequently as a circuit program because the fatigued muscles need longer to recover.

If you want to rehabilitate an injured muscle, your program would be similar to the circuit training program of higher repetitions and lower weights. However, a rehabilitation program, unlike a circuit training program, focuses on working the injured muscle group.

Limitations

It is extremely important to check with your doctor before beginning a weight training program, particularly if you have any physical limitations or are over 30. If you have musculoskeletal problems, check with an orthopaedist to make sure that the program will not aggravate those problems.

✔ **Quick Tip**

An exercise professional, like a certified athletic trainer, a sports physical therapist, an exercise physiologist, or a strength and conditioning coach, can help you design a program that's suitable for your needs.

Part Six

Sports Nutrition For Young Adults

Chapter 45

Eating Before And Between Athletic Events

Food consumed before and between athletic events can have a significant impact on an individual's ability to perform. Many people have their own ideas about what foods to consume around athletic events. Some of these ideas may be good. However, many foods consumed by athletes before and between events are inappropriate and may harm the athlete's performance. This chapter outlines the proper aspects of eating close to performance time.

Body Functions

A basic understanding of certain bodily functions can be helpful in learning the important components of a good pre-event meal.

Digestion. Athletic performance will be better if virtually no food is in the stomach or small intestines at the time the event is being performed. All food must be digested in the stomach and small intestines before being absorbed into the body and, thus, clear the gastrointestinal tract. However, the time needed for digestion varies due to factors such as the carbohydrate, fat, and protein content of the meal as well as the size of the meal. For example, carbohydrates are relatively easy to digest. Carbohydrates can generally be

About This Chapter: Text in this chapter is from "Sports Nutrition For Young Adults: Eating Before and Between Athletic Events," by Robert E. Keith, © 1998, reprinted with permission from the Alabama Cooperative Extension System–Alabama A&M and Auburn Universities.

digested and absorbed in about three to four hours. However, fat and protein require a much longer time, approximately five to seven hours, to digest and absorb. The size of the meal also can influence the overall time needed for digestion and absorption. Large meals may require many hours to clear the gastrointestinal tract, whereas, smaller meals may be digested in just a couple of hours. Nervousness often associated with athletic events also can impair normal digestion and absorption of food.

Blood Supply. An average-size adult will have about five quarts of blood circulating throughout the body. Children have less, the amount depending on the size of the child. Following ingestion of a meal, blood will be diverted from areas of the body with low needs to the stomach and intestinal area. This extra blood helps the processes of digestion and absorption of the food that has been eaten. During exercise, large amounts of blood are diverted to the working muscles and to the skin for sweat production and cooling. In this process blood is actually shunted away from the gastrointestinal tract. Thus, digestion and absorption of food can be impaired during exercise because the digestive system receives less blood instead of more. Therefore, it is advantageous to the athlete to have the digestive and absorptive processes virtually complete by the time exercise starts. There should be little or no food in the stomach and small intestine at the time of exercise.

Liver Carbohydrate. The liver is capable of storing carbohydrate (called glycogen). This liver carbohydrate can be released to the blood and is a major source of blood glucose

> ### ♣ It's A Fact!!
> ### Components Of A Good Pre-Event Meal
>
> - The meal should be consumed 2 to 4 hours before the event.
>
> - The meal should be high in carbohydrate content with small amounts of fat and protein.
>
> - Generally, foods should be somewhat bland. Spicy, gas-producing, and other irritating foods should be avoided.
>
> - The meal should be low in dietary fiber.
>
> - The meal should be small in size—less than 1,000 calories.
>
> - Dilute, non-caffeinated drinks should be consumed. Alcoholic beverages should be avoided.

(blood sugar). If the blood glucose concentration drops too low, working muscle and brain, which rely on the glucose for energy, can be deprived of this fuel source and not function properly. This would be detrimental to the person who is exercising. The liver can store enough carbohydrate to supply the brain and resting muscles for about 12 to 15 hours. Working muscle will use up liver carbohydrate much faster. Thus, making sure liver carbohydrate stores are at maximum levels would be important for an athlete about to enter an event.

Components Of A Good Pre-Event Meal

Certain components of a proper pre-event meal can be important to performance. The meal should clear the gastrointestinal tract by the time the event starts. The meal should be able to enhance liver carbohydrate stores, and the meal should help support hydration in the athlete.

Timing. Because virtually all food should be cleared from the gastrointestinal tract prior to exercise, timing of the meal becomes an important issue. Pre-event meals should be consumed from 2 to 4 hours before exercise. This allows ample time for a proper pre-event meal to be cleared. If the meal is consumed longer than 4 hours before the event, then the athlete may become hungry. Foods eaten less than 2 hours before exercise may not have time to be digested and absorbed. This can actually hurt performance.

Composition of the meal. Carbohydrate foods clear the stomach and small intestines faster than high protein or high fat foods. Thus, pre-event meals should consist primarily of high carbohydrate-type foods. Small amounts of protein and fat are acceptable. Items such as breads, cereals, pasta, pancakes, rice, fruits and fruit juices, and low fat yogurt are all examples of foods that could be used in a pre-event meal. Foods such as steaks, eggs, french fries, hamburgers, hot dogs, nuts, and bacon are high in fat or protein and should be minimized in meals eaten before competition.

Bland foods. Foods eaten before competition generally should be somewhat bland in taste. Spicy foods with pepper or chili powder and foods such as onions, cabbage, broccoli, and beans should be avoided. These foods tend to stimulate the gastrointestinal tract, produce gas, and could cause problems when eaten before athletic events. While a small amount of a carbonated beverage is probably acceptable, consumption of large quantities of these beverages should be avoided due to possible gas production.

Dietary fiber. Normally, it would be a good practice to include foods with ample dietary fiber in one's diet. However, some types of dietary fiber can stimulate defecation and having to go to the bathroom during an athletic event is not advantageous. Foods high in fiber, such as beans, various types of bran, nuts, and raw vegetables, should be minimized during the hours or day prior to a major competition.

Meal size. As previously mentioned, large meals take a long time to be digested and absorbed. Large meals eaten the day before an athletic event would be acceptable; however, large meals should not be consumed on the day of an event, before the competition. Consumption of large pre-event meals will virtually guarantee that food will still be in the stomach and small intestines at the time of competition. This can cause minor to serious discomfort for the athlete. It is recommended that pre-event meals not exceed 1,000 calories. Often the meal may be only 500 to 600 calories. For example, a turkey sandwich made with white bread, mustard, and a small amount of lettuce and tomato would contain approximately 350 calories. Add a glass of apple juice (120 calories) and a cup of flavored yogurt (220 calories) and you have a pre-event meal of almost 700 calories. A breakfast of two 6-inch pancakes (200 calories), 2 pats of margarine (90 calories), 4 ounces of syrup (100

> ✔ **Quick Tip**
> **Pre-Event High Carbohydrate Foods**
>
> Toast and jelly
>
> Spaghetti with tomato sauce
>
> Bread
>
> Macaroni
>
> Low fat yogurt
>
> Sherbet
>
> Skim milk
>
> Pancakes with syrup
>
> Bagels
>
> Low fiber cereals
>
> Thick-crust cheese pizza
>
> Rice
>
> Baked potato
>
> Canned fruit
>
> Puddings
>
> Applesauce
>
> Bananas
>
> Grits
>
> Fruit juices
>
> Waffles
>
> Cream of wheat
>
> English muffins

calories), and an 8-ounce glass of orange juice (120 calories) would provide a total of 510 calories.

Beverages. The consumption of ample quantities of fluid in the hours before competition is encouraged. This will insure that the athlete does not go into the event in a dehydrated state. Beverages such as low fat or skim milk or fruit juices can be consumed up 2 hours before the event. Water and sports drinks should be consumed 2 hours or less before the start of the event. Consumption of carbonated beverages should be minimized in the pre-event period as these types of beverages may result in excessive belching and stomach discomfort before exercise. Consumption of caffeine-containing beverages such as coffee, tea, and cola also should be avoided during this time. Caffeine has a diuretic action that can increase urine output and possibly contribute to dehydration. Caffeine consumption also can increase the frequency of defecation. Alcoholic beverages should be avoided. Alcohol has a diuretic action similar to caffeine. In addition, alcohol consumption beyond minimal amounts can have adverse effects on performance.

Adverse Effects Of Improper Pre-Event Meals

Improper pre-event nutrition can harm the athlete in several ways. If meals before competition are taken too far in advance or are low in carbohydrates, then the athlete could go into the event feeling hungry and perhaps with blood sugar values that are lower than optimum. Low fluid consumption in the hours before an event can result in the athlete's being dehydrated. This would adversely influence performance, especially on hot, humid days. Most adverse effects of pre-event meals are associated with food still remaining in the stomach and intestines when physical activity begins. This

---

✔ **Quick Tip**

Possible Adverse Symptoms Of An Improper Pre-Event Meal

- Nausea
- Intestinal cramps
- Belching
- Low blood sugar

- Vomiting
- Flatulence
- Diarrhea or the urge to defecate
- Dehydration

food can cause numerous gastrointestinal problems. All of these side effects could cause the athlete to perform less than optimally. Even if symptoms are not severe, the athlete's performance is probably being compromised.

Eating Between Events

Many athletes may have to perform several times during a day. Multiple matches in tennis and two or three soccer games in a day are not unusual. Guidelines for eating between these events generally are not different from those for pre-event meals. This is especially true if there are at least 2 hours between events. The between-events meal then becomes a pre-event meal. Often the time between events is less than 2 hours. In these cases a full meal cannot be consumed. Instead, a small, high-carbohydrate snack will need to be consumed along with adequate fluid intake from sports drinks and water. Generally, in these situations the athlete would not want to consume more than about 300 calories. The main focus is to keep the athlete hydrated and not feeling hungry, yet still leave the gastrointestinal tract empty when competition begins.

Eating In Restaurants

If possible, it is probably best to eat pre-event meals at home and to bring between-events snacks with you the day of the event. This allows better control

---

✔ Quick Tip
Between-Events Snack Foods

Oatmeal raisin cookies	Fig/Apple/Strawberry Newtons
Graham crackers	Saltine crackers
Pretzels	Low fat yogurt
Animal crackers	Raisins
Bread	Bananas
Canned peaches	Applesauce
Low fat puddings	Poptarts
Vanilla wafers	Sports drinks

by the athlete of food choices, volume, timing, etc. However, eating foods from or at home is not always possible and athletes must choose foods from restaurant menus. As much as possible the same guidelines should be followed when eating out (timing, composition, and size of meal). Most restaurants will offer some lower fat foods. For example, choose a grilled chicken sandwich with honey mustard instead of a hamburger with mayonnaise and cheese. Choose orange juice or water instead of a carbonated drink. If eating Mexican food, choose a basic bean burrito without sour cream and cheese. If eating Italian, spaghetti with just a tomato sauce would be better than a spicy meat sauce. A thick-crust cheese and mushroom pizza would be better than a thin-crust pepperoni, sausage, and peppers pizza. In a Chinese restaurant eat mostly rice with just a little of the other dishes. These are just a few examples of proper pre-event menu choices in various restaurants. With a little knowledge and forethought choosing good pre-event meals from restaurants can be accomplished.

> **☞ Remember!!**
>
> To play your best, it is important to eat well keeping in mind appropriate types and amounts of food to eat before or between competitions.

Chapter 46

Hydration: The Importance Of Water In The Body

Proper nutrition is fundamental to fitness and performance. Although many athletes carefully regulate their diet, they may pay little attention to their body's fluid needs. They often misunderstand and, as a result, underplay the importance of water to good nutrition.

Young athletes are not as efficient at body temperature regulation as adults are, they risk overheating and the consequent onset of heat-related illnesses. It is imperative that young athletes drink enough fluids to perform at their best and to reduce the dangerous risks of dehydration during prolonged physical activity.

The Importance Of Water In The Body

The body is comprised of about 60 percent water, and much of that water is located inside lean muscle tissue. Water is needed by the body because it regulates the processes and chemical reactions of every living cell. If each cell is to complete the reactions demanded for performance at optimal speed, movement, and endurance, the body must have adequate access to fluid. Some of the functions of water include:

About This Chapter: Text in this chapter is from "Sports Nutrition For Young Adults: Hydration," by Robert E. Keith and Leslie Wade, © 1997, reprinted with permission from the Alabama Cooperative Extension System–Alabama A&M and Auburn Universities.

- transporting protein, amino acids, carbohydrates, vitamins, minerals, and oxygen to cells.

- being part of the structure of the chemical compounds in the body.

- aiding in the digestion and absorption of nutrients.

- aiding in the repair and replacement of old tissues.

- helping flush the system of toxic wastes.

- helping to maintain constant body temperatures by providing perspiration for cooling and blood circulation for warming.

- lubricating and cushioning the joints and tissues of the body.

♣ **It's A Fact!!**
Through normal perspiration, respiration, and urination, the body can lose up to half a gallon of water a day. Actively training athletes can lose even more!

Water Balance

Water Input. Water needed by the body comes from a variety of sources and is provided by food, drink, and metabolism. In addition to water itself, beverages such as milk, sports drinks, and juices contain large amounts of water. Other foods also contain rich supplies of water. Fresh fruit and vegetables generally contain a lot of water (some contain as much as 95 percent water), while protein foods such as beef and eggs can contain up to 50 percent water. Water also is released in the body as foods are broken down and metabolized for energy.

Water Output. To ensure proper hydration, fluid lost must not exceed fluid consumed. The body can lose up to half a gallon of water a day through normal perspiration, respiration, and excretion processes. During prolonged physical activity, water losses increase due to increased breathing and sweating. In fact, during heavy exercise, an athlete can lose between 2 and 4 quarts of sweat (6 to 8 pounds of body weight) in just one hour! The body's digestive system can only absorb about 1 quart of fluid per hour, so an athlete must consume fluids before, during, and after exercise to replace fluid losses and minimize dehydration.

Water Losses On Hot, Humid Days

High temperatures increase the rate of water lost through perspiration. Exercising in hot, humid climates presents yet another concern: the body's ability to sweat efficiently is reduced because the sweat on the skin meets resistance evaporating. The air is already filled with moisture, which makes it difficult for the sweat to evaporate. As a result, the body cannot cool itself properly, and internal body temperature can rise to dangerous levels.

Other factors can increase the rate of fluid loss. These must be avoided or minimized to stop the onset of rapid dehydration:

- excessive clothing, padding, and taping.

- competing in environmental conditions to which the athlete is un-accustomed.

- intense levels of solar radiation (bright sunshine).

- increased intensity of exercise.

- increased duration of exercise.

- failure to consume fluids every 15 to 20 minutes during practice (an athlete needs to drink even if he/she does not feel thirsty).

Athletes must consider these factors that increase the rate of fluid loss and use extreme caution when training on sunny, hot, and humid days. These combined factors present the most dangerous environmental conditions for athletes. They encourage the rapid onset of dehydration and quickly raise internal body temperature.

The Effects Of Dehydration

Dehydration is a net loss of water and fluids from the body, caused by an imbalance in the body's supply and demand. The first symptom of dehydration is fatigue. Other early symptoms of dehydration include:

- thirst

- headache

- dry or cotton mouth

- dizziness or lightheadedness
- weakness
- rapid heartbeat
- dry, flushed skin
- muscle cramps

During physical activity, body heat rises very quickly due to the working muscles. One of the major functions of fluids is to maintain core body temperatures, so as body heat rises, the body compensates by sweating. As the sweat evaporates, the skin and the blood (which is traveling through vessels near the surface of the skin) are cooled. This cooled blood then flows back to the body's core, thereby decreasing internal body temperature.

The body cannot properly cool itself when dehydration occurs. Serious heat-related injuries or illnesses, such as heat exhaustion and heat stroke, can result when excessive fluid is lost and not replaced during exercise and the body temperature increases. Symptoms of heat exhaustion include dizziness, weakness, rapid pulse, low blood pressure, headache, and elevated body temperature. Symptoms of heat stroke can include sudden cessation of sweating, clumsiness or stumbling, disorientation, vomiting, and loss of consciousness. Death can occur with heat stroke.

Dehydration reduces one's endurance and increases one's risk for heat-related illnesses, such as heat exhaustion and heat stroke. When the body becomes dehydrated, athletic performance can be greatly hindered. A water loss equal to 5 percent of body weight can reduce muscular work capacity by 20 to 30 percent. Table 46.1 shows the effects of dehydration on performance as measured by percent body weight lost as fluid during exercise.

Monitoring Hydration

Thirst is not a good indicator of the need for water intake because exercise blunts the thirst mechanism. When thirst does become detectable, fluid stores have already been depleted, and the early stages of dehydration are apparent. At the point of thirst, the body has already lost up to 2 percent of its body weight in fluid, a loss which has been shown to impair thermoregulation and reduce work capacity by 10 to 15 percent.

The color and amount of urine excreted are good indicators of the body's state of hydration. Urine should be clear and in large quantities, and urination should occur frequently throughout the day. Highly concentrated urine is usually a sign of dehydration.

Body weight lost during periods of exercise is another excellent indication of the amount of fluid lost. It is important that the athlete weigh before and after activity to monitor fluid loss. For every pound of body weight lost, 2 cups (16 ounces) of fluid must be consumed for hydration. Because the

---

♣ It's A Fact!!

Table 46.1. How Your Body Reacts When You Lose Fluids During Exercise

Percent Weight Loss	Effects On The Body
1 to 2	Increase in core body temperature
3	Significant increase in body temperature with aerobic exercise
5*	Significant increase in body temperature with a definite decrease in aerobic ability and muscular endurance
	Possible 20 to 30 percent decrease in strength and anaerobic power
	Susceptibility to heat exhaustion
6	Muscle spasms, cramping
10 or more	Excessively high core body temperature
	Susceptibility to heat stroke
	Heat injury and circulatory collapse with aerobic performance

* With a 5 percent body weight loss, an athlete will need at least 5 hours to rehydrate.

body can only absorb about 1 quart of water every hour, the athlete must drink fluids before, during, and after exercise to guard against the risks of dehydration. In fact, fluid replacement must continue at least 24 hours after vigorous, sustained activity to restore lost fluids and electrolytes. Table 46.2 presents a well-accepted model for hydration before, during, and after exercise.

What Is The Best Fluid To Drink?

For most athletes, cold water is an acceptable source of fluid replacement. Drinking cool or cold water is best because water enters the bloodstream and tissues rapidly and helps cool the interior of the body.

In long-distance events (those lasting 60 minutes or more) diluted fruit juices (one part juice to one part water) or sports drinks are preferred because they supply glucose, the body's main source of energy, as well as small amounts of sodium. Sodium has been shown to possibly increase the rate of water and carbohydrate absorption from the digestive tract and to encourage fluid retention after exercise.

♣ **It's A Fact!!**

Table 46.2. How Much Fluid To Drink When You're Exercising

Time	Amount To Drink
1 to 2 hours and 30 minutes before exercise	2 cups (16 ounces) of cold fluid
5 to 15 minutes before exercise	1 to 2 cups (8 to 15 ounces) of cold fluid
Every 15 to 20 minutes during exercise	1/2 to 3/4 cup of fluid even if not thirsty
Immediately following exercise	2 cups (16 ounces) of cold water for each pound of body weight lost
After exercise and the next day	Drink fluids liberally. May take up to 36 hours to completely rehydrate.

☞ Remember!!

Water is the single most important nutrient needed by young athletes. If athletes exercise when they are dehydrated, they will not perform at an optimal level and will risk the onset of dangerous heat-related illness. Moreover, because the young athletes may not be as efficient at body temperature regulation as adults, the danger of dehydration and increased body temperature should be of primary concern to the performing athlete and the coaching staff.

Another advantage of drinking sports drinks is that the taste will actually encourage the athlete to drink. In fact, a recent study has shown that the ingestion of a sports drink by 9- to 12-year-old exercising boys resulted in a nearly two-fold increase in fluid consumption when compared to plain water.

Athletes should not drink full strength fruit juices and other highly concentrated drinks. These create feelings of fullness and can cause cramping.

Athletes also should avoid fluids containing caffeine or alcohol. These have diuretic effects; that is, they promote the excretion of water from the body, causing the body to lose more fluid in the urine that is actually provided by the beverage. This loss of water, in turn, impairs temperature regulation, lowering the athlete's defense against heat-related illnesses. In addition, caffeine can cause stomach upset, nervousness, sleeplessness, headaches, and irritability.

Chapter 47

Be Smart About Sports Supplements

If you're a competitive athlete or a fitness buff, improving your sports performance is probably on your mind. Spending tons of time in the gym or at practice may offer results (along with a pile of sweaty laundry), but it's no shortcut, and teens with busy lives may be looking for fast, effective results.

Some people think that taking drugs known as sports supplements could improve their performance without so much hard work. But do sports supplements really work? And are they safe?

What Are Sports Supplements?

Sports supplements (also referred to as ergogenic aids) are products used to enhance athletic performance. They come in different forms, including vitamins, synthetic (manmade) drugs, and hormones, most of which are available over the counter without a prescription.

Some people think that supplements help them develop more muscle mass, increase strength, and build stamina. Other people use sports supplements

About This Chapter: Text in this chapter is from "Sports Supplements." This information was provided by KidsHealth, one of the largest resources online for medically reviewed health information written for parents, kids, and teens. For more articles like this one, visit www.KidsHealth.org, or www.TeensHealth.org. © 2002 The Nemours Center for Children's Health Media, a division of The Nemours Foundation. Reprinted with permission.

to lose weight. If you're thinking about using sports supplements, you're not alone. Many teens who see sports medicine doctors when they want to improve their performance have questions about how supplements work and whether they're safe.

Most of the foods you see on the shelves of your local grocery store and the drugs your doctor prescribes for you are regulated by a government agency called the Food and Drug Administration (FDA). The FDA ensures that many foods, beverages, and drugs adhere to certain safety standards. But sports supplements aren't regulated by the FDA, and no sports supplements have been tested on kids and teens. That means that scientists and doctors don't know whether supplements are safe or effective for teens to use.

Lots of sports organizations have developed policies on sports supplements. The National Football League (NFL), the National Collegiate Athletic Association (NCAA), and the International Olympic Committee (IOC) have banned the use of steroids, creatine, ephedra, and androstenedione by their athletes, and competitors who use them face fines, ineligibility, and suspension from their sports.

Common Supplements And How They Affect the Body

Whether you hear about sports supplements from your teammates in the locker room or the sales clerk at your local vitamin store, chances are you're not getting the whole story about how supplements work and the risks you take by using them.

Anabolic steroids are hormones that help the body build muscle tissue and increase muscle mass. Steroids, also known as roids or juice, are similar to the male hormone testosterone, which is produced naturally in larger amounts in guys' bodies and smaller amounts in girls' bodies. When a person takes steroids, the body's muscle tissue is stimulated to grow, producing larger and stronger muscles.

But steroids can have some unwelcome, serious side effects—such as high blood pressure and heart disease, liver damage and cancer, urinary and bowel problems, strokes and blood clots, and sleep problems. A person who takes steroids may develop bigger muscles, but he or she is also at risk for baldness and severe acne. Guys who take juice can suffer from infertility, breast and nipple enlargement, and problems having an erection. Girls may find themselves with deeper voices, smaller breasts, menstrual problems, and an increase in facial and body hair.

Steroids can also have emotional effects on the user, such as severe mood swings, aggressive behavior, irritability, and depressive or suicidal thoughts. Teens who inject steroids with infected needles are also at risk for HIV or hepatitis.

Androstenedione, more commonly known as andro, is another popular nutritional supplement. When a person takes andro, the body may convert it to testosterone, which is necessary for muscle development. When it's taken in large doses, andro is said to increase muscle mass, although studies haven't shown that andro is particularly effective. Scientists don't know exactly how much andro the body absorbs, and the long-term effects of andro use haven't been determined. What is known is that andro can cause hormone imbalances in people who use it. Andro use may have the same effects as taking anabolic steroids and may lead to such dangerous side effects as testicular cancer, infertility, stroke, and an increased risk of heart disease.

Another sports supplement you may have heard about is **human growth hormone (hGH).** Doctors may prescribe growth hormone for some teens who have certain hormone or growth problems to help them develop normally. But growth hormone can also be abused by athletes who want to build muscle mass. Many athletes still use growth hormone even though several sports organizations (such as the NCAA) have banned it. Teen athletes who abuse growth hormone may have impaired development and altered hormone levels.

In a recent survey of high school senior athletes, about 44% said they had tried or currently used **creatine** to enhance athletic performance. Creatine is already manufactured by the body in the liver, kidneys, and pancreas, and it occurs naturally in foods such as meat and fish. If a person takes creatine supplements, the extra creatine is stored in the muscles, and some people think that it gives them an energy boost during workouts or competitions.

✔ Quick Tip

Tips For Dealing With Athletic Pressure And Competition

Advertisements for sports supplements often use persuasive before and after pictures that make it look easy to get a muscular, toned body. But remember—the goal of supplement advertisers is to make money by selling more supplements. Because sports supplements are not regulated by the FDA, sellers are not required to provide information about their dangerous side effects. Teens and kids may seem like an easy sell on supplements because they may feel dissatisfied or uncomfortable with their still-developing bodies, and many supplement companies try to convince teens like you that supplements are an easy solution.

Don't waste your hard-earned allowance or pay from your after-school job on expensive and dangerous supplements. Instead, try these tips for getting better game:

- **Make down time a priority.** Some studies show that teens need more than 8 hours of sleep a night—are you getting enough? If you come home from practice to a load of homework, try doing as much homework as possible on the weekend to free up your nights for sleep. If you have an after-school job that's interfering with your ZZZs, consider cutting back on your hours during your sports season.

- **Try to R-E-L-A-X.** Your school, work, and sports schedules may have you sprinting from one activity to the next, but taking a few minutes to relax can be helpful. Meditating or visualizing your success during the next game may improve your performance; sitting quietly and focusing on your breathing can give you a brief break and prepare you for your next activity.

- **Chow down on good eats.** Fried, fat-laden, or sugary foods will interfere with your performance in a major way. Instead, focus on eating foods such as lean meats, whole grains, vegetables, fruits, and low-fat dairy products. Celebrating with the team at the local pizza place after a big game is fine once in a while, but for most meals and snacks choose healthy foods to keep your body weight in a healthy range and your performance at its best.

- **Eat often.** Sometimes teens skip breakfast or have an early lunch and then try to play a late afternoon game. But they quickly wear out because they haven't had enough food to fuel their activity. Not eating enough may place teens at risk for injury or muscle fatigue. So make sure to eat lunch on practice and game days. If you feel hungry before the game, pack easy-to-carry, healthy snacks in your bag, such as fruit, bagels, or string cheese.

- **Avoid harmful substances.** Drinking, smoking, or doing drugs are all-around bad ideas for athletes. Smoking will diminish your lung capacity and ability to breathe, alcohol will make you sluggish and tired, and drugs will impair your hand-eye coordination and reduce your alertness. And you can kiss your team good-bye if you get caught using these substances—many schools have a no-tolerance policy for athletes.

- **Train harder and smarter.** If you get out of breath easily during your basketball game and you want to increase your endurance, improving your cardiovascular conditioning is key. If you think that more leg strength will help you excel on the soccer field, consider weight training to increase your muscle strength. Before changing your program, though, get advice from your doctor. You can't expect results overnight, but improving your strength and endurance with hard work will be a lot safer for your body in the long run.

- **Consult a professional.** If you're concerned about your weight or whether your diet is helping your performance, talk to your doctor or a registered dietitian who can evaluate your nutrition and steer you in the right direction. Coaches can help you too, by helping you focus on weak spots during practice. And if you're still convinced that supplements will help you, talk to your doctor or a sports medicine specialist. The doc will be able to offer alternatives to supplements based on your body and sport.

☞ Remember!!

Supplements cannot improve sports performance. Only hard work, good nutrition, and proper rest help you to improve your sports performance.

Available over the counter in pill, powder, or gel form, creatine is one of the most popular nutritional supplements, and teens make up a large portion of the supplement's users. Teens who take creatine usually take it to improve strength, but the long-term and short-term effects of creatine use haven't been studied in teens and kids. Research has not shown that creatine can increase endurance or improve aerobic performance—but it may leave teens prone to muscle cramps and tears. And there have been several reports of creatine use leading to seizures or kidney failure.

Fat burners (sometimes known as thermogenics) are a recent addition to the sports supplement market. Fat burners are often made with an herb called **ephedra**, also known as ephedrine or ma huang. Ephedra is a stimulant found in over-the-counter pills such as Metabolife, Ripped Fuel, and Yellow Jacket, and it speeds up the nervous system and increases metabolism. Some teens use fat burners to lose weight or to increase energy—but using products containing ephedrine is a bad idea for anyone. Ephedra-based products can be one of the most dangerous supplements. They can cause an irregular heartbeat (known as an arrhythmia), dehydration, fainting, and occasionally even death.

Many products containing ephedrine have been taken off the shelves because of their dangerous effects on health, but many fat burners still contain ephedra. The NCAA and the IOC have banned the use of ephedrine.

Will Supplements Make Me A Better Athlete?

Sports supplements haven't been tested on teens and kids. But studies on adults show that the claims of many supplements are weak at best. Most won't make you any stronger, and none will make you any faster or more skillful.

Many factors go into your abilities as an athlete—including your diet, how much sleep you get, genetics and heredity, and your training program—but the fact is that using sports supplements may put you at risk for serious health conditions. So instead of turning to supplements to improve your performance, concentrate on eating the best nutrition and following a serious weight-training and aerobic-conditioning program.

Chapter 48

Are Steroids Worth The Risk?

Dominic, like many of his classmates, wanted to be a great ball player. Just being good wasn't enough—he wanted to be the best. He dreamed of playing professional baseball someday, but he knew there was intense competition for positions on major league teams. His girlfriend, Deborah, was also a highly competitive athlete. Deborah's appearance and her performance were very important to her. Deborah wanted to stand out compared to other girls in high school, and she wanted to have what she thought was the ideal body.

Because of the pressure they felt to excel, Dominic and Deborah toyed with the idea of taking steroids. They thought steroids might give them the edge they needed to push their bodies past their natural limits. They had heard rumors about the bad side effects of using steroids, but they didn't know how dangerous steroids really are. Read on to find out the truth about taking steroids.

What Are Steroids?

Steroids, sometimes referred to as roids or juice, are very closely related to certain hormones. The body produces steroids to support certain functions such as fighting disease and promoting growth.

About This Chapter: Text in this chapter is from "Are Steroids Worth the Risk?" This information was provided by KidsHealth, one of the largest resources online for medically reviewed health information written for parents, kids, and teens. For more articles like this one, visit www.KidsHealth.org. or www.TeensHealth.org. © 1999 The Nemours Center for Children's Health Media, a division of The Nemours Foundation. Reprinted with permission.

Anabolic steroids are artificially produced hormones that are similar to testosterone. **Testosterone** (pronounced: teh-stoss-tuh-rone) is a natural male sex hormone produced in the human body. Although testosterone is a male hormone, girls' bodies produce smaller amounts of it as well. Testosterone promotes masculine traits that guys develop during puberty, such as deepening of the voice and the growth of body hair. Testosterone levels also affect how aggressive a person is and how much sex drive he or she has. Athletes sometimes take anabolic steroids because they can help to increase muscle mass and body strength.

Steroids can be taken in the form of pills, powders, or injections. Some types of steroids have medical uses and are available by prescription or in the form of dietary supplements. Dietary supplements that contain steroids often make claims that are false and very little is known about the long-term effects on the body of some of these substances.

How Do Anabolic Steroids Work?

Anabolic steroids stimulate muscle tissue to grow and bulk up by mimicking the effect of testosterone on the body. Steroids have become popular because they may improve endurance, strength, and muscle mass. But research has not shown that they improve skill, agility, or performance.

Dangers Of Steroids

Anabolic steroids cause many different types of problems. Less serious side effects include acne, purple or red spots on the body, swelling of legs and

✎ Weird Words

Steroids: Closely related to hormones, they fight disease and promote growth.

Anabolic steroids: Artificially produced hormones that are similar to testosterone.

Testosterone: A natural male sex hormone produced in both males and females.

feet, persistent bad breath, and less commonly jaundice or yellowing of the skin. Other side effects are:

- premature balding

- dizziness

- mood swings including anger, aggression, and depression

- nausea

- vomiting

- trembling

- high blood pressure that can damage the heart or blood vessels

- aching joints

- greater chance of injuring muscles

- liver damage

- shortening of final adult height

Risks for girls include:

- facial hair growth

- masculine trait development and loss of feminine body characteristics, such as shrinking of the breasts

- menstrual cycle changes

Risks for guys include:

- testicular shrinkage

- pain when urinating

- breast development

- impotence (inability to get an erection)

- sterility (inability to have children)

> **✔ Quick Tip**
>
> Steroid users who inject the drugs with a needle may be at greater risk for contracting HIV (human immunodeficiency virus), the virus that causes AIDS, if they share needles with other users. They are also at greater risk for contracting hepatitis, a disease of the liver. This is particularly scary because it can be impossible to tell if your friend or an athlete on your team is sick. It's not enough to take their word for it; sharing needles is never safe.

Anabolic steroids are so controversial because of all the health risks associated with them. Most are illegal and are banned by professional sports organizations and medical associations. If an athlete is caught using steroids, his or her career can be destroyed.

Some people combine or stack anabolic steroids with other drugs. Because it is difficult to understand how the drugs interact, there is the possibility of taking a deadly combination. Just as many medications should not be taken together, anabolic steroids have the same potential for negative interactions. Emergency departments have reported cases of vomiting, tremors, dizziness, and even coma (unconsciousness) when patients were admitted after taking combinations of steroids.

Steroids can also have serious psychological side effects. Some users become aggressive or combative developing roid rage—extreme, uncontrolled bouts of anger caused by long-term steroid use. Others experience irritability, paranoia, and severe depression when they try to stop taking steroids.

> **☞ Remember!!**
> ## Alternatives to Steroids
> Being a good athlete means training the healthy way: eating the right foods, practicing, and strength training without the use of drugs. Not only will you be improving your sports performance, you'll also be taking good care of your body.

Some of the long-term effects of steroids may not show up for many years. Lyle Alzado, a former Los Angeles Raiders defensive lineman, believed his prolonged use of steroids caused the rare form of brain cancer that affected his central nervous system before he died. If users could see the results of their steroid use in 5, 10, or 25 years, would they still take them? Probably not.

Part Seven

Sport Safety Guidelines For Active Teens

Chapter 49

Prevent Baseball And Softball Injuries

Each year, more than 125,000 baseball and softball players under age 15 are injured badly enough to seek treatment in hospital emergency departments. Hundreds of thousands of adults receive minor injuries in these sports. Many of the injuries can be prevented if players wear safety gear and if additional safety measures are added to the game.

Tips For Preventing Baseball And Softball Injuries

To avoid injuries while playing baseball or softball, follow these safety tips from the American Academy of Pediatrics, the Centers for Disease Control and Prevention (CDC), the Consumer Product Safety Commission, and other sports and health organizations.

- Before you start a training program or play competitive baseball or softball, go to the doctor for a physical exam. The doctor can help assess any special injury risks you may have.

- Make sure you wear all the required safety gear every time you play and practice. Always wear a helmet when batting, waiting to bat, or running the bases. Helmets should have eye protectors, either safety goggles or face guards. Shoes with molded cleats are recommended

About This Chapter: Text in this chapter is from "Baseball and Softball Safety," SafeUSA™, www.safeusa.org, Centers for Disease Control and Prevention, 2002.

(most youth leagues prohibit the use of steel spikes). If you are a catcher, you will need additional safety gear: catcher's mitt, face mask, throat guard, long-model chest protector, and shin guards.

- If you are a pitcher, make sure pitching time is limited. Little League mandates time limits and requires rest periods for young pitchers.

- Warm-up and stretch before playing.

- Do not play through pain. If you get injured, see your doctor. Follow all the doctor's orders for recovery, and get the doctor's permission before you return to play.

- Make sure first aid is available at all games and practices.

- Talk to and watch your coach. Coaches should enforce all the rules of the game, encourage safe play, and understand the special injury risks that young players face. Make sure your coach teaches players how to

---

✔ Quick Tip

Conclusions From The U.S. Consumer Product Safety Commission (CPSC) Study

- Baseball protective equipment currently on the market may prevent, reduce, or lessen the severity of more than 58,000 injuries or almost 36 percent of an estimated 162,100 hospital emergency-room-treated, baseball-related injuries occurring to children each year.

- Softer-than-standard balls may prevent, reduce, or lessen the severity of the 47,900 ball impact injuries to the head and neck.

- Batting helmets with face guards may prevent, reduce, or lessen the severity of about 3,900 facial injuries occurring to batters in organized play.

- Safety release bases that leave no holes in the ground or parts of the base sticking up from the ground when the base is released may prevent, reduce, or lessen the severity of the 6,600 base-contact sliding injuries occurring in organized play.

Source: U.S. Consumer Product Safety Commission News Release, June 4, 1996.

avoid injury when sliding (prohibits headfirst sliding in young players), pitching, or dodging a ball pitched directly at them.

- Above all, keep baseball and softball fun. Putting too much focus on winning can make you push too hard and risk injury.

Encourage your league to use breakaway bases. These bases, which detach when someone slides into them, can prevent many ankle and knee injuries in both children and adults. Leagues with players 10 years old and under should alter the rules of the game to include the use of adult pitchers or batting tees. Remember, you don't have to be on a baseball diamond to get hurt. Make sure you wear safety gear and follow safety rules during informal baseball and softball games, too.

Who Is Affected?

In the United States, more than 33 million people participate in organized baseball and softball leagues. Nearly 6 million of these players are 5 to 14 years old. Even though these sports are not considered contact sports, they are associated with a large number of injuries. Hospital emergency departments treat more than 95,000 baseball-related injuries and 30,000 softball-related injuries among players under age 15 each year. The number of injuries among adults is also high, with as many as 8 percent of players sustaining injuries each year.

The majority of injuries in baseball and softball are minor, consisting mostly of abrasions (scrapes), sprains, strains, and fractures. Many of these injuries are to the ankle and knee. Eye injuries are also common in baseball. In fact, baseball is the leading cause of sports-related eye injuries in children. Catastrophic injuries in baseball and softball are rare. They occur most often when players are struck in the head or chest with a ball or a bat. On average, 3 children under age 15 die each year from baseball-related injuries.

Baseball can lead to injuries caused by overusing a certain body part. Pitchers commonly suffer overuse injuries in their elbows or shoulders. As many as 45 percent of pitchers under age 12 have chronic elbow pain, and among high school pitchers, the percentage rises to 58 percent. To prevent these injuries, Little League Baseball, Inc., has set a limit of six innings of pitching per week and requires pitchers to rest between appearances. Teaching proper pitching mechanics can also prevent serious overuse injuries.

Helmets and safety equipment for catchers have brought about reductions in injuries. Little League Rule 1.7 says, "A catcher's helmet must meet NOCSAE specifications and standards." Other safety gear has been added

---

☞ Remember!!
Additional Baseball/Softball Safety Information

American Academy of Orthopaedic Surgeons
6300 North River Rd.
Rosemont, IL 60018-4262
Toll-Free: 800-346-AAOS (2267)
Fax On Demand: 800-999-2939
Website: www.aaos.org

Through the public information link on the AAOS home page, you can access fact sheets on injury prevention for many popular sports, including baseball.

American Academy of Pediatrics
141 Northwest Point Blvd.
Elk Grove Village, IL 60007-1098
Phone: 847-434-4000
Fax: 847-434-8000
Website: www.aap.org

American Red Cross
2025 East Street N.W.
Washington, DC 20006
Phone: 703-248-4222
Fax: 202-303-4498
Website: www.redcross.org

The American Red Cross offers advice on conditioning young athletes.

more recently, including eye protectors and face masks on helmets. Chest protectors and softer balls are also being studied for their protective effect.

Making changes to the playing field and the rules of the game can also prevent injuries. Sliding into the base causes more than 70 percent of recreational softball injuries and nearly one-third of baseball injuries. Using bases that break away upon impact can prevent 1.7 million injuries per year. Adding

Brain Injury Association of America
105 North Alfred St.
Alexandria, VA 22314
Toll-Free: 800-444-6443
Phone: 703-236-6000
Website: www.biausa.org
E-mail: familyhelpline@biausa.org

BIA's fact sheet about sports and concussion safety provides data on brain injuries for several sports, including baseball.

U.S. Consumer Product Safety Commission
4330 East-West Highway
Bethesda, MD 20814-4408
Toll-Free: 800-638-2772
Phone: 301-504-6816
Fax: 301-504-0124 and 301-504-0025
Website: www.cpsc.gov
E-mail: info@cpsc.gov

National SAFE KIDS Campaign
1301 Pennsylvania Ave. N.W., Suite 1000
Washington, DC 20004
Phone: 202-662-0600
Fax: 202-393-2072
Website: www.safekids.org

Visit the SAFE KIDS home page to access fact sheets on sports and recreation injuries, or call 202-662-0600.

screens or fencing to the dugout and eliminating the on-deck circle protects players from wild pitches, foul balls, and flying bats.

✔ **Quick Tip**

Baseball/Softball-Specific Guidelines

- Most injuries in baseball and softball involve the throwing arm and shoulder, but these injuries usually result through a gradual process. Athletes should not abuse the throwing arm by overusing it.

- Players should incorporate conditioning and stretching exercises for the shoulder into their overall program.

- It is to the player's advantage to warm-up and cool-down the throwing arm properly to minimize the risk of injuries.

- Condition all shoulder muscles, emphasizing muscles in the back of the shoulder that are required to stop the pitching motion. Muscles in the front of the arm are naturally stronger—shoulder injuries can result from weaker muscles in the back.

Source: Text excerpted with permission from "Minimizing the Risk of Injury in High School Athletics," a brochure from the National Athletic Trainers' Association (NATA) © 2003 NATA.

References

The data and safety tips in this chapter were obtained from the following sources:

American Academy of Orthopaedic Surgeons. *Baseball*. Available at http://www.aaos.org/wordhtml/pat_educ/baseball.htm. Accessed July 8, 1999.

American Academy of Orthopaedic Surgeons Seminar (Sullivan J, Grana W, editors). The Pediatric Athlete. Park Ridge, IL: *The Academy*, 1990:141,149-151,259.

American Academy of Pediatrics. Risk of injury from baseball and softball in children 5 to 14 years of age. *Pediatrics* 1994;93(4):690-692.

American Academy of Pediatrics. Sports Medicine: Health care for young athletes. Elk Grove Village, IL: *The Academy*, 1991:148-150.

American Red Cross. *Red Cross gears up to help prevent sports injuries this spring: coaches advised on proper conditioning of young athletes.* News release, May 7, 1998.

Caine D, Caine C, Lindner K, editors. Epidemiology of Sports Injuries. Champaign, IL: *Human Kinetics*, 1996:63-85.

CDC. Sliding-associated injuries in college and professional baseball - 1990-1991. *Morbidity and Mortality Weekly Report* 1993;42(12):223,229-230.

Institute for Preventative Sports Medicine. Softball injuries: Phase I of a study on the costs, causes and prevention of recreational softball injuries. Available at http://users.aol.com/wwwipsm/pubs/softball_I.html. Accessed July 7, 1999.

U.S. Consumer Product Safety Commission. *Baseball safety.* CPSC publication #329. Washington, DC: The Commission.

U.S. Consumer Product Safety Commission. Reducing youth baseball injuries with protective equipment. *Consumer Product Safety Review* 1996;1(1):1-4.

Chapter 50

Basketball Safety

Each year, more than 200,000 young people under age 15 are treated for basketball-related injuries in hospital emergency departments. Many of these injuries can be prevented if players condition and train properly and follow the rules of the game. A safe playing environment also lowers the risk of injury.

Tips For Preventing Basketball Injuries

To avoid sports injuries, follow these safety tips from the American Academy of Orthopaedic Surgeons, the National SAFE KIDS Campaign, and other sports and health organizations.

- Before you start a training program or play competitive basketball, go to the doctor for a physical exam. The doctor can help assess any special injury risks you may have.

- Make sure you wear all the required safety gear every time you play and practice. Knee and elbow pads protect against scrapes and bruises, and mouth guards prevent serious dental injuries. Eye protection is recommended (eye injuries account for about 2 percent of injuries,

About This Chapter: Text in this chapter is from "Basketball Safety," SafeUSA™, www.safeusa.org, Centers for Disease Control and Prevention, 2002.

according to the National Collegiate Athletic Association). If you wear glasses, talk to the eye doctor about sports eyewear.

- Warm-up and stretch before playing.

- Do not to play through pain. If you get injured, see your doctor. Follow all the doctor's orders for recovery, and get the doctor's permission before you return to play.

- Make sure first aid is available at all games and practices.

- Coaches should enforce all the rules of the game, encourage safe play, and understand the special injury risks that young players face. They should never allow players to hold, block, push, trip, or charge opponents.

> **✔ Quick Tip**
>
> At the high school and recreational levels, basketball injuries occur more frequently during practice; college players are injured more often during games.

- Inspect the court for safety. Baskets and boundary lines should not be close to walls, fences, bleachers, or water fountains. The goals and the walls behind them should be padded. If you play outside, make sure the court is free of holes and debris.

- Above all, keep basketball fun. Putting too much focus on winning can make you push too hard and risk injury.

Who Is Affected?

Basketball is a popular sport, especially among children and young adults. But the sport carries a risk for injury, whether played in an organized league or with friends on a local park court. More than 200,000 young people under age 15 are treated in hospital emergency departments each year for basketball-related injuries. This makes basketball the fourth leading cause of injury in both unorganized settings and organized community team sports.

Injuries to basketball players are usually minor, mostly sprains and strains. The ankle and knee are the most common sites of injury, followed by the lower back, hand, and wrist. Eye injuries also occur frequently, as a result of being hit with fingers or elbows.

Girls and women appear to have a higher rate of injury than boys and men. And many of the injuries female players sustain are more serious than those of their male counterparts (e.g., knee injuries).

Additional Basketball Safety Resources

American Academy of Orthopaedic Surgeons
6300 North River Rd.
Rosemont, IL 60018-4262
Toll-Free: 800-346-AAOS (2267)
Fax On Demand: 800-999-2939
Website: www.aaos.org

Through the public information link on the AAOS home page (www.aaos.org), you can access fact sheets on injury prevention for many popular sports, including basketball.

National Athletic Trainers Association
2952 Stemmons Frwy.
Dallas, TX 75247-6196
Phone: 214-637-6282
Fax: 214-637-2206
Website: www.nata.org
E-mail: webdude@nata.org

On NATA's home page (www.nata.org), you'll find a link to injury information, including statistics and prevention tips.

National SAFE KIDS Campaign
1301 Pennsylvania Ave. N.W., Suite 1000
Washington, DC 20004
Phone: 202-662-0600
Fax: 202-393-2072
Website: www.safekids.org

Visit the SAFE KIDS home page (www.safekids.org) to access fact sheets on sports and recreation injuries, or call 202-662-0600.

National Youth Sports Safety Foundation

One Beacon St., Suite 3333
Boston, MA 02108
Phone: 617-277-1171
Fax: 617-722-9999
Website: www.nyssf.org
E-mail: NYSSF@aol.com

NYSSF (www.nyssf.org) has a variety of fact sheets on sports safety available for purchase.

☞ **Remember!!**

Basketball Specific Guidelines

- Players should focus on conditioning exercises for the total body, including upper and lower extremities.

- Players should focus on good warm-up and stretching prior to any ballistic movements.

- Footwear should fit properly to minimize the risk of ankle- and foot-related injuries.

- Replace footwear when the shock absorption is no longer adequate.

Source: Text excerpted with permission from "Minimizing the Risk of Injury in High School Athletics," a brochure from the National Athletic Trainers' Association (NATA) © 2003 NATA.

References

The data and safety tips in this fact sheet were obtained from the following sources:

American Academy of Orthopaedic Surgeons. *Basketball.* Available at http://www.aaos.org/wordhtml/pat_educ/basketba.htm. Accessed July 7, 1999.

American Academy of Pediatrics. Sports Medicine: Health care for young athletes. Elk Grove Village, IL: *The Academy*, 1991:152,169.

Caine D, Caine C, Lindner K, editors. Epidemiology of Sports Injuries. Champaign, IL: *Human Kinetics*, 1996:86-97.

Chapter 51

Football Injury Prevention

Each year, more than 150,000 football players under age 15 seek treatment for injuries in hospital emergency rooms. Football injuries, many of them serious, can be prevented if players use all safety gear properly and follow the rules of the game.

Tips for Preventing Football Injuries

To avoid injury while playing football, follow these safety tips from the American Academy of Pediatrics, the American Academy of Orthopaedic Surgeons, the Centers for Disease Control and Prevention, and other sports and health organizations.

- Before you start a training program or play competitive football, go to the doctor for a physical exam. The doctor can help assess any special injury risks you may have.

- Make sure you wear all the required safety gear every time you play and practice. All tackle football players must wear: a helmet; pads for the shoulders, hips, tailbone, and knees; thigh guards; and a mouth guard with a keeper strap. Talk to your coach to find out what kind of cleats are recommended or required in your league. If you wear glasses, talk to your eye doctor about special eyewear for sports.

About This Chapter: Text in this chapter is from "Football Safety (American)," SafeUSA™, www.safeusa.org, Centers for Disease Control and Prevention, 2002.

- Warm-up and stretch before playing.

- Do not play through pain. If you get injured, see your doctor. Follow all the doctor's orders for recovery, and get the doctor's permission before you return to play. This is especially important for brain injuries—getting a second brain injury before the first one has healed can be fatal.

- Make sure first aid is available at all games and practices.

- Coaches should enforce all the rules of the game. They should never allow illegal blocking, tackling from behind, or spearing. Coaches should also encourage safe play and understand the special injury risks that young players face.

- Above all, keep football fun. Putting too much focus on winning can make you push too hard and risk injury.

Whether you play football on an organized team or with a few friends in the park, there are still injury risks. Unfortunately, few people who play in backyard football games follow the safety rules observed in league play. Set rules for informal play, including these:

- Wear helmets and pads.

- Play only with children of similar size and age.

- Play on grass, never in the street or in a parking lot.

- Stick to touch or flag football— they can be less dangerous than tackle.

> **✎ Weird Words**
>
> Illegal Blocking: Pulling a football player down by the knees or grabbing the face mask.
>
> Spearing: Using the top of the helmet to tackle when playing football.

Who Is Affected?

Studies have shown that 15 to 20 percent of players age 8 to 14 are injured during the football season. More than 150,000 football players under age 15 are treated in hospital emergency departments each year. Among tackle football players on high school teams, the injury rate has been reported as high as 64 percent.

Sprains and strains are the most frequent injuries among players of all age groups. For young children, injuries to the arms, hands, and shoulders are most common; older players most often injure the lower extremities. Knee injuries, which total approximately 92,000 each year, often lead to chronic knee pain.

Concussions make up about 5 percent of reported football injuries. A player who has sustained a concussion is four to six times more likely to sustain another one, and getting a second brain injury before the first one has healed can prove fatal. As seen in the boxing profession, repeated concussions sustained over a long period of time can lead to serious impairments.

All football leagues, from Pop Warner to professional, require safety equipment and prohibit tackling from behind and spearing (using the top of the helmet to tackle). Before these safety measures were in place, many more football players sustained disabling injuries. These measures have also reduced deaths among football players by more than 75 percent.

✔ Quick Tip

You can help reinforce these rules by setting a good example. When you play football—or any other sport—always follow the rules and wear appropriate safety gear.

Safety Resources

American Academy of Orthopaedic Surgeons

6300 North River Rd.
Rosemont, IL 60018-4262
Toll-Free: 800-346-AAOS (2267)
Fax On Demand: 800-999-2939
Website: www.aaos.org

The AAOS fact sheet on football provides a list of equipment required by most youth football leagues.

Brain Injury Association of America

105 North Alfred St.
Alexandria, VA 22314
Toll-Free: 800-444-6443
Phone: 703-236-6000
Website: www.biausa.org; E-mail: familyhelpline@biausa.org

BIA's fact sheet about sports and concussion safety provides data on brain injuries for several sports, including football.

National Athletic Trainers Association

2952 Stemmons Frwy.
Dallas, TX 75247-6196
Phone: 214-637-6282
Fax: 214-637-2206
Website: www.nata.org
E-mail: webdude@nata.org

On NATA's home page (www.nata.org), you'll find a link to injury information, including statistics and prevention tips.

National SAFE KIDS Campaign

1301 Pennsylvania Ave. N.W., Suite 1000
Washington, DC 20004
Phone: 202-662-0600
Fax: 202-393-2072
Website: www.safekids.org

Visit the SAFE KIDS home page (www.safekids.org) to access fact sheets on sports and recreation injuries.

National Youth Sports Safety Foundation

One Beacon St., Suite 3333
Boston, MA 02108
Phone: 617-277-1171
Fax: 617-722-9999
Website: www.nyssf.org; E-mail: NYSSF@aol.com

NYSSF (www.nyssf.org) has a variety of fact sheets on sports safety available for purchase.

References

The data and safety tips in this chapter were obtained from the following sources:

American Academy of Orthopaedic Surgeons. *Football*. Available at www.aaos.org/wordhtml/pat_educ/football.htm. Accessed July 6, 1999.

American Academy of Pediatrics. Sports Medicine: Health care for young athletes. Elk Grove Village, IL: *The Academy*, 1991:150-152.

Caine D, Caine C, Lindner K, editors. Epidemiology of Sports Injuries. Champaign, IL: *Human Kinetics*, 1996:41-62.

CDC. Sports-related recurrent brain injuries—United States. *Morbidity and Mortality Weekly Report* 1994;46(10):224-227.

National Pediatric Trauma Registry. *Football Injuries*. NPTR fact sheet #5. March 1994. Available at www.nemc.org/rehab/factshee.htm. Accessed July 7, 1999.

☞ Remember!!
Football Specific Guidelines

- Intentional spearing of opponents should be discouraged.

- Blocking below the waist should be minimized during practice.

- Block and tackle with the head up to reduce the risk of neck injuries.

- In addition to total strengthening and conditioning, football-specific conditioning exercises should strengthen the neck to allow players to keep their heads firmly erect while making contact during blocks or tackles.

- Make sure the practice and playing areas are safe. Look for holes, broken glass, and other hazards on and around the practice field, game field, and blocking sleds.

- Ample fluid replacement should be available at all times.

Source: Text excerpted with permission from "Minimizing the Risk of Injury in High School Athletics," a brochure from the National Athletic Trainers' Association (NATA) © 2003 NATA.

Chapter 52

Gymnastics Safety

Hospital emergency departments treat more than 25,000 injured gymnasts under age 15 each year. Many of these injuries can be prevented if athletes and trainers know about the special injury risks associated with the sport and if safety measures and equipment are put into place.

Tips for Preventing Gymnastics Injuries

To avoid gymnastics injuries, follow these safety tips from the American Academy of Pediatrics, the American Academy of Orthopaedic Surgeons, the National SAFE KIDS Campaign, and other sports and health organizations.

- Before you start a gymnastics training program, go to the doctor for a physical exam. The doctor can help assess any special injury risks you may have.

- Make sure you wear all the required safety gear every time you compete or practice. Gymnasts may need wrist guards and hand grips; special footwear, and pads may also be required.

- Do not play through pain. If you get injured, see your doctor. Follow all the doctor's orders for recovery, and get the doctor's permission before you return to the sport.

About This Chapter: Text in this chapter is from "Gymnastics Safety," SafeUSA™, www.safeusa.org, Centers for Disease Control and Prevention, 2002.

- Make sure first aid is available at all competitions and practices.

- Talk to and watch your coach. Coaches should emphasize safety and understand the special injury risks that young gymnasts face.

- Inspect the facilities where you train and compete. Equipment should be in good condition and spaced far enough apart to avoid collisions. Floors should be padded, and mats should be secured under every apparatus. Safety harnesses should be used when you do new or difficult moves.

- Insist that you have spotters when learning new skills or doing difficult moves. Spotters should be present during practice and competition—they can help catch you if you fall.

- If you have any concerns about difficult moves, tell you coach. Don't let the coach push you to do things you are not ready for.

- Above all, keep gymnastics fun. Putting too much focus on winning can make you push too hard and risk injury.

Who Is Affected?

In the U.S., more than 600,000 children take part in school-sponsored and club-level gymnastics competitions. Some gymnasts start training at an early age (as young as 4 or 5 years old) and practice for several hours each day. With the high physical demands of gymnastics—and the increasing levels of difficulty—comes a high risk of injury.

The majority of gymnastics-related injuries are mild to moderate, with sprains, strains, and stress fractures being most common. Ankles and knees are the most frequent sites of injury, typically resulting from landings and dismounts. Injuries to the lower back are also common. Although acute injuries are rarely severe, as many as half of all injuries lead to chronic pain, and bone fractures in young athletes can cause long-term physical problems.

Floor exercises are the most common cause of injury, due to the large number of bends, twists, and landings required in those routines. Other factors that increase the risk of injury are trying moves that are too complicated for one's skill level, not using safety harnesses or spotters, getting over-tired, and spending long hours practicing.

Of special concern among female gymnasts is improper diet and eating disorders, such as anorexia nervosa and bulimia. The emphasis on a slender physique can lead some female gymnasts to lower their food intake so much that they deprive their bodies of essential nutrients. Studies have found that these athletes have lower bone density and a greater incidence of stress fractures.

Additional Gymnastics Safety Resources

American Academy of Pediatrics
141 Northwest Point Blvd.
Elk Grove Village, IL 60007-1098
Phone: 847-434-4000
Fax: 847-434-8000
Website: www.aap.org

American Academy of Orthopaedic Surgeons
6300 North River Rd.
Rosemont, IL 60018-4262
Toll-Free: 800-346-AAOS (2267)
Fax On Demand: 800-999-2939
Website: www.aaos.org

☞ Remember!!
To avoid gymnastic injuries, know your skill level, use safety harnesses and spotters, and rest when you are tired.

Through the public information link on the AAOS home page (www.aaos.org), you can access fact sheets on injury prevention for many popular sports, including gymnastics.

National Athletic Trainers Association

2952 Stemmons Frwy.
Dallas, TX 75247-6196
Phone: 214-637-6282
Fax: 214-637-2206
Website: www.nata.org
E-mail: webdude@nata.org

On NATA's home page (www.nata.org), you'll find a link to injury information, including statistics and prevention tips.

National SAFE KIDS Campaign

1301 Pennsylvania Ave. N.W., Suite 1000
Washington, DC 20004
Phone: 202-662-0600
Fax: 202-393-2072
Website: www.safekids.org

Visit the SAFE KIDS home page (www.safekids.org) to access fact sheets on sports and recreation injuries or call 202-662-0600.

National Youth Sports Safety Foundation

One Beacon St., Suite 3333
Boston, MA 02108
Phone: 617-277-1171
Fax: 617-722-9999
Website: www.nyssf.org
E-mail: NYSSF@aol.com

The Winter 1998 issue of NYSSF's *Sidelines* included an article on gymnastics injuries. To request a copy, contact NYSSF.

References

The data and safety tips in this fact sheet were obtained from the following sources:

American Academy of Orthopaedic Surgeons Seminar (Sullivan J, Grana W, editors). The Pediatric Athlete. Park Ridge, IL: *The Academy*, 1990:138.

American Academy of Pediatrics. Sports Medicine: Health care for young athletes. Elk Grove Village, IL: *The Academy*, 1991:158-159.

Caine D, Caine C, Lindner K, editors. Epidemiology of Sports Injuries. Champaign, IL: *Human Kinetics*, 1996:213-246.

Raney E. Child and adolescent gymnastics: How to avoid injury. *Hughston Health Alert*. Available at http://www.hughston.com/hha/a.gym.htm. Accessed July 9, 1999.

Zetaruk M, Mitchell W. Gymnastics injuries. *Sidelines* 1998;7(2):1-2. (*Sidelines* is a publication of the National Youth Sports Safety Foundation.)

Chapter 53

Running Injury-Free

Running Advice From The American Podiatric Medical Association

Nowhere is the miracle of the foot more clear than watching the human body in motion. The combination of 26 bones, 33 joints, 112 ligaments, and a network of tendons, nerves, and blood vessels all work together to establish the graceful synergy involved in running. The balance, support, and propulsion of a jogger's body all depend on the foot. But before entering a fitness regimen that includes jogging, don't forget to make certain your body's connection with the ground is in proper working order.

See Your Podiatrist

It is a good idea for a beginning jogger to visit a podiatric physician before starting an exercise program. Your podiatrist will examine your feet and identify potential problems, discuss conditioning, prescribe an orthotic device that fits into a running shoe (if needed), and recommend the best style of footwear for your feet.

About This Chapter: Text in this chapter is reprinted with permission from *Your Podiatric Physician Talks About Running and Your Feet*, a brochure produced by the American Podiatric Medical Association, www.apma.org, © 1999 APMA. Reprinted by permission.

Frequent joggers ought to see a podiatrist regularly to check for any potential stress on the lower extremities. Anyone, regardless of age, should check with a doctor if a cardiac condition, weight problem, or other medical complication already exists.

The Importance Of Stretching

Before beginning an exercise regimen, proper stretching is essential. If muscles are properly warmed up, the strain on muscles, tendons, and joints is reduced.

Stretching exercises should take 5-10 minutes, and ought to be conducted in a stretch/hold/relax pattern without any bouncing or pulling. It is important to stretch the propulsion muscles in the back of the leg and thigh (posterior), and not forget the anterior muscles. Some effective stretching exercises include:

- **The wall push-up.** Face a wall from three feet away, with feet flat on the floor, and knees locked. Lean into the wall, keeping feet on the floor and hold for 10 seconds as the calf muscle stretches, then relax. Do not bounce. Repeat five times.

- **The hamstring stretch.** Put your foot, with knee straight and locked, on a chair or table. Keep the other leg straight with knee locked. Lower your head toward the knee until the muscles are tight. Hold to a count of 10 then relax. Repeat five times, then switch to the other leg.

- **Lower back stretch.** In a standing position, keep both legs straight, feet spread slightly. Bend over at the waist and attempt to touch the palms of your hands to the floor. Hold the stretch for 10 seconds and repeat 10 times.

> **✎ Weird Words**
>
> Podiatrist: A medical doctor specializing in feet.
>
> Pronation: Rolling in and down, of the foot.
>
> Orthoses or Orthotics: Arch supports—shoe inserts—prescribed by a podiatrist.
>
> Shin Splints: Pain at the front and inside of the lower leg caused by running on hard surfaces, overstriding, muscle imbalance, or overuse.

Proper Footwear

Shoe choice should be determined by weight, foot structure, and running regimen. Keep in mind that all shoes have a different shape, and sizes and widths are not uniform from shoe to shoe.

♣ It's A Fact!!

During a 10-mile run, the feet make 15,000 strikes, at a force of three to four times the body's weight.

Consider whether an orthotic device will be placed in your shoe, and whether your running style is flat-footed or on the balls of the feet. Shoes should provide cushioning for shock absorption, and ought to be able to fully bend at the ball of the foot area. Visit the shoe store in the afternoon, when the feet are slightly swollen, and wear thick running socks when trying shoes on.

Training Tips

Systematic exercises must progress slowly from easy to rigorous to prevent debilitating muscle strain or more serious injury. The best and safest way to start a running program is with a four-day-per-week conditioning program for 12-16 weeks.

Begin with two sets of two-minute jogs interspersed with five minutes of fast walking. If muscles are stiff, walk only; have an easy day if you're in pain. As the weeks progress, gradually increase the number of minutes jogged per set to 20 minutes. Spend at least five workouts at each new level attained.

By the 16th week, you should be able to run two sets of 20 minutes each, with a five-minute walk before, between, and after. Make adjustments for heat and altitude, and don't be frustrated if you think your pace is too slow. Remember, a disciplined regimen will decrease your chances of injury.

Proper foot hygiene can also prevent injuries. Keeping feet powdered and dry is important, especially to the jogger suffering from blisters. Blisters can be prevented by application of petroleum jelly or creams to the feet where they occur.

Aches And Pains Of Running

Even with the best preparation, aches and pains are an inevitable result of a new jogging regimen. If the pain subsides with slow easy exercise, you may continue, but if it gets worse, stop the activity and rest. If it persists, see your podiatrist.

The most common pain associated with jogging is known as runner's knee, a catch-all for jogging-related knee pain. One of the most common causes of runner's knee is excessive pronation, or rolling in and down, of the foot. Orthoses (arch supports—shoe inserts) prescribed by your podiatrist are the best way to alleviate the problem. Occasionally, rubber pads in the arch of the shoe will help.

Shin splints, which painfully appear at the front and inside of the leg, are caused by running on hard surfaces, overstriding, muscle imbalance, or overuse. Treatment includes changing running technique or insertion of an orthotic device in the shoe.

☞ **Remember!!**
Track And Field Specific Guidelines

- Stretching is key to minimizing the risk of injury in every event.

- Conditioning programs should concentrate on muscular strength, muscular endurance, and flexibility. Individual event training should be emphasized.

- All athletes involved in running events should work to maintain year-round cardiovascular endurance.

- Before and after each event, athletes should warm-up and cool-down, stretch, and hydrate with proper fluids.

- Special attention should be paid to the nutritional needs of the endurance athlete.

Source: Text excerpted with permission from "Minimizing the Risk of Injury in High School Athletics," a brochure from the National Athletic Trainers' Association (NATA) © 2003 NATA.

Chapter 54

Reduce Soccer Injuries

More than 200,000 youths under age 15 are treated each year in hospital emergency departments, doctors' offices, clinics, and outpatient centers for injuries related to soccer. Many injuries can be prevented if players wear proper safety gear and follow the rules of the game. Increasing the safety of the goal posts can also reduce the number of injuries.

Tips For Preventing Soccer Injuries

To avoid injury while playing soccer, follow these safety tips from the American Academy of Pediatrics, the American Academy of Orthopaedic Surgeons, the U.S. Consumer Product Safety Commission, and other sports health organizations.

- Before you start a training program or enter a competition, go to the doctor for a physical exam. The doctor can help assess any special injury risks you may have.

- Make sure you wear all the required safety gear every time you play and practice. Wear shin guards during every game and every practice. Shoes with molded cleats or ribbed soles are recommended.

About This Chapter: Text in this chapter is from "Soccer Safety," SafeUSA ™, www.safeusa.org, Centers for Disease Control and Prevention, 2002.

- Warm-up and stretch before playing. Don't shoot goals before warming up.

- Do not play through pain. If you get injured, see your doctor. Follow all the doctor's orders for recovery, and get the doctor's permission before you return to play.

- Make sure first aid is available at all games and practices.

- Follow the rules. Coaches and referees should enforce all the rules of the game. For example, most leagues prohibit sliding tackles from behind, which can result in serious injury to players.

♣ **It's A Fact!!**

More than 23 percent of high school soccer players, regardless of gender, are likely to sustain at least one time-loss injury during a season.

Source: Text excerpted with permission from "Minimizing the Risk of Injury in High School Athletics," a brochure from the National Athletic Trainers' Association (NATA) © 2003 NATA.

- Talk to and watch your coach. Coaches should enforce all the rules of the game, encourage safe play, and understand the special injury risks that young players face.

- Ask your doctor and coach whether it's safe for you to head the ball and, if so, make sure you know how to head the ball correctly to avoid head and neck injury.

- Don't climb on the goal posts or hang or swing from the crossbar.

- Above all, keep soccer fun. Putting too much focus on winning can make you push too hard and risk injury.

Make sure the field and equipment are safe. Work with coaches, city officials, and parents, and other players to improve safety.

- Encourage your league to use waterproof, synthetic balls instead of leather ones. Leather balls can become waterlogged and very heavy, making them dangerous for play.

- Make sure movable soccer goals are anchored to the ground at all times, not just during play. Goals have been known to tip over in strong winds or when climbed on, causing severe injuries.

Who Is Affected?

With about 40 million amateur players, soccer is the most popular sport worldwide. It is also a sport associated with a fairly high rate of injury. In the U.S., more than 200,000 young people each year are injured badly enough to seek medical treatment.

For players under 12 years old, the injury rate in soccer is very low—less than 1 percent—but the injury rate rises with age. Nearly 8 percent of high school soccer players are injured in a season, and among community leagues, nearly 9 percent of players 19 years old and younger sustain injuries. Older participants sustain more frequent and severe injuries than young players, and girls are injured more often than boys. Most injuries are caused by illegal plays, poor field conditions, or heading the ball incorrectly.

Injuries in soccer are usually mild—sprains, strains, and contusions (bruises)—and mostly affect the lower extremities. The most common site of injury is the ankle, followed closely by the knee. Acute head injuries are rare, accounting for about 5 percent of injuries. Many of the most severe injuries are related to soccer goal posts. Goal posts have been responsible for at least 22 deaths in the last 20 years, and hospital emergency departments treat about 90 goal-related injuries each year. Most of these deaths and injuries have been caused by hitting one's head on the goal post or being hit or crushed by a falling goal post.

> **✔ Quick Tip**
>
> If the goal posts on your field(s) don't have padding, talk to school or park authorities about adding pads. Studies have shown that padding on goal posts greatly reduces the risk of serious injury caused by a player's head hitting the post.

Injuries can be prevented if players wear shin guards, warm-up before play, and follow the rules of the game. Changes in equipment can also greatly enhance injury prevention efforts. Most notably, the addition of padding to goal posts can reduce the number and severity of head injuries. Laboratory testing has shown that padding reduces the force of hitting the post by 31 to 63 percent. Anchoring movable goal posts to the ground at all times, even when not in use, can also greatly reduce some of the most serious injuries. The National Federation of State High School Associations' Soccer Rules Committee now requires that soccer goals be anchored. The international soccer association (FIFA [Fédération Internationale de Football Association]) is also considering making this change to its rules.

Additional Soccer Safety Resources

American Academy of Orthopaedic Surgeons
6300 North River Rd.
Rosemont, IL 60018-4262
Toll-Free: 800-346-AAOS (2267)
Fax On Demand: 800-999-2939
Website: www.aaos.org

Through the public information link on the AAOS home page, you can access fact sheets on injury prevention tips for many popular sports, including soccer.

Brain Injury Association of America
105 North Alfred St.
Alexandria, VA 22314
Toll-Free: 800-444-6443
Phone: 703-236-6000
Website: www.biausa.org
E-mail: familyhelpline@biausa.org

BIA's fact sheet about sports and concussion safety provides data on brain injuries for several sports, including soccer.

National Athletic Trainers Association
2952 Stemmons Frwy.
Dallas, TX 75247-6196
Phone: 214-637-6282
Fax: 214-637-2206
Website: www.nata.org
E-mail: webdude@nata.org

👉 **Remember!!**

Soccer Specific Guidelines

- Players should be encouraged to wear appropriate shin guards during practice and play.

- Provide fluids on the sidelines throughout practice and games. Although soccer requires non-stop play with no time outs, athletes should be encouraged to come to the sidelines or touch line where they can replenish fluids without penalty.

- Warm-up for approximately 15 minutes, beginning for half that time without a ball. Warm-up exercises should include light jogging and stretching. Without these warm-ups, the explosive action of shooting can result in strained muscles.

- Adhere to the rules of the game when tackling.

- Although soccer does not provide time outs, injuries should be evaluated immediately to ensure the athlete is not worsening the injury.

Source: Text excerpted with permission from "Minimizing the Risk of Injury in High School Athletics," a brochure from the National Athletic Trainers' Association (NATA) © 2003 NATA.

At www.nata.org, you'll find a link to injury information, including statistics and prevention tips.

National Youth Sports Safety Foundation

One Beacon St.
Suite 3333
Boston, MA 02108
Phone: 617-277-1171
Fax: 617-722-9999
Website: www.nyssf.org
E-mail: NYSSF@aol.com

NYSSF (www.nyssf.org) has a variety of fact sheets on sports safety available for purchase.

U.S. Consumer Product Safety Commission

4330 East-West Highway
Bethesda, MD 20814-4408
Toll-Free: 800-638-2772
Phone: 301-504-6816
Fax: 301-504-0124
Additional Fax: 301-504-0025
Website: www.cpsc.gov
E-mail: info@cpsc.gov

Safety standards set by the CPSC and the soccer goal industry can reduce the risk of soccer goal tip-overs and associated injuries.

References

Data and safety tips in this fact sheet were obtained from the following sources:

American Academy of Orthopaedic Surgeons. *Public information on soccer.* Available at www.aaos.org/wordhtml/pat_educ/soccer.htm. Accessed July 1999.

American Academy of Orthopaedic Surgeons Seminar (Sullivan J, Grana W, editors). The Pediatric Athlete. Park Ridge, IL: *The Academy,* 1990:141.

American Academy of Pediatrics. Sports Medicine: Health care for young athletes. Elk Grove Village, IL: *The Academy,* 1991:154-155.

Bir C, Cassatta S, Janda D. *An analysis and comparison of soccer shin guards* (abstract). The Institute for Preventative Sports Medicine web site. Available at www.ipsm.org. Accessed July 1999.

Caine D, Caine C, Lindner K, editors. Epidemiology of Sports Injuries. Champaign, IL: *Human Kinetics,* 1996:387-398.

CDC. Injuries associated with soccer goalposts–United States, 1979-1993. *Morbidity and Mortality Weekly Report* 1994;43(9):153-155.

Janda D, Bir C, Wild B, Olson S, Hensinger R. *A laboratory and field testing analysis of a preventive intervention* (abstract). The Institute for Preventative Sports Medicine web site. Available at www.ipsm.org.

U.S. Consumer Product Safety Commission. *New standard for soccer goals helps prevent tip-over deaths linked to unanchored goals.* News release, May 4, 1999.

U.S. Consumer Product Safety Commission. *CPSC warns consumers: anchor soccer goals to prevent tip-over.* News release, March 29, 1996.

Chapter 55

Timely Tips For Tennis Types

Tennis players of all skill levels can improve their health along with their game by using some simple measures for conditioning, technique, injury prevention, and equipment.

Conditioning And Skills

- To improve your heart and lung conditioning, consider a running program. Running three to five times a week will help you sustain the stamina for a top level of play through long matches.

- Get expert instruction in both conditioning and technique. The pros will not only help you with technique, but also provide you with a fitness program to suit your physical condition and level of play.

- Work on all-around flexibility and strength. Consider consulting a sports physiotherapist or medical professional who can recommend a program to suit your body type.

Preventing Injury

- Warm-up before starting to play, without fail. And remember that a warm-up means getting warm. Start with brisk walking or easy jogging to

About This Chapter: Text in this chapter is reprinted with permission from Nesbitt, L. "Timely Tips for Tennis Types," *Physician and Sportsmedicine* 1998, 26 (5), 107-108. © 1998 The McGraw-Hill Companies. All rights reserved. Reviewed in June 2003 by Dr. David A. Cooke, MD, Diplomate, American Board of Internal Medicine.

get your muscles warm, then stretch for several minutes. Consult a qualified instructor and develop your own warm-up routine, centering on muscles that come into play during a tennis match.

- If you are prone to ankle sprains, tape up with the proper athletic product, or consult a sports shop or healthcare professional for an ankle brace designed for tennis. (For advice on other injuries common in tennis, see "Court Trials: Coping With Common Tennis Injuries" at the end of this chapter.)

- Calf muscles can get tight in tennis. Do lots of runner's stretches before, between, and after matches. These are especially good for women who spend time in high- heeled shoes.

- Drink lots of water before, during, and after your match. Avoid caffeine, alcohol, and drinks that are high in sugar.

- Ongoing sore feet or legs in tennis may be a result of a mechanical foot imbalance. This can often be corrected by taping, an off-the-shelf orthotic insert, or a custom-made orthotic device prescribed by a healthcare professional.

Equipment

- Wear tennis shoes for stability and cushioning (see "Selecting Tennis Shoes," in this chapter). Don't wear running shoes, which are designed for forward motion and don't protect as well against an ankle sprain.

- Socks have improved. Try those for tennis that wick away perspiration and reduce friction. Reduced friction can help you avoid blisters.

- Choose the right racket.[1] Your arm should not get tired swinging it. Mid-level string tension will absorb shock but give good power. And as you grasp the handle, a finger's width should separate the tip of your middle finger from the crease at the base of your thumb. [[1]Reference: Harding WG III: Elbow pain in young tennis players: selecting the right racket, learning good technique. *Phys Sportsmed* 1991;19(9):135-136.]

- Keep a couple of small adhesive bandages in your bag in case you need them for foot or hand blisters.

Selecting Tennis Shoes

Wear shoes that are designed specifically for racket sports and support your feet well. Replace worn-out tennis shoes. Patches or other repairs are temporary at best, and excessively worn shoes can affect both your feet and your playing style. Never play in improperly fitted or borrowed shoes.

When buying shoes, look for those that support the arch firmly and allow room to move your toes. At the store, try tennis shoes on and practice some on-court moves to make sure they fit and feel comfortable. As a rule, more expensive shoes are of better quality, but not always. Look for:

- Reinforcement at the toe to protect your foot and minimize wear when the toe drags on the court;

- A well-padded sole at the ball of the foot, which is where most pressure is exerted;

- Sturdy sides of the shoe for stability during side-to-side motions;

> ✔ Quick Tip
> **Game Point**
>
> Tennis is a great way to get muscles working, enjoy time with a friend or three, and test your ability. The tips provided can help you ace the sport without double-faulting on your body.

- A well-cushioned heel for absorbing jarring forces;

- Ample room in the toe box to prevent blisters; and

- A firm and well-padded heel counter (back and sides of heel) for support.

Court Trials: Coping With Common Tennis Injuries

Even if they take precautions to avoid injury, tennis players sometimes get hurt. Here are pointers on how to deal with some of the most common tennis problems.

Corns and calluses. Corns and calluses indicate pressure, friction, and imbalance of the foot. If you have calluses, place 1/8-inch or 1/4-inch moleskin or felt on each side of the callus to reduce pressure until you can get proper medical help. Do not use commercial acid corn cures because they can lead to skin irritation and infection.

Because most corns and calluses are signs of some underlying mechanical problem, they cannot be eliminated permanently until the problem itself is corrected. Seek professional attention. Simple corrective procedures can relieve disabling problems.

Tennis leg. Sudden movements of the foot and leg may result in tennis leg, or a muscle tear deep within the calf. Never play with calf muscle pain. Seek medical help.

Tennis elbow. Bending the elbow during a backhand swing, an improper racket, and weak muscles can all contribute to pain in the elbow.[2] If you have persistent elbow pain, take a break from tennis for a few weeks. Icing can also help. If the pain continues, see a physician, who may prescribe an elbow strap, strengthening exercises, and other measures. [2Reference: Case WS: Acing tennis elbow. *Phys Sportsmed* 1993;21(7):21-22.]

> ☞ **Remember!!**
>
> This information is not intended as a substitute for medical treatment. Before starting an exercise program, consult a physician.

Tennis toe. Tennis toe is characterized by severe, throbbing pain beneath the toenail. Symptoms include vague swelling of the toe and purple discoloration under the nail. The discoloration is from bleeding, which may appear as vertical streaks beneath the nail.

The condition usually affects the big toe or the one next to it. Tennis toe is often caused by modern tennis shoes, which give such good traction that the foot is forced to the front of the shoe during sudden stops, thus traumatizing the nail. Shoes should have a finger's width of room in front of the toes.

Initially, you can use cold packs and painkillers like aspirin to provide relief if the pain is severe. Placing a 1/8-inch-thick felt pad on the skin behind the base of the nail can help you prevent or cope with the problem, as can trimming the nail. Medical care can also help.

When to stop, when to resume. Swelling, stress, and strain won't necessarily mean you have to stop playing altogether. You may just have to scale back. Assessment and treatment by a medical professional can pave the way to pain-free playing.

Don't try to return to full tennis activity immediately after an injury or other forced layoff. Return gradually, and slow down if you feel pain. Get professional advice if you're unsure of how to resume your program.

—by Lloyd Nesbitt, DPM

Dr. Nesbitt is a podiatrist in private practice in Toronto.

Chapter 56

In-Line Skates And Skateboards

Each year, more than 100,000 people are treated in hospital emergency departments for injuries related to in-line skating, and nearly 40,000 seek emergency treatment for skateboarding injuries. The majority of these patients are under age 25. Many injuries can be prevented if skaters wear proper safety gear and avoid risky skating behavior.

Injury Prevention Tips For In-line Skaters And Skateboarders

To avoid injuries while in-line skating and skateboarding, follow these safety tips from the American Academy of Pediatrics, the Centers for Disease Control and Prevention (CDC), the U.S. Consumer Product Safety Commission, and other sports and health organizations.

- Make sure you wear all the required safety gear every time you skate. All skaters should wear a helmet, knee and elbow pads, and wrist guards. If you do tricks or play roller hockey, make sure to wear heavy-duty gear.

- Check your helmet for proper fit. The helmet should be worn flat on the head, with the bottom edge parallel to the ground. It should fit snugly and

About This Chapter: Text in this chapter is from "Skates and Skateboards Safety," SafeUSA™, www.safeusa.org, Centers for Disease Control and Prevention, 2002.

should not move around in any direction when you shake your head.

- Choose in-line skates or a skateboard that best suits your ability and skating style. If you are a novice, choose in-line skates with three or four wheels. Skates with five wheels are only for experienced skaters and people who skate long distances. Choose a skateboard designed for your type of riding—slalom, freestyle, or speed. Some boards are rated for the weight of the rider.

- Find a smooth skating surface; good choices are skating trails and driveways without much slope (but be careful about children skating into traffic). Check for holes, bumps, and debris that could make you fall. Novice in-line skaters should start out in a skating rink where the surface is smooth and flat and where speed is controlled.

> ### ♣ It's A Fact!!
>
> Irregular riding surfaces account for more than half of the skateboarding injuries caused by falls. Wrist injury is the number one injury, usually a sprain or a fracture. Skateboarders who have been skating for less than a week suffered one-third of the injuries. When experienced riders suffered injuries, it was usually from falls that were caused by rocks and other irregularities in the riding surface.
>
> Source: Reprinted from "Skateboarding," a fact sheet produced by the National Safety Council. © 2001. Permission to reprint granted by the National Safety Council, a membership organization dedicated to protecting life and promoting health. For more information, visit the website of the National Safety Council at www.nsc.org.

- Don't skate in areas with high pedestrian or vehicle traffic. Children should not skate in the street or on vehicle parking ramps.

- Never skitch. Skitching is the practice of holding on to a moving vehicle in order to skate very fast. People have died while skitching.

- If you are new to in-line skating, lessons from an instructor certified by the International In-line Skating Association may be helpful. These lessons show proper form and teach how to stop. Check with your local parks and recreation department to find a qualified instructor.

- If you get injured while skating, see your doctor. Follow all the doctor's instructions for your recovery, and get the doctor's permission before you start skating again.

Who Is Affected?

Millions of people in the U.S.—the majority of them under age 25—take part in in-line skating and skateboarding as a form of recreation and exercise. But these sports can be dangerous, especially when safety precautions are ignored. Each year, more than 100,000 skaters are injured seriously enough to need medical care in hospital emergency departments, doctors' offices, clinics, and outpatient centers. Most of these injuries occur when skaters lose control, skate over an obstacle, skate too fast, or perform a trick.

While most skating injuries are minor or require only outpatient care, 36 fatalities have been reported since 1992. Thirty-one of those skating deaths

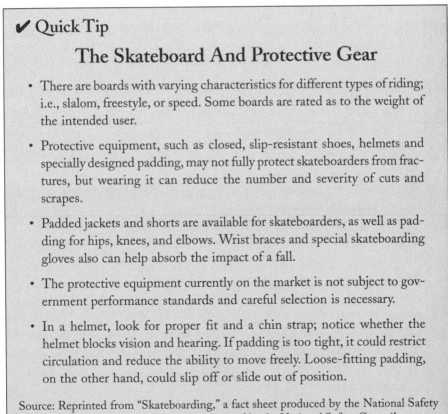

✔ **Quick Tip**

The Skateboard And Protective Gear

- There are boards with varying characteristics for different types of riding; i.e., slalom, freestyle, or speed. Some boards are rated as to the weight of the intended user.

- Protective equipment, such as closed, slip-resistant shoes, helmets and specially designed padding, may not fully protect skateboarders from fractures, but wearing it can reduce the number and severity of cuts and scrapes.

- Padded jackets and shorts are available for skateboarders, as well as padding for hips, knees, and elbows. Wrist braces and special skateboarding gloves also can help absorb the impact of a fall.

- The protective equipment currently on the market is not subject to government performance standards and careful selection is necessary.

- In a helmet, look for proper fit and a chin strap; notice whether the helmet blocks vision and hearing. If padding is too tight, it could restrict circulation and reduce the ability to move freely. Loose-fitting padding, on the other hand, could slip off or slide out of position.

Source: Reprinted from "Skateboarding," a fact sheet produced by the National Safety Council. © 2001. Permission to reprint granted by the National Safety Council, a membership organization dedicated to protecting life and promoting health. For more information, visit the website of the National Safety Council at www.nsc.org.

were from collisions with motor vehicles. Among all age groups, 63 percent of skating injuries are fractures, dislocations, sprains, strains, and avulsions (tears). More than one-third of skating injuries are to the wrist area, with two-thirds of these injuries being fractures and dislocations. Approximately 5 percent are head injuries.

Safety gear has been shown to be highly effective in preventing injuries among skaters. Pads can reduce wrist and elbow injuries by about 85 percent and knee injuries by 32 percent. Although studies have not determined the degree to which helmets reduce head injuries among skaters, helmets have been shown to be highly protective among bicyclists.

Despite the proven safety benefits and relative low cost of helmets and pads, many skaters don't wear them. Nearly two-thirds of injured in-line skaters and skateboarders were not wearing safety gear when they crashed. One study found that one-third of skaters wear no safety gear, and another one-third use only some of the recommended safety equipment. Teens are least likely to wear all the safety gear. Nine out of ten beginning skaters wear all the safety gear, but studies have shown that many skaters shed the helmet and pads as they gain experience.

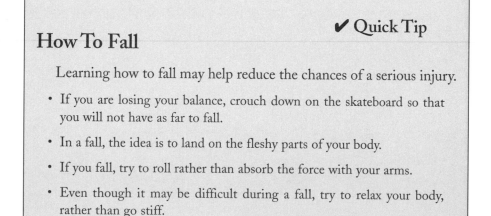

✔ **Quick Tip**

How To Fall

Learning how to fall may help reduce the chances of a serious injury.

- If you are losing your balance, crouch down on the skateboard so that you will not have as far to fall.
- In a fall, the idea is to land on the fleshy parts of your body.
- If you fall, try to roll rather than absorb the force with your arms.
- Even though it may be difficult during a fall, try to relax your body, rather than go stiff.

Source: Reprinted from "Skateboarding," a fact sheet produced by the National Safety Council. © 2001. Permission to reprint granted by the National Safety Council, a membership organization dedicated to protecting life and promoting health. For more information, visit the website of the National Safety Council at www.nsc.org.

Tips For Using A Skateboard

- Give your board a safety check each time before you ride.

- Always wear safety gear.

- Never ride in the street.

- Obey the city laws. Observe traffic and areas where you can and cannot skate.

- Don't skate in crowds of non-skaters.

- Only one person per skateboard.

- Never hitch a ride from a car, bicycle, etc.

- Don't take chances; complicated tricks require careful practice and a specially-designated area.

- Learn to fall—practice falling on a soft surface or grass.

Source: Reprinted from "Skateboarding," a fact sheet produced by the National Safety Council. © 2001. Permission to reprint granted by the National Safety Council, a membership organization dedicated to protecting life and promoting health. For more information, visit the website of the National Safety Council at www.nsc.org.

Additional In-Line Skates and Skateboarding Safety Resources

American Academy of Pediatrics
141 Northwest Point Blvd.
Elk Grove Village, IL 60007-1098
Phone: 847-434-4000
Fax: 847-434-8000
Website: www.aap.org

American Academy of Orthopaedic Surgeons
6300 North River Rd.
Rosemont, IL 60018-4262
Toll-Free: 800-346-AAOS (2267)
Fax On Demand: 800-999-2939
Website: www.aaos.org

Through the public information link on the AAOS home page, you can access fact sheets on a variety of popular sports, including in-line skating.

Brain Injury Association of America
105 North Alfred St.
Alexandria, VA 22314
Toll-Free: 800-444-6443
Phone: 703-236-6000
Website: www.biausa.org
E-mail: familyhelpline@biausa.org

BIA's fact sheet on sports and concussion safety provides data on brain injuries for several sports, including in-line skating.

U.S. Consumer Product Safety Commission
4330 East-West Highway
Bethesda, MD 20814-4408
Toll-Free: 800-638-2772
Phone: 301-504-6816
Fax: 301-504-0124 and 301-504-0025
Website: www.cpsc.gov
E-mail: info@cpsc.gov

CPSC offers kids advice on skateboard and in-line skating safety.

National SAFE KIDS Campaign
1301 Pennsylvania Ave. N.W., Suite 1000
Washington, DC 20004
Phone: 202-662-0600
Fax: 202-393-2072
Website: www.safekids.org

Visit the SAFE KIDS home page to access fact sheets on sports and recreation injuries.

National Youth Sports Safety Foundation
One Beacon St., Suite 3333
Boston, MA 02108
Phone: 617-277-1171
Fax: 617-722-9999
Website: www.nyssf.org
E-mail: NYSSF@aol.com

NYSSF has a variety of fact sheets on sports safety available for purchase.

References

The data and safety tips in this fact sheet were obtained from the following sources:

American Academy of Orthopaedic Surgeons. *Injuries from in-line skating*. Position statement. Available at www.aaos.org/wordhtml/papers/position/inline.htm. Accessed July 8, 1999.

American Academy of Pediatrics. In-line skating injuries in children and adolescents. *Pediatrics* 1998;101(4):720-721.

CDC. Toy safety–United States, 1984. *Morbidity and Mortality Weekly Report* 1985;34(5):755-6, 761-2.

National Pediatric Trauma Registry. *Falls while skating or skateboarding.* NPTR fact sheet #9. April 1999. Available at www.nemc.org/rehab/factshee.htm. Accessed July 7, 1999.

Schieber R, Branche-Dorsey C, Ryan G. Comparison of in-line skating injuries with rollerskating and skateboarding injuries. *JAMA* 1994;271(23):1856-1858.

Schieber R, Branche C. In-line skating injuries: Epidemiology and recommendations for prevention. *Sports Medicine* 1995;19(6):427-432.

U.S. Consumer Product Safety Commission. *CPSC projects sharp rise in in-line skating injuries.* News release, June 21, 1995. Available at www.cpsc.gov/cpscpub/prerel/prhtml95/95135.html. Accessed July 12, 1999.

U.S. Consumer Product Safety Commission. *Safety commission warns about hazards with in-line roller skates: Safety alert.* CPSC document #5050. Available at www.cpsc.gov/cpscpub/pubs/5050.html. Accessed July 12, 1999.

U.S. Consumer Product Safety Commission. *Holiday skateboard and rollerskates safety.* Available at www.cpsc.gov/kids/skate.html. Accessed July 12, 1999.

Chapter 57

Prevent Ski And Snowboard Injuries

Safety On The Slopes

Millions of people ski, snowboard, and sled each year in the United States. These cold weather activities, which can be exhilarating, also result in many injuries each year. By developing skills with a qualified instructor and supervising young children while they participate in these activities, you can help reduce the risk of injury.

You can reduce the chance of becoming injured while skiing, snowboarding, and sledding if you follow these safety tips from the American Academy of Orthopaedic Surgeons, the National Ski Areas Association, SAFE KIDS, and the U.S. Consumer Product Safety Commission.

Skiing And Snowboarding

Preparation:

• Before you get out on the slopes, be sure you're in shape. You'll enjoy the sports more and have lower risk of injury if you're physically fit.

About This Chapter: Text in this chapter is from, "Winter Sports Injury Prevention: Safety on the Slopes," SafeUSA™, www.safeusa.org, Centers for Disease Control and Prevention, 2002.

- Take a lesson (or several) from a qualified instructor. Like anything, you'll improve the most when you receive expert guidance. And be sure to learn how to fall correctly and safely to reduce the risk of injury.

- Don't start jumping maneuvers until you've had proper instruction on how to jump and have some experience. Jumps are the most common cause of spinal injuries among snowboarders.

- Obtain proper equipment. Be sure that your equipment is in good condition and have your ski or snowboard bindings adjusted correctly at a local ski shop.

- Wear a helmet to prevent head injuries from falls or collisions. Skiers and snowboarders should wear helmets specifically designed for these sports.

♣ **It's A Fact!!**
One study showed that helmet use by skiers and snowboarders could prevent or reduce the severity of nearly half of head injuries to adults and more than half of head injuries to children less than 15 years old.

- When buying skiwear, look for fabric that is water and wind-resistant. Look for wind flaps to shield zippers, snug cuffs at wrists and ankles, collars that can be snuggled up to the chin and drawstrings that can be adjusted for comfort and to keep the wind out.

- Dress in layers. Layering allows you to accommodate your body's constantly changing temperature. For example, dress in polypropylene underwear (top and bottoms), which feels good next to the skin, dries quickly, absorbs sweat, and keeps you warm. Wear a turtleneck, sweater, and jacket.

- Be prepared for changes in the weather. Bring a headband or hat with you to the slopes (60 percent of heat-loss is through the head) and wear gloves or mittens.

- Protect your skin from the sun and wind by using a sun screen or sun block. The sun reflects off the snow and is stronger than you think, even on cloudy days!

Responsibility Code For Skiers

The National Ski Areas Association endorses a responsibility code for skiers. This code can be applied to snowboarders also. The following are the code's seven safety rules of the slopes:

1. Always stay in control and be able to stop or avoid other people or objects.

2. People ahead of you have the right of way. It is your responsibility to avoid them.

3. You must not stop where you obstruct a trail or are not visible from above.

4. Whenever starting downhill or merging into a trail, look uphill, and yield to others.

5. Always use devices to help prevent runaway equipment.

6. Observe all posted signs and warnings. Keep off closed trails and out of closed areas.

7. Prior to using any lift, you must have the knowledge and ability to load, ride, and unload safely.

• Always use appropriate eye protection. Sunglasses or goggles will help protect your vision from glare, help you to see the terrain better, and help shield your eyes from flying debris.

When You're On The Slopes

• The key to successful skiing and snowboarding is control. To have it, you must be aware of your technique and level of ability, the terrain, and the skiers and snowboarders around you.

• Take a couple of slow ski or snowboard runs to warm-up at the start of each day.

• Ski or snowboard with partners and stay within sight of each other, if possible. If one partner loses the other, stop and wait.

• Stay on marked trails and avoid potential avalanche areas such as steep hillsides with little vegetation. Begin a run slowly. Watch out for rocks and patches of ice on the trails.

• Be aware of the weather and snow conditions and how they can change. Make adjustments for icy conditions, deep snow powder, wet snow, and adverse weather conditions.

• If you find yourself on a slope that exceeds your ability level, always leave your skis or snowboard on and side step down the slope.

- If you find yourself skiing or snowboarding out of control, fall down on your rear end or on your side, the softest parts of your body.

- Drink plenty of water to avoid becoming dehydrated.

- Avoid alcohol consumption. Skiing and snowboarding do not mix well with alcohol or drugs. Beware of medicines or drugs that impair the senses or make you drowsy.

- If you're tired, stop and rest. Fatigue is a risk factor for injuries.

The Problem

According to the National Sporting Goods Association, nearly 10 million persons participate in alpine skiing more than once a year and up to 2.5 million snowboard each year. Skiing, snowboarding, and sledding can be

---

✔ Quick Tip

Common Ski and Snowboard Injuries

Skiing: The most common injuries in downhill skiing are to the knee, shoulder, and thumb. Because of the long twisting lever arm of the ski, tears of the anterior cruciate ligament (ACL) and medial collateral ligament (MCL) are the most common knee injuries. Impact from moguls or jumps can cause chipping of the surface of the knee (articular cartilage). Shoulder injuries occur with tumbling falls, causing either dislocations or rotator cuff tears. If the pole gets caught between the thumb and forefinger, a tear of the ulna collateral ligament of the thumb may occur. Ski injuries may be prevented by proper pre-season conditioning and proper falling technique.

Snowboarding: Knee injuries are less common with snowboarding than in skiing due to the fixed position of the legs. Unfortunately, most of the force from falling is therefore taken by the upper limbs and back. Common snowboarding injuries are wrist fractures, shoulder injuries, clavicle fractures, and spine injuries.

Source: Jeffrey L. Halbrecht, MD, Institute for Arthroscopy and Sports Medicine, San Francisco, CA, www.iasm.com © 2001, reprinted with permission.

great fun and are terrific ways to exercise. But they can also be risky. The U.S. Consumer Product Safety Commission (CPSC) estimates that 84,200 skiing injuries and 37,600 snowboarding injuries were treated in hospital emergency rooms in the United States in 1997, including approximately 17,500 head injuries. However, the most common skiing-related injuries are knee and ankle sprains and fractures. While most skiing and snowboarding injuries occur among adults, the majority of sledding-related injuries are among children 5-14 years old. More than 14,500 children in this age group were treated for sledding-related injuries in the United States in 1997.

The estimated number of skiing-related injuries declined by more than 25 percent from 1993 to 1997, partly because of improvements in ski equipment, such as redesigned bindings. However, during that same period, snowboarding injuries nearly tripled and the number of head injuries from snowboarding increased five-fold.

A CPSC study found there were 17,500 head injuries associated with skiing and snowboarding in 1997. This study estimated that 7,700 head injuries, including 2,600 head injuries to children, could be prevented or reduced in severity each year by using skiing or snowboarding helmets. The study also showed that helmet use could prevent about 11 skiing- and snowboarding-related deaths annually. As a result of these findings, CPSC recommends skiers and snowboarders wear helmets specifically designed for these activities to prevent head injuries from falls and collisions.

Additional Ski And Snowboard Safety Resources

American Academy of Orthopaedic Surgeons
6300 North River Rd.
Rosemont, IL 60018-4262
Toll-Free: 800-346-AAOS (2267)
Fax On Demand: 800-999-2939
Website: www.aaos.org

Through the public information link to patient education on the AAOS home page, you can access fact sheets on injury prevention for many sports, including skiing and sledding.

American Academy of Pediatrics

141 Northwest Point Blvd.
Elk Grove Village, IL 60007-1098
Phone: 847-434-4000
Fax: 847-434-8000
Website: www.aap.org

AAP has safety tips for the winter holidays (including tips on outdoor sports) at www.aap.org.

✔ **Quick Tip**

Snowboarders: wrist guards and knee pads can help protect you when you fall.

National Safety Council

1121 Spring Lake Drive
Itasca, IL 60143-3201
Phone: 630-285-1121
Fax: 630-285-1315
Website: www.nsc.org

NSC's website provides winter sport injury prevention information.

National Ski Areas Association

133 S. Van Gordon St., Suite 300
Lakewood, CO 80228
Phone: 303-987-1111
Fax: 303-986-2345
Website: www.nsaa.org
E-mail: nsaa@nsaa.org

NSAA is the trade association for ski area owners and operators. Suggestions for safe skiing and snowboarding can be found on their website.

National Ski Patrol

133 S. Van Gordon St., Suite 100
Lakewood, CO 80228
Phone: 303-988-1111
Fax: 303-988-3005
Website: www.nsp.org

NSP is a nonprofit membership association providing education services about emergency care and safety to the public and mountain recreation industry.

National SAFE KIDS Campaign
1301 Pennsylvania Ave. N.W., Suite 1000
Washington, DC 20004
Phone: 202-662-0600
Fax: 202-393-2072
Website: www.safekids.org

U.S. Consumer Product Safety Commission
4330 East-West Highway
Bethesda, MD 20814-4408
Toll-Free: 800-638-2772
Phone: 301-504-6816
Fax: 301-504-0124 and 301-504-0025
Website: www.cpsc.gov
E-mail: info@cpsc.gov

Information about CPSC's study of the impact of using helmets to prevent head injuries to skiers and snowboarders can be accessed at www.cpsc.gov.

☞ **Remember!!**

Before you hit the slopes, put safety first—use proper equipment, know the responsibility code, and stay in control.

References

The data and safety tips in this fact sheet were obtained from the following sources:

American Academy of Orthopaedic Surgeons. *Skiing*. Available at www.aaos.org/wordhtml/pat_educ/skiing.htm. Accessed December 10, 1999.

American Academy of Orthopaedic Surgeons. *Sledding Safety*. Available at www.aaos.org/wordhtml/papers/position/sledding.htm. Accessed December 10, 1999.

Caine D, Caine C, Lindner K, editors. Epidemiology of Sports Injuries. Champaign, IL: *Human Kinetics*, 1996:29-40.

National Ski Areas Association. *Ski and Snowboarding Tips*. Available at www.nsaa.org.

National Ski Areas Association. *Your Responsibility Code*. Available at www.nsaa.org.

SAFE KIDS. *Sports and Recreational Activity Injury*. Available at www.safekids.org.

U.S. Consumer Product Safety Commission. *CPSC Staff Recommends Use of Helmets for Skiers, Snowboarders to Prevent Head Injuries*. Available at www.cpsc.gov Accessed December 10, 1999.

Chapter 58

Enjoy Safe Biking

Bicycling is one of the most popular ways to get around, whether for recreation, sport, or transportation. An estimated 57 million Americans ride bikes ranging from high performance, 18-speed, touring models to dirt bikes equipped with balloon tires—and dozens of variations in between.

With millions of cyclists on the roads—the same roads occupied by millions of motor vehicles that are larger, heavier, and faster than bikes—the National Safety Council believes that defensive driving applies to people who pedal with their feet to travel, as well as to those who push on the gas pedal. Because about 900 bicyclists were killed and some 70,000 suffered disabling injuries (1999 statistics), it is clear that taking precautions in traffic and wearing protective equipment are a cyclist's best shields against unintentional injuries.

The Council offers the following tips for safe and enjoyable bicycling:

• Obey traffic rules. Get acquainted with ordinances. Cyclists must follow the same rules as motorists.

About This Chapter: Text in this chapter is reprinted from "Enjoy Safe Bicycling," a fact sheet produced by the National Safety Council. © 2001. Permission to reprint granted by the National Safety Council, a membership organization dedicated to protecting life and promoting health. For more information, visit the website of the National Safety Council at www.nsc.org.

- Know your bike's capabilities. Remember that bicycles differ from motor vehicles; they're smaller and can't move as fast. But, they can change direction more easily, stop faster, and move through smaller spaces.

- Ride in single file with traffic, not against it. Bicycling two abreast can be dangerous. Bicyclists should stay as far right on the pavement as possible, watching for opening car doors, sewer gratings, soft shoulders, broken glass, and other debris. Remember to keep a safe distance from the vehicle ahead.

- Make safe turns and cross intersections with care. Signal turns half a block before the intersection, using the correct hand signals (left arm straight out for left turn; forearm up for right turn). When traffic is heavy and the cyclist has to turn left, it is best to dismount and walk the bicycle across both streets at the crosswalks.

- Never hitch on cars. A sudden stop or turn could send the cyclist flying into the path of another vehicle.

- Before riding into traffic: stop, look left, right, left again, and over your shoulder.

- Always be seen. During the day, cyclists should wear bright clothing. Nighttime cycling is not advised, but if riding at night is necessary, retroreflective

---

✔ Quick Tip

Bicycle-Related Head Injuries

Bicycle-related head injuries account for about:

- 500 deaths per year

- 17,000 hospitalizations

- 153,000 emergency department visits

- Two-thirds of bicycle-related deaths

- One-third of non-fatal bicycle injuries

There is:

- One head injury death every 15 hours

- One emergency department visit due to head injury every 3 minutes

Cost of bicycle-related head injuries:

- Costs society more than $3 billion in 1991

- 32% of bicycle-related head injury deaths in 1992 were children aged 5-14 years

Source: National Bicycle Safety Network, Centers for Disease Control and Prevention (CDC) 2002.

♣ It's A Fact!!
Factors In Bicycle-Related Injuries and Deaths

Age is a factor for bicycle-related injuries and deaths:

- Rate of injury is highest for children aged 5-15 years
- Rate of death is highest for children aged 10-14 years

Gender is a factor for bicycle-related injuries and deaths:

- Males are 2.4 times more likely to be killed per bicycle trip.

Helmet use is a factor. Universal helmet use could:

- Save one life each day
- Prevent one head injury every 4 minutes

---

clothing, designed to bounce back motorists' headlight beams, will make cyclists more visible.

- Make sure the bicycle has the right safety equipment: a red rear reflector; a white front reflector; a red or colorless spoke reflector on the rear wheel; an amber or colorless reflector on the front wheel; pedal reflectors; a horn or bell; and a rear view mirror. A bright headlight is recommended for night riding.

- Wear a helmet. Head injuries cause about 85 percent of all bicycling fatalities. The Council strongly urges all cyclists to wear helmets. The first body part to fly forward in a collision is usually the head, and with nothing but skin and bone to protect the brain from injury, the results can be disastrous.

- In March 1999, the U.S. Consumer Product Safety Commission (CPSC) issued a uniform, mandatory federal safety standard for all bike helmets. All helmets manufactured or imported for sale in the U.S. must carry a label or sticker stating that they meet the requirements of the new standard. Cyclists who currently have a helmet that meets the ASTM, ANSI, or Snell standards do not need to rush out to buy a new one; these helmets provide adequate protection. However, when it's time to replace a helmet because it has been outgrown or damaged in a crash, buying a helmet that meets the CPSC standard is recommended. The helmet should fit securely and should be worn low and near the eyebrows—not back on the forehead.

A properly designed helmet has four characteristics:

- a stiff outer shell designed to distribute impact forces and protect against sharp objects;

- an energy-absorbing liner at least one-half inch thick;

- a chin strap and fastener to keep the helmet in place; and,

- it should be lightweight, cool in hot weather, and fit comfortably.

☞ Remember!!

There is no limit to the fun and healthful exercise gained from bicycling. Being careful, always, will give riders safer trips and greater peace of mind.

Chapter 59

Scuba Diving Safety

What Is Recreational Scuba Diving?

Recreational scuba diving is defined as pleasure diving to a depth of 130 feet without decompression stops.

Several scuba-certifying agencies offer training for divers, from beginners to experts. Three of the agencies are the Professional Association of Diving Instructors (PADI), the National Association of Underwater Instructors (NAUI) and Scuba Schools International (SSI). Basic classes involve classroom instruction and training in a pool and open water settings. The most popular courses last from 4 to 8 weeks.

What Are The Most Common Problems Of Scuba Diving?

The most common medical problems are simple middle ear squeezes. Squeezes cause pain in your ears. The pain is caused by the difference in pressure between the air spaces of your ears and mask, and higher water pressure as you go deeper into the water. Squeezes that affect the inner ear or sinuses are less common.

Cuts, scrapes, and other injuries to the arms and legs can be caused by contact with fish and other marine animals, certain species of coral and hazards such as exposed sharp metal on wrecks or fishing line.

♣ **It's A Fact!!**

How Common Are Medical Problems In Scuba Diving?

Fortunately, serious medical problems are not common in recreational scuba divers. While there are millions of dives each year in the Unites States, only about 90 deaths are reported each year worldwide. In addition, fewer than 1,000 divers worldwide require recompression therapy to treat severe dive-related health problems.

What Dangerous Medical Conditions Are Possible When I Am Diving?

- **Inner ear barotrauma.** This condition may happen if you had trouble clearing during a dive. The result is severe dizziness and hearing loss.

- **Pulmonary barotrauma.** This condition is the result of improper breathing during the ascent to the surface, or occasionally, from diving with a respiratory tract infection. Symptoms include chest pain, shortness of breath, and hoarseness.

- **Arterial gas embolism (AGE).** This is a type of pulmonary barotrauma in which bubbles enter the circulation and travel to the brain. Symptoms such as numbness or tingling of the skin, weakness, paralysis, or even loss of consciousness may occur. This is a very serious diving injury.

- **Decompression sickness (the bends).** This condition occurs during ascent and on the surface of the water. Inert nitrogen gas that is dissolved in body tissues and blood comes out of solution and forms bubbles in the blood. The bubbles can injure various body tissues and may block blood vessels. The most common signs of severe decompression sickness are dysfunction of the spinal cord, brain, and lungs.

Remember: If you should develop any of the symptoms on this list during a dive or after a dive, you should get medical care immediately.

How Can I Lower My Risk Of Medical Problems?

Most severe dive-related injuries and deaths happen in beginning divers. To be safe, always dive within the limits of your experience and level of training. Good rules to follow for safe diving include:

1. Never try a dive you're not comfortable with. During descent, you should gently equalize your ears and mask. At depth, never dive outside the parameters of the dive tables or your dive computer.

2. Never hold your breath while ascending. You should always ascend slowly while breathing normally.

3. Become familiar with the underwater area and its dangers. Learn which fish, coral, and other hazards to avoid so that injuries do not occur. Be aware of local tides and currents.

4. Never panic under water. If you become confused or afraid during a dive, stop, try to relax, and think the problem through. You can also get help from your dive buddy or dive master.

5. Never dive without a buddy.

6. Always plan your dive, then always dive your plan.

7. Always stay within the no-decompression limits.

8. Be sure that your diving equipment can handle the dive you have planned and that the equipment is working well.

9. Don't drink alcohol before diving.

10. Never dive while taking medicine unless your doctor has said it's safe.

11. Diving can be dangerous if you have certain medical problems. Ask your doctor how diving may affect your health.

12. Cave diving is dangerous and should only be attempted by divers with proper training and equipment.

13. If you don't feel well or if you are in pain after diving, go to the nearest emergency room immediately.

14. Don't fly for 12 hours after a no-decompression dive, even in a pressurized airplane. If your dive required decompression stops, don't fly for at least 24 hours.

What Should I Do In A Diving Emergency?

If you or one of your dive buddies has an accident while diving, or if you would like to discuss a potential diving-related health problem, call the Divers Alert Network (DAN) emergency telephone line (919-684-8111). DAN is located at Duke University Medical Center in Durham, NC. Doctors, emergency medical technicians, and nurses are available 24 hours a day to answer your questions. If needed, they will direct you to the nearest hyperbaric chamber or other appropriate medical facility.

What Is A Hyperbaric Chamber?

A hyperbaric chamber is a facility where you are placed under increased pressure. It's similar to being underwater. This can often help injury from arterial gas embolism or decompression sickness by shrinking bubbles and allowing them to pass through your blood vessels.

Additional Information About Recreational Scuba Diving

Divers Alert Network (DAN)
The Peter B. Bennett Center
6 West Colony Place
Durham, NC 27705
Toll-Free: 800-446-2671
Fax: 919-490-6630
Diving Emergencies: 919-684-8111 (Remember to call local EMS first, then DAN)
Website: www.diversalertnetwork.org
E-mail: dan@diversalertnetwork.org

Underwater Medicine Associates

P.O. Box 481
Bryn Mawr, PA 19010
Phone: 610-896-8806
Fax: 610-896-2883
Website: www.scubamed.com
E-mail: sandy@scubamed.com

Diving Medicine Online

31681 Shoal Water Drive
Ono Island, AL 36561
Phone: 251-980-1384
Fax: 309-424-2744
Website: www.scuba-doc.com
E-mail: scubadoc@scuba-doc.com

Ernest S. Campbell, MD, FACS writes and maintains Diving Medicine Online. Visit the website for answers to your scuba diving medical questions.

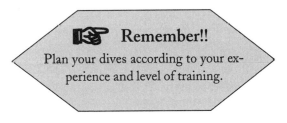

Remember!!
Plan your dives according to your experience and level of training.

Part Eight

Resources For Help And Additional Information

Chapter 60

Directory Of Resources About Sports Injuries In Teens

The following organizations can provide additional information about the treatment and prevention of sports injuries. For your convenience in locating contact information for specific organizations, they are listed alphabetically.

American Academy of Orthopaedic Surgeons
6300 North River Rd.
Rosemont, IL 60018-4262
Toll-Free: 800-346-AAOS (2267)
Fax On Demand: 800-999-2939
Website: www.aaos.org

American Association of Oral and Maxillofacial Surgeons
9700 W. Bryn Mawr Avenue
Rosemont, IL 60018-5701
Phone: 847-678-6200
Fax: 847-678-6286
Website: www.aaoms.org

American Academy of Pediatrics
141 Northwest Point Boulevard
Elk Grove Village, IL 60007-1098
Phone: 847-434-4000
Fax: 847-434-8000
Website: www.aap.org
E-mail: cfc@aap.org

About This Chapter: Resources were compiled from many sources deemed accurate. Contact information was current as of July 2003.

American College of Rheumatology
1800 Century Place, Suite 250
Atlanta, GA 30345
Phone: 404-633-3777
Fax: 404-633-1870
Website: www.rheumatology.org
E-mail: acr@rheumatology.org

American College of Sports Medicine
401 W. Michigan Street
Indianapolis, IN 46202-3233
Phone: 317-637-9200
Fax: 317-634-7817
Website: www.acsm.org
E-mail: publicinfo@ascm.org

American Orthopaedic Foot and Ankle Society
2517 Eastlake Avenue E., Suite 200
Seattle, WA 98102
Phone: 206-223-1120
Fax: 206-223-1178
Website: www.aofas.org
E-mail: aofas@aofas.org

American Orthopaedic Society for Sports Medicine
6300 N. River Road, Suite 500
Rosemont, IL 60018
Toll-Free: 877-321-3500
Phone: 847-292-4900
Fax: 847-292-4905
Website: www.sportsmed.org
E-mail: aossm@aossm.org

American Physical Therapy Association
1111 North Fairfax Street
Alexandria, VA 22314-1488
Toll-Free: 800-999-2782
Phone: 703-684-2782
Website: www.apta.org

American Podiatric Medical Association
9312 Old Georgetown Rd.
Bethesda, MD 208114-1621
Toll-Free: 800-ASK-APMA (275-2762)
Phone: 301-571-9200
Fax: 301-530-2752
Website: www.apma.org

American Red Cross
2025 East Street N.W.
Washington, DC 20006
Phone: 703-248-4222
Fax: 202-303-4498
Website: www.redcross.org

Arthritis Foundation
1330 West Peachtree Street
Atlanta, GA 30309
Toll-Free: 800-283-7800
Phone: 404-872-7100 or call your local chapter (listed in the telephone directory)
Website: www.arthritis.org
E-mail: arthritis@finelinesolutions.com

Bicycle Helmet Safety Institute

4611 Seventh Street South
Arlington, VA 22204-1419
Phone: 703-486-0100
Website: www.helmets.org
E-mail: info@helmets.org

Brain Injury Association of America

105 North Alfred St.
Alexandria, VA 22314
Toll-Free: 800-444-6443
Phone: 703-236-6000
Website: www.biausa.org
E-mail: familyhelpline@biausa.org

Divers Alert Network (DAN)

The Peter B. Bennett Center
6 West Colony Place
Durham, NC 27705
Toll-Free: 800-446-2671
Fax: 919-490-6630
Diving Emergencies: 919-684-
8111 (Remember to call local EMS
first, then DAN)
Website: www.diversalertnetwork.org
E-mail: dan@diversalertnetwork.org

Diving Medicine Online

31681 Shoal Water Drive
Ono Island, AL 36561
Phone: 251-980-1384
Fax: 309-424-2744
Website: www.scuba-doc.com
E-mail: scubadoc@scuba-doc.com

Institute for Arthroscopy and Sports Medicine

2100 Webster St., Suite 331
San Francisco, CA 94115
Phone: 415-923-0944
Fax: 415-923-5896
Website: www.iasm.com
E-mail: jhalbrecht@iasm.com

National Athletic Trainers Association (NATA)

2952 Stemmons Frwy.
Dallas, TX 75247-6196
Phone: 214-637-6282
Fax: 214-637-2206
Website: www.nata.org
E-mail: webdude@nata.org

National Center for Injury Prevention and Control

Centers for Disease Control and
Prevention (CDC), Mailstop K65
4770 Buford Highway N.E.
Atlanta, GA 30341-3724
Phone: 770-488-1506
Fax: 770-488-1667
Website: www.cdc.gov/ncipc
E-mail: CHCINFO@cdc.gov

National Collegiate Athletic Association (NCAA)

P.O. Box 6222
Indianapolis, IN 46206-6222
Phone: 317-917-6222
Fax: 317-917-6888
Website: www.ncaa.org

National Institute of Arthritis and Musculoskeletal and Skin Diseases (NIAMS)

National Institutes of Health
1 AMS Circle
Bethesda, MD 20892-3675
Toll-Free: 877-22-NIAMS (266-4267)
Phone: 301-495-4484
Fax: 301-718-6366
TTY: 301-565-2966
Website: www.niams.nih.gov
E-mail: niamsinfo@mail.nih.gov

National SAFE KIDS Campaign

1301 Pennsylvania Ave. N.W.
Suite 1000
Washington, DC 20004
Phone: 202-662-0600
Fax: 202-393-2072
Website: www.safekids.org

National Safety Council

1121 Spring Lake Drive
Itasca, IL 60143-3201
Phone: 630-285-1121
Fax: 630-285-1315
E-mail: info@nsc.org
Website: www.nsc.org

National Ski Areas Association

133 S. Van Gordon St., Suite 300
Lakewood, CO 80228
Phone: 303-987-1111
Fax: 303-986-2345
Website: www.nsaa.org
E-mail: nsaa@nsaa.org

National Ski Patrol

133 S. Van Gordon St., Suite 100
Lakewood, CO 80228
Phone: 303-988-1111
Fax: 303-988-3005
Website: www.nsp.org

National Youth Sports Safety Foundation

One Beacon St., Suite 3333
Boston, MA 02108
Phone: 617-277-1171
Fax: 617-722-9999
Website: www.nyssf.org
E-mail: NYSSF@aol.com

Prevent Blindness America

500 East Remington Road
Schaumburg, IL 60173
Toll-Free: 800-331-2020
Fax: 847-843-8458
Website: www.preventblindness.org

Safety Equipment Institute

1307 Dolley Madison Blvd.
Suite 3A
McClean, VA 22101
Phone: 703-442-5732
Fax: 703-442-5756
Website: www.SEInet.org
E-mail: info@SEInet.org

Snell Memorial Foundation

3628 Madison Avenue
Suite 11
North Highlands, CA 95660
Toll-Free: 888-SNELL99 (763-
5599)
Phone: 916-331-5073
Fax: 916-331-0359
Website: www.smf.org
E-mail: info@smf.org

Underwater Medicine Associates

P.O. Box 481
Bryn Mawr, PA 19010
Phone: 610-896-8806
Fax: 610-896-2883
Website: www.scubamed.com
E-mail: sandy@scubamed.com

U.S. Consumer Product Safety Commission

4330 East-West Highway
Bethesda, MD 20814-4408
Toll-Free: 800-638-2772
Phone: 301-504-6816
Fax: 301-504-0124 and 301-504-
0025
Website: www.cpsc.gov
E-mail: info@cpsc.gov

Chapter 61

Suggested Reading For Active Teens

Books

The American Physical Therapy Association Book of Body Maintenance and Repair, by Marilyn Moffat, Terry Boles, Steve Vickery, and the American Physical Therapy Association, Henry Holt & Company, Inc.; 1999. 288 pp.

The Complete Waterpower Workout Book: Program for Fitness, Injury Prevention, and Healing, by Lynda Huey, with Robert Forster and Pete Romano, Random House Trade Paperbacks; 1993. 400 pp.

The Female Athlete's Body Book: How to Prevent and Treat Sports Injuries in Women and Girls, by Gloria Beim and Ruth Winter, McGraw-Hill/Contemporary Books; 2003. 272 pp.

Orthopedic & Athletic Injury Evaluation Handbook, by Chad Starkey, Jeffrey L. Ryan, and Clifton L. Taulbert, Henry Holt & Company, Inc.; 1999. 288 pp.

Sports Injuries: A Self-Help Guide, by Vivian Grisogono, John Murray Pubs Ltd.; 1989. 294 pp.

About This Chapter: Information in this chapter was compiled from sources deemed accurate. The resources listed in this chapter are intended to serve as a starting point for further research. They represent a sampling of available material; this list is not complete. Inclusion does not constitute endorsement.

Sports Injury Prevention and Rehabilitation, by Eric Shamus and Jennifer Shamus, McGraw-Hill/Appleton & Lange; 2001. 513 pp.

The Sports Medicine Bible for Young Athletes, by Lyle J. Michell with Mark Jenkins, Scourcebooks Trade; 2001. 288 pp.

Strength & Power for Young Athletes, by Wayne Westcott and Avery D. Faigenbaum; Human Kinetics; 2000. 200 pp.

Sports Nutrition

Feeding the Young Athlete: Sports Nutrition Made Easy for Players and Parents, by Cynthia Lair with Scott Murdoch Ph.D., Moon Smile Press; 2002. 112 pp.

Running

Explosive Running: Using the Science of Kinesiology to Improve Your Performance, by Michael Yessis, Ph.D, McGraw-Hill/Contemporary Books; 2000. 192 pp.

Running Injury-Free: How to Prevent, Treat and Recover from Dozens of Painful Problems, by Joe Ellis and Joe Henderson, Rodale Press; June 1994. 272 pp.

Runner's World Complete Book of Running: Everything You Need to Know to Run for Fun, Fitness, and Competition, by Amby Burfoot, Rodale Press; 1999. 320 pp.

Runner's World Complete Book of Women's Running: The Best Advice to Get Started, Stay Motivated, Lose Weight, Run Injury-Free, Be Safe, and Train for Any Distance, by Dagny Scott Barrios, Dagny Scott, Amby Burfoot, Rodale Press; 2000. 308 pp.

Brochures

Available from the American College of Sports Medicine: Single copies of these brochures are available free of charge by sending a self-addressed, stamped, business-size envelope to: ACSM National Center, P.O. Box 1440, Indianapolis, IN 46206-1440.

- "Eating Smart, Even When You're Pressed for Time"

- "Fitting Fitness In, Even When You're Pressed for Time"

- "Female Athlete Triad: Amenorrhea, Eating Disorders, and Osteoporosis"

- "Exercise-Induced Asthma"

- "Nutrition, Training, and Injury Prevention Guidelines: A guide for soccer players"

- "Nutrition and Sports Performance: A guide for physically active young people"

- "Sprains, Strains, and Tears"

- "What Is an Exercise Physiologist?"

Contact for a free copy of the following brochures from The Arthritis Foundation. Write to: The Arthritis Foundation, P.O. Box 7669, Atlanta, GA 30357-0669 or call 800-283-7800.

- "2003 Walking Guide" Item No: 810-0503AA

- "Safe or Sorry: What Parents Need to Know about Kids and Sports Injuries" Item No: 550-9360Al

On-Line Reading

These websites offer information about treatment and prevention of sports injuries.

AAOS On-Line Service: Your Orthopaedic Connection
http://orthoinfo.aaos.org

American Orthopaedic Society for Sports Medicine (AOSSM)
http://www.sportsmed.org

ESPN.com Training Room
http://espn.go.com/TrainingRoom

Institute for Arthroscopy and Sports Medicine, San Francisco
http://www.iasm.com

MedFact's SportsDoc
http://www.medfacts.com/sprtsdoc.htm

The Physician and Sportsmedicine Online
http://www.physsportsmed.com

SportsMedicine.Com
http://www.sportsmedicine.com

SportsMedWeb
http://riceinfo.rice.edu/~jenky

Index

Index

Page numbers that appear in *Italics* refer to illustrations. Page numbers that have a small 'n' after the page number refer to information shown as Notes at the beginning of each chapter. Page numbers that appear in **Bold** refer to information contained in boxes on that page (except Notes information at the beginning of each chapter).